MATTY
AN AMERICAN HERO

MATTY

AN AMERICAN HERO

Christy Mathewson of the New York Giants

RAY ROBINSON

New York   Oxford
OXFORD UNIVERSITY PRESS
1993

Oxford University Press

Oxford New York Toronto
Delhi Bombay Calcutta Madras Karachi
Kuala Lumpur Singapore Hong Kong Tokyo
Nairobi Dar es Salaam Cape Town
Melbourne Auckland Madrid

and associated companies in
Berlin Ibadan

Published by Oxford University Press, Inc.,
200 Madison Avenue, New York, New York 10016

Oxford is a registered trademark of Oxford University Press

Library of Congress Cataloging-in-Publication Data
Robinson, Ray, 1920 Dec. 4-
Matty: An American Hero : Christy Mathewson of the New York Giants /
Ray Robinson.
p. cm. Includes index.
ISBN 0-19-507629-X
1. Mathewson, Christy, 1880–1925.
2. Baseball players—United States—Biography.
I. Title.
GV865.M37R63 1993
796.357'092—dc20 [B] 92-40974

Lines from Dulce et Decorum Est by Wilfred Owen reprinted by
permission of New Directions Publishing Corp.

9 8 7 6 5 4 3 2 1

Printed in the United States of America
on acid-free paper

To Mike Schacht and Don Honig,
who encouraged me
to write about Matty

Acknowledgments

During the course of my research on Matty many people—friends, associates, total strangers, old-time fans—generously provided me with information and insights without which this book could not have been written. I'd like to thank each one of them for their kindness and hope I am not overlooking anyone who responded to my requests.

In no particular order, here are those who wrote to me, spoke to me, and cooperated in so many ways: Betty Cook of Lewisburg, a neighbor of Jane Mathewson, who became her closest "relative" in Jane's last years; Marsha Scott Gori, Bradley Tufts, and Doris Dysinger of Bucknell's splendid staff; Bob Carman of Lafayette College; Susan Avery and Mary Ann Rubino of the New York Lung Association; Jerry Beatty, whose father covered Matty for the press; Lawrence Ritter; Donald Honig; Ed Linn; David Wise; George Vecsey; Pete Hamill; Jack Newfield; Meg Dooley; Michael Gershman; Paul A. Dickard; Marty Appel; Faigi Rosenthal of the New York *Daily News* Library; Steve Robinson; Paul Jablow; Dr. Lloyd Feinberg, a collector of Matty memorabilia; Marc Okkonen; Bob Peterson; Richard Egan; Dr. Ira Cohen; Dr. Robert Samuelson; Leo Trachtenberg; Mike Schacht; Harold Rosenthal; Keith Sutton, former sports editor of the Wayne (Pa.) *Independent*, and Marty Myer, the current sports editor; Graham R. Lobb; Debra Dagavarian-Bonar; Eric Rolfe Greenberg; and Ira Berkow.

To all those wonderful people at Baseball's Hall of Fame and Museum at Cooperstown, New York, including Tom Heitz, Bill Deane, Pat Kelly, Bob Browning and summer intern Gretchen Curtis, my thanks for their help and hospitality.

Special thanks to Claudia Ebeling of Lewisburg, who lives two blocks from Matty's grave and who, in a delightful letter, told me in great detail about Matty's ghost-written books and of two deceased relatives who used to talk avidly of the days when they took the train from Reading to Philadelphia to see Matty pitch.

Thanks also to Grace Van Lingen, the sprightly 82-year-old daughter of Henry Mathewson, Matty's brother. To this day Grace Van Lingen speaks of "my Uncle Christy, who made certain that I had enough money to attend Bucknell and Syracuse." She was "in awe of him, as a little girl, and always found him warm and attentive, though reserved."

Another interesting informant was 98-year-old Jacques Coe, who was born in Amsterdam and came to Brooklyn in 1902. "Whenever Mathewson pitched, my father would give me 25 cents to sit in the bleachers," Coe wrote. "My best memory of him is that he threw without question the fewest bases on balls of any pitcher that I have ever seen. Whenever I see a pitcher these days who cannot seem to find home plate Christy Mathewson always comes to mind." The 90-year-old Henry Goldwater informed me that his father was a good friend of Matty. "I played baseball at the University of Michigan," recalled Goldwater, "but I was told by Matty that my fingers were too small ever to make a good pitcher."

A veritable library of books, including Matty's own priceless *Pitching in a Pinch*, were of significant help in developing a view of Matty and his time. They were: *The Baseball Story* by Fred Lieb; *Baseball America* by Donald Honig; *The Image of Their Greatness* by Lawrence Ritter and Donald Honig; *The World Series Encyclopedia* edited by Don Schiffer; *Baseball's Famous Pitchers* by Ira Smith; *The Giants of the Polo Grounds* by Noel Hynd; *The Real McGraw* by Arthur Mann; *The Tumult and the Shouting* by Grantland Rice; *The Imperial Diamond* by Lee Lowenfish; *The Glory of Their Times* by Lawrence Ritter; *The Greatest Giants of Them All* by Arnold Hano; *The Greatest Sports Stories from the New York Times* edited by Allison Danzig and Peter Brandwein; *The Legendary Champions* by Rex Lardner; *The Pitch That Killed* by Mike Sowell; *Great Times* by J. C. Furnas; *The Hero in America* by Dixon Wecter; *Red: A Biography of Red Smith* by Ira Berkow; *Sport: Mirror of American Life* by Robert H. Boyle; *The World of Damon Runyon* by Tom Clark; *Ty Cobb* by Charles Alexander; *Woodrow Wilson* by August Heckscher; *Stengel: His Life and Times* by Robert Creamer; *Baseball* by Robert Smith; *Eight Men Out* by Eliot

Asinof; Union County Heritage; *The Boston Braves* by Harold Kaese; *The Physics of Baseball* by Robert K. Adair; Wayne County Sports History, 1871–1972; "Mathewson" (an article in *Sport Magazine*) by Ed Linn; *My Greatest Day in Baseball* as told to John P. Carmichael; *The Epic of New York City* by Edward Robb Ellis; *The Celebrant* by Eric Rolfe Greenberg; *Our Game* by Charles Alexander; *The Ultimate Book of Baseball* by Daniel Okrent; *Ring* by Jonathan Yardley; *The Legend of Hobey Baker* by John Davies; *The Days of McGraw* by Joseph Durso; *Casey at the Bat* by Ernest Lawrence Thayer, afterword by Donald S. Hall; *The New York Giants* by Frank Graham; *The Greatest Pitchers of All Time* by Donald Honig; *The Baseball Fan's Guide to Spring Training* by Mike Shatzkin and Jim Charlton; *Fathers Playing Catch With Sons* by Donald S. Hall; *The Baseball Encyclopedia* by Joseph Reichler; *Heroes of the World Series* by Al Silverman; *The Unforgettable Season* by G. H. Fleming; *Book of Sports Legends* edited by Joseph Vecchione; *The Baseball Hall of Fame* by Gerald Astor; *Heroes* by Joe McGinniss; *Everything Baseball* by James Mote; *The Cincinnati Reds* by Lee Allen; *Baseball's Hall of Fame* by Robert Smith; *Baseball: America's Diamond Mind* by Richard C. Crepeau; *Superstars of Baseball* by Bob Broeg; *Christy Mathewson: Baseball's Greatest Pitcher* by Gene Schoor; *The Ballplayers* by Mike Shatzkin; *Heywood Broun* by Richard O'Connor; *Heywood Broun* by Dale Kramer; *No-Hitters* by Phil Pepe; *Tuberculosis* by Saul Solomon; *A Life: Damon Runyon* by Jimmy Breslin; *The World Series: A Pictorial History* by John Devaney; *Baseball: The Early Years* by Harold Seymour; *The Baseball Player—An Economic Study* by Paul M. Gregory; *My Life in Baseball* by Ty Cobb with Al Stump; *The Best of the Athletic Boys* by Jack Newcombe; *The American Diamond* by Branch Rickey; *My All-Time All-Stars* edited by Tom Meany; *The New York Times Book of Baseball History* foreword by Red Smith.

I would also like to express my appreciation to my agent, Jay Acton, a true baseball aficionado who is doing impressive work in trying to restore baseball to the inner cities (RBI is the happy acronym for the organization) and to Sheldon Meyer of Oxford University Press for grasping immediately the singular role that Matty played in baseball history.

Every book needs its Xerox machine. Once again, my friend,

Bob Witten, placed his office equipment at my disposal, with Marianna Sorshek cranking the pages out when I needed them.

To Phyllis, who had only a vague knowledge of Christy Mathewson when I broached the subject, my gratitude for her devotion and encouragement. And for always being there.

New York City   Ray Robinson
September 1992

Contents

Show me a hero and I will write
you a tragedy.
                    —F. Scott Fitzgerald

Without heroes we are all plain people
and don't know how far we can go.
          —Bernard Malamud, *The Natural*

MATTY
AN AMERICAN HERO

1

HEROES

WHEN Christy Mathewson, possibly the most accomplished pitcher of all time, was born in the tiny town of Factoryville, Pennsylvania, in 1880, there were few, if any, athletic heroes. Americans were still content to exult in those individuals who had won renown as warriors, like the Alamo's Davy Crockett, the successful failure, Robert E. Lee, or the earthy Ulysses S. Grant, who had commanded and killed well, or as politicians, who had succeeded in winning elections. The hero could hardly be one who had devoted his life to the mind, the spirit, or to games.

"Certain occupations," wrote Robert Penn Warren, "are not heroic—artists, scholars, scientists, philosophers, physicians—need not apply here for a pedestal."

Rather, it was that person, presumably strong, courageous, and noble, who could command the public imagination. More often than not, it was through service to the people that one became a hero. The quintessential American hero had always been George Washington, the architect of his country's gestating democracy. Glacial and removed, to some rather inhuman, General Washington bespoke dignity and strength. He was the warrior hero whose roots could be traced back to the Greek mythology of Achilles and Ulysses.

At the turn of the twentieth century, when the modern era of baseball is said to have gotten under way, the accepted heroes were men such as inventors Henry Ford and Thomas A. Edison, or statesmen such as Washington, Lincoln, and Jefferson, although the latter struck some people as being entirely too cerebral. Benjamin Franklin, the plain man who rose to undreamed-of heights in his nation's service, was an Horatio Alger in the flesh. "With a little luck," wrote author Dixon Wecter, "you might be a Franklin, but Washington is clearly what you could never be."

When Christy Mathewson first appeared on the scene, as a pitcher for the New York Giants, athletes had not yet won much acclaim as role models. John L. Sullivan, the Boston Strong Boy, was recognized far and wide as the heavyweight champion of the world. But he was also known as a hard-swearing braggart and drunk. When he exclaimed out loud that he could "lick any son of a bitch in the house," he was believed. But his bluster and unquenchable thirst prevented him from being adopted as a national hero.

In baseball circles, some ballplayers were, indeed, perceived as virile, rugged men—and types like John J. McGraw and Connie Mack won plaudits for generalship and tactics. But the extra dimension of herohood didn't attach to them. There were players who were written about as larger than life and were said to be generous to their friends and mothers. But for the most part, too many of them spit on the carpet or threw up in public to allow any in their profession to be canonized.

Tyrus Raymond Cobb was the most proficient hitter and base-stealer of his generation, but he had the temperament of an angry warthog. Volatile, insanely competitive, and paranoid (character traits that, in more recent times, have been attributed to the accidental killing of his beloved father by his mother), Cobb jumped on friend and foe alike. He had wide and grudging respect—but he was no man's hero.

Adrian Constantine "Cap" Anson was the first ballplayer to amass 3000 hits in the late 1880s. A fierce bench jockey and umpire-baiter, Anson was also a practicing racist and bigot, although that wasn't held against him at the time. A genius of sorts at baseball strategy, Anson also helped to popularize baseball. But he failed to popularize himself. Cornelius McGillicuddy won fame as the gentle, courtly manager Connie Mack. He was the early version of "baseball class," even if he did resort to tipping catcher's bats and employing some of the game's chronic drunkards (Rube Waddell, for example). But since when do managers become heroes to anyone, either their own players or the outside world? John McGraw, Mack's scrappy competition in the National League, and the man who would be fortunate enough to become Mathewson's manager, had a dark side that often overrode his exceptional baseball mind. Fans wanted him on their side—but he was no hero.

Other dominant ballplayers of that era had idiosyncrasies and defects that diminished them. John "Honus" Wagner, everyone's all-time shortstop, was as intelligent, decent, and hard-working as any man could be. But he was thick-handed, big-bellied and, despite his skills, somewhat awkward to look at. Napoleon Lajoie, a wonderful second baseman, was of French-Canadian extraction (which probably ruled him out to begin with) but he, too, was a somewhat uninspiring figure, and slow afoot.

By 1900 ballplayers, in the order of their social acceptance, were lower even than circus clowns, itinerant actors, and train robbers. On the whole, they were crude, roistering, disreputable folks full of foul oaths and beery smells. Few would have recommended them for entrance into a decent caravansary.

"They were mostly young and uneducated," Stephen Jay Gould has written. "Hardly any of those early players went to college and few finished high school. Baseball, for all its mythological hyping, really took root as a people's sport in America. Rube, the nickname of so many early players, reflected a common background."

Some ballplayers were locals, bred in the area in which they played the professional game. But many were off the farms or out of mills and factories. They arrived mostly from the South, Southwest and Midwest, often carrying the traditional crumbling suitcases and meager vocabularies.

Wahoo Sam Crawford, an outfielder from 1899 to 1917, acknowledged that players were not looked on too fondly in polite circles. "We were considered pretty crude," he said.

Davy Jones, an outfielder for the Cubs and Tigers at the turn of the century and a man reputed to be a calming influence on the tempestuous Cobb, told *The Glory of Their Times* author Lawrence S. Ritter that "in those days a lot of people looked upon ballplayers as bums . . . they were thought to be too lazy to work for a living." Jones added that he was going with a girl when he decided to become a professional ballplayer and her parents refused to let her see him any more.

When pitcher Rube Marquard first decided to become a ballplayer, his father threatened never to talk to his son again. "Why would a grown man want to become a player and wear those funny suits," snarled Marquard's Dad. "Go out and get yourself an education!"

Innumerable stories circulated about the distasteful adven-
tures of ballplayers—drinking, women-chasing, gambling, and all
other manner of uncouth activities. Eddie Cantor, the comic who
starred in the Ziegfeld Follies, said that to many people "a baseball
player was the king of loafers." But while the game these ruffians
played became increasingly popular among people from all walks
of life, there continued to be a strangely schizophrenic reaction to
its practitioners. Men, women, and little boys enjoyed rooting for
the home team, and sometimes betting on them. They talked and
argued about the relative merits of their favorites and collected National League baseball player cards, which were first issued in the
1880s (the American League didn't come into existence until 1901).
But these same people generally held ballplayers in contempt for
their bad manners and unwholesome habits.

Deprived of real-life baseball heroes, many were drawn to one
transcendent athletic saint, even before Mathewson made his proud
appearance on the scene. That was Frank Merriwell of Fardale
Academy and Yale. The hitch was that Merriwell never truly existed, being a fictitious character created out of the imagination of
a writer named Gilbert Patten.

From 1896 to 1914 Merriwell was the beau ideal of millions
who read about his singular exploits and feats of derring-do in *TipTop
Weekly*, the most popular five-cent novel of its era. Merriwell played
every sport under the sun. He was a dominant pitcher in baseball,
a superb halfback in football, a powerful stroke on the crew (in his
spare time he also coached the freshman crew), and he was also a
whiz in boxing, lacrosse, golf, track, and billiards. More important,
Merriwell possessed a spotless character: he didn't drink or smoke,
stood for truth, justice, family, loyalty, duty, patriotism, friendship, right over wrong. He was anti-snob, anti-bully, and pro-
tolerance. In short, he represented the heroic residue of late nine-
teenth-century passions.

A spindly small-town boy from Corinna, Maine, Patten was as
physically fragile as Merriwell was vigorous and robust. Patten never
attended Yale, or any college, for that matter, but that failed to
deter him from spawning over 20,000 words a week about his athletic paragon. Under the writing name of Burt L. Standish, Patten
turned himself inside out in the process of creating Merriwell;
Merriwell was everything he was not.

The given name of Frank Merriwell, Patten once explained,
was based on the hero's characteristics—clean as a hound's tooth,

above-board, merry, frank. The "well" on Merriwell suggested Frank's abounding physical health.

Not surprisingly, many were captivated by the figure that Patten created. The future President Woodrow Wilson, plagued by illness through his life, was a part-time coach of Princeton's undefeated football team in 1878. He was much drawn to Merriwell. Jack Dempsey, from the coal mines of Manassa, Colorado, and one day to upend the giant Jess Willard for the heavyweight title of the world, was an avid reader of the Merriwell books. Dan Parker, a crusading New York sports editor, constantly dipped into Merriwell as a youth and liked to think the young man was real. Among all the distinguished as well as obscure people who devoured Merriwell was the young Christy Mathewson, soon to emerge as the real-life version of his own mythical hero.

The word "hero" comes from the Greek word *heros*, which means the embodiment of composite ideals. Yet the Greeks always knew their gods were not perfect; they knew they were fallible and possessed character flaws. Many Americans, however, preferred to view Mathewson as a hero without warts. In this public thirst for a saint among ballplayers Mathewson became someone entirely apart from his own rowdy fraternity. He was an idealized, cardboard figure—the first to come from the baseball ranks.

Mathewson was as handsome as the matinee idol of his time, William Faversham (who played Romeo to Maude Adams' Juliet), and could have posed for Arrow collar ads. Everyone conceded he was a striking figure in his Giants baseball uniform. Off the field, with his neatly pressed tweedy suit, carefully knotted tie, wavy brown hair parted precisely in the middle and alert, blue eyes, Matty could have been taken for an aspiring law student or businessman. A public relations wizard could have invented Mathewson.

No player before his time—or after—(that includes Babe Ruth, Ty Cobb, Ted Williams, Mickey Mantle, Willie Mays, and Stan Musial) ever captured the public fancy the way Matty did. It is no exaggeration to suggest that he was truly loved by most fans, even those who despised John McGraw and the Giants ball club. Millions worshipped him and spoke his name reverently. Some couldn't discern the difference between myth and reality. They actually confused Matty with Merriwell. "Men and women of all classes held Mathewson up as a role model for their children and, no doubt, secretly regarded him as one for themselves," wrote Jonathan Yardley.

In assessing Matty's qualities one must avoid an excess of "trolley car nostalgia," as Martin Amis has written, for the endless superlatives led to his deification. However, there was no escaping the fact that during his life Matty's reputation extended far beyond the boundaries of his sport.

If we choose to exclude Walter Johnson, Matty was the greatest pitcher of his era. But Johnson, decent and shy as he was, never won the affection of a nation. Matty was worshipped; Johnson was only liked.

"Hero worship is the national disease that does most to keep the grandstands filled and the playgrounds empty," wrote Ring Lardner, the acidulous baseball writer, following the exposure of the Black Sox Scandal of 1919. Lardner felt he'd been violated by those White Sox players whom he had befriended in his years spent traveling with the club. However, since Matty had always been a special hero and pal of Lardner, the humorist never had cause to change his mind about the one man that he admired above all others in baseball.

Today it is difficult for personalities in any sport to be regarded as heroes or role models. The relentless, often prurient eye of TV and other branches of the media, the ubiquitous intrusions of investigative journalists, the invasion of private lives by sportswriters once content to report solely on hits, runs, and errors, all tend to reduce current sports stars into ordinary human beings—some decent, kind, many sleazy, narcissistic, corrupt, and ignorant.

It's a safe prediction that no sports figure will ever again approach the hold that Matty once had on America in the early days of the twentieth century. A watershed figure, he defined baseball in a new, acceptable way for millions. With his brains, demeanor, and attractive personality, plus his achievements on the field, he was the first authentic sports hero—certainly the first baseball hero. His chief accomplishment, perhaps, was that he came close to living up to his popular image.

2

GROWING UP IN
FACTORYVILLE

I N 1880 Factoryville, Pennsylvania, no longer
  boasted the single cotton factory that had originally won the hamlet its name. Many of the town's 650 inhabi-
tants detested the name of Factoryville and agitated, from time to
time, to change it, but to no avail.

To the north of Factoryville, in northeastern Pennsylvania, were
the towering coal bunkers of Scranton, with Carbondale to the east.
Lewisburg, site of Bucknell University since the school's founding
by a cadre of Baptists in 1846, was 75 miles to the west. Nestled
among green hills on the edge of the great anthracite coal region
of the state, Factoryville was protected from the black desola-
tion of grime and cinder that made the territory to the south so forbidding.

Thus isolated from the busy outside world, Factoryville was
known for little but its solitude until the twelfth day of August,
1880, when Christopher Mathewson was born there. A Republican
from Ohio, James A. Garfield, had been elected President that year,
over W. S. Hancock, continuing the domination of Abraham Lincoln's party in the White House since the end of the Civil War. A
year later, when Mathewson was one year old, Garfield was assas-
sinated by a disgruntled office seeker. Douglas MacArthur, destined to become a military hero of two great wars, was also born
in 1880, as was Helen Keller, who became a hero to the deaf and
unsighted. Damon Runyon, a future recorder of many of Mathew-

son's deeds on the island of Manhattan, was also born that year, in Manhattan, Kansas.

In 1880, the fledgling National League, having been born four years earlier in a Grand Central Hotel room in New York City, had eight teams—New York, Boston, Chicago, Louisville, Hartford, Philadelphia, Cincinnati, and St. Louis. When baseball's senior league was founded, New York's streets, hitherto dark, were lit by electricity for the first time, there was no radio or television to illuminate the event, and the United States had some 87,000 railroad miles in which to carry these new professional ballplayers.

Baseball had its roots in the 1840s in America, although General Abner Doubleday, its reputed founder, had nothing to do with it. Rather it was a gentleman named Alexander Cartwright who devised the rules, even deciding there should be 90 feet between bases. However, Cartwright also prescribed that there should be 50 feet from pitcher to catcher, thus giving pitchers of that day a definite edge over batters. No doubt Mathewson would have benefited considerably from that minimal distance.

With the coming of the Civil War, when bedraggled soldiers of the Union and Confederacy played their own version of baseball, as an antidote to boredom and butchery, the game grew in popularity. Legend had it that Abe Lincoln himself delighted in playing this game, even preferring it to his beloved rail-splitting. That hardly lessened the appeal of the game, even if such stories sounded as meretricious as the ones related earlier about George Washington and cherry trees.

By the time Mathewson was born baseball had spread to rock-studded sandlots, cow pastures (on which ancient fecal deposits often were employed as bases), county fairgrounds, and recreational parks. There were summer resort teams, with mostly college athletes filling out the rosters, thus jeopardizing their amateur status. Many small businesses in the mining, mill, and factory towns put together teams, thus reinforcing a working-class image for the game. These local teams often were the source of considerable civic pride. The muscular, as well as the anemic, were attracted to play, for it was felt that baseball required more than physique.

If baseball had emerged as the pastime of the common man, football, played since early colonial times, seemed the province of the elitists. Many young men in eastern colleges engaged in football; the first intercollegiate game had been played in 1869 between Princeton and Rutgers, with 25 players on each side. Walter Camp, Yale '80, was the game's prime innovator, and he fully understood that the game's reputation of mayhem and savagery was not about to win many converts, unless changes were made.

Of Scotch descent (during Matty's lifetime there was constant speculation that he was of Scandinavian origin), the Matteson (changed later to Mathewson) family settled in Rhode Island in the early seventeenth century. Some years later a company of settlers from that community journeyed west, into the hills around Factoryville, and put down roots there. Having been cotton manufacturers in their home surroundings, they meant to follow the same occupation in Pennsylvania. They built a factory, which stood for many years until the remains started to rust and crumble. But the machinery they brought with them was never used; as far as anyone knows, they never manufactured any cotton. The area was simply too isolated for such activity. A tranquil village before the arrival of the Mathewsons, Factoryville would always remain so.

When the Mathewsons first came to Factoryville, Gilbert Bailey Mathewson, born in 1847, helped his parents build a modest log cabin. Before long, when many young men from the North answered the call of President Lincoln, Gilbert donned his kepi and the dark blue of the Union forces and joined up.

As the last echoes of the Civil War's bugles faded away, Gilbert returned to Factoryville. In the early 1870s he married Minerva I. Capwell. A pleasant-faced woman with cool, refined manners, Minerva was eight years younger than Gilbert and came from a moneyed pioneer family in the area.

Though Gilbert was resolutely opposed to time-wasting, he had a sense of humor when the occasion warranted it and was known as a jack-of-all-trades, with a penchant for carpentering. At one time he occupied himself in the post office at Washington, Pennsylvania, southwest of Factoryville.

Ultimately Gilbert became a gentleman farmer, tending to his house, his garden, his apple orchard, and his hens. He was certain he and his growing family wouldn't be better off anyplace else than Factoryville, where people enjoyed the comfortable surroundings and the healthful climate.

In 1880 Christopher was the first born. Cyril died in infancy in 1882. Christine arrived in 1884 and Jane in 1888. Two boys, Henry, born in 1886, and Nicholas, in 1890, rounded out the family. All five children shared the large physiques of their parents, being big-boned, strong, and seemingly without problems.

Gilbert Mathewson once explained how Matty wound up with the name of Christopher. "His uncle, who was also named Christopher, wanted the name perpetuated," said Gilbert, "so he settled for a thousand dollars on Matty, when we consented to name him Christopher. It was a long name, as well as a somewhat uncommon one at the time but it was shortened to Christy and it seemed to take."

The Mathewson home that replaced the log cabin was situated in a valley, with a winding shallow brook running not far from it. A neighbor recalled how instructions were given to anyone searching for the Mathewson ancestral abode: "It's over the crick, up Main Street, 'til you come to the second cross road, then over the railroad tracks to a square house on the left."

In the rear of the wooden Victorian house was an apple orchard and to one side of the orchard was a garden, where Gilbert Mathewson passed much of his time. A small enclosed yard contained a number of Wyandotte hens that came from a blooded stock, imported from England. Beyond the yard was a barn, where cows, chickens, and pigs were kept.

The Mathewson parents were regarded as sober folk who raised their family in a religious atmosphere. They were a church-going people, tied to the Baptist faith, which sometimes could be rigid and stern. Gilbert and Minerva—she especially—looked upon drinking and smoking as national evils, habits not to be cultivated. If cultivated, they were to be given up immediately. However, Gilbert was known to "take a nip now and then," even though, in deference to Minerva, who heartily endorsed the policies of the Women's Christian Temperance Union, he never encouraged the habit for his sons.

Many of those living in the Factoryville area went to work in the mines as soon as they came of age. Since the Mathewsons had no wish for Christy to follow that path, they fervently hoped their son would become a preacher. The career of a baseball player for Christy was as far from their minds as Factoryville was from Los Angeles. Aware of how ballplayers were regarded—ungentlemanly louts, that's what they were!—Gilbert and Minerva wanted nothing of that for their son.

Along with a strong attachment to their religion, the Mathewsons also possessed a devotion to education and learning. Christy's grandmother had established Keystone Academy, a junior preparatory college in Factoryville. All of the boys, including Christy, would eventually attend Keystone.

The earliest sign that Christy might not be headed straight for the pulpit occurred when he was just four years old. Minerva Mathewson once related how little Christy always insisted on playing with the older boys in the neighborhood. "They tried to discourage him by telling him he wasn't big enough to play with them," she said. "But Christy said he *was* big enough. He then proved it by throwing a rag ball over the roof of our barn to a waiting catcher on the other side in a game that the youngsters used to call 'hailey over.' "

A few minutes later Christy appeared before his mother, tears streaming down his face. "He was scared," said Mrs. Mathewson, "because he had broken Mrs. Reynolds' window. Well, I told him, you'll just have to pay Mrs. Reynolds. Go over and ask her how much it is and then take the money out of your little bank. It took Christy a long time to save up the dollar that the broken window cost. But it taught him a sense of responsibility."

In Christy's own recollections of that growing-up period he acknowledges taking to baseball the way most young boys played at being pirates or Indian hunters. "But I don't think I was much above the average of the other kids my age in Factoryville," he said. Christy had a cousin, older than himself, who studied the theory of throwing. "I used to throw flat stones with him," said Christy, "and got to be good at it. When I was nine I could throw a stone farther than any of my chums. Then I'd go out in the woods and throw at squirrels and blackbirds. I always used round stones, as these could be thrown more accurately."

Before he was twelve years old Christy played the outfield and also tried his hand at second base. However, he always wanted to pitch, perhaps because *everyone* wanted to pitch. He realized that batting cross-handed, as he did, put a heavy handicap on his talents as a hitter, so he was determined to pitch for the town team and also at Keystone Academy.

In 1895, the same year that Babe Ruth was born in Baltimore, Christy received his baptism of fire as a play-for-pay pitcher. As a 15-year-old pitching against tough coal-mine kids of 18, 19, and 20 years old, he earned one dollar a game with Factoryville's team. In his first effort he faced Mills City, an adjoining town even less densely populated than Factoryville. He pitched for two solid hours, striking out everybody at least once, and won the game on his own hit. The final score was 19–17.

Christy was then taken on a ten-mile trip to play against another local team. There were other occasions when he had to walk from one starting pitching assignment to another when horse-drawn transportation was not readily available. A number of times he hired out—for the same dollar-a-game he'd originally received from his Factoryville friends—to Mills City. While committing this minor act of heresy, Christy pitched the first shutout of his life.

"I guess it was quite an accomplishment," he reminisced years later, "considering the rather nondescript team that played behind me."

It was clear that the residents of Factoryville and other tiny communities in Pennsylvania were much taken with baseball by this time. Cobb, the future Georgia Peach, was just a child. John McGraw was still several years away from imposing his truculent presence on the Baltimore Orioles, the best ball club of the era, and Connie Mack had only just begun, in Pittsburgh, his lengthy managerial career. This was, indeed, baseball in its mewling infancy. But the message of this enticing village game was spreading like a wild fever.

There was no doubt that the game was more rousing, livelier, and quicker than the foreign sport of cricket, and, much to its advantage, baseball was divorced from the class-consciousness of its British counterpart. There was also, providing another large measure of difference from games like football, no clock to end or hurry along baseball's action, no fixed boundary of time when the hostilities had to come to a halt. Baseball was a timeless adventure; you played until nine innings came and went, and, if there was no winner after nine innings, the game proceeded into extra innings. Theoretically a ball game, no matter where it was played, might endure forever. Could anyone discover a better pastime than that? Twenty-seven outs had to be charged against a side before it went down to defeat, but the game did not run against time.

Baseball also appealed to so many primal, fundamental instincts—hitting a ball, throwing a ball, catching a ball, chasing after a ball, watching a ball. Could spitting on a ball, which many pitchers were already doing, be included in that litany? And one couldn't discount the yelling, screaming, and cheering that went on on the sidelines—even the unsportsmanlike cursing-out of umpires.

And wasn't baseball, in this burgeoning democracy, which was constantly being proclaimed by its politicians, truly the most democratic of all sports? Couldn't a man playing this game, even if he was a ruffian or drunkard, win recognition for a few transient moments, in his home locality?

A few years after Matty's teenage beginnings as a pitcher, Ernest Lawrence Thayer, a San Francisco newspaperman, would write an eternal ballad to baseball called "Casey at the Bat." The inglorious Mudville club of Thayer's poem might have been Factory-ville, Mills City, Scranton, or any other town or village. Thayer's "writhing pitcher, grinding the ball into his hip," as he faced Casey, "with ten thousand eyes upon him," could surely have been young Matty, as he went about his early mound apprenticeship.

Already a strapping right-handed pitcher of six foot, one and a half inches and 196 pounds, Matty came to be known in northeastern Pennsylvania as "Husk." When he walked to the mound for his dollar, surrounded by barking dogs, slumbrous horses, and buggies full of town supporters, he bent to his task with great relish. He exhibited unusual maturity, even in his teen years, for he already understood that it wasn't necessary to strike out every batter, or use his best pitch in situations that hardly demanded it. His earnestness and intelligence, combined with his good looks (an early observer enthused over him for having a "St. Gaudens head"), strong, thick shoulders, and upright posture (even if he was somewhat knock-kneed), gave him an image that was bound to grow.

Strangely, when he started classes at Keystone, Matty's reputation as a football player even surpassed his role on the mound. His specialty was kicking, a part of the game that Matty seemed to take to naturally. The foot played an important role in the gridiron game of the late 1890s, and Matty became quite adept at drop-kicking the ball in place or on the run. There were college field-goal kickers such as Alex Moffat of Princeton, who could kick with either foot at distances of up to 70 yards. In 1898 Pat O'Dea of Wisconsin, considered the most effective kicker in the college ranks, beat Northwestern with a 62-yarder.

At Keystone Matty was hardly up to those achievements, but his drop-kicking did bring him some notice. He generally played center or in the backfield, at fullback. In addition, he was on the basketball team, which he found to be excellent exercise and an interesting sport, barely in its incipient stages.

Playing football and basketball at Keystone, along with baseball, Matty surprisingly acknowledged that he preferred football. Baseball, argued Matty, might be a far better game from the standpoint of the spectator, but he submitted that he would rather play football, if it came down to that. A reason for such a reaction might have been the fact that at Keystone he didn't take the mound until his final year, when he became captain. He had played in the outfield, which might have given him far less enjoyment and certainly less control of events.

While at Keystone Matty picked up extra cash in the summer

by playing baseball. Although his family was better off than many in the region, Matty was encouraged by his parents to earn extra money to get through school. This wouldn't have jeopardized his amateur standing, either, for in those times rules governing such matters as professionalism and amateurism were considerably more lax than they were to become. Players of ability often played semi-pro baseball under assumed names, then returned to school, where they resumed their "amateur" careers.

"I was obliged to play baseball in the summer," said Matty. The fact that he did served to change his perspective on his future life, for he had been heading either for the ministry or a career in forestry.

Offered a verbal contract of twenty dollars a month plus board if he'd pitch for Honesdale, a town of less than 5000 located near the New York border, Matty seized the opportunity. So the summer of 1898 was spent in a Honesdale uniform, as was the summer of 1899. Honesdale had a team in the Orange County League, which also included clubs from Chester, Goshen, and Port Jervis. On July 16, 1898, the Wayne *Independent* noted that "a young man named Mathewson" was signed by the Honesdale Reds. The paper also wrote that Honesdale had fared well with Matty, winning the championship in 1898. Honesdale played 48 games that season, and Matty won 8 out of 11 games that he started. The team was called the "greatest ever assembled in Honesdale." On July 18, 1899, Matty pitched his last game for Honesdale, a 14–6 triumph over Port Jervis. The Port Jervis union claimed that Matty "probably never pitched a finer game." In addition, he connected for five of Honesdale's 21 hits. Newspapers in the area agreed that he was "one of the best pitchers ever to wear a Honesdale uniform, an all-around athlete with good habits."

On July 15, 1899, before enrolling at Bucknell University and within a day or so before America's intervention in Cuba came to an end, terminating the expansionist episode known as the Spanish-American War, Matty joined Taunton in the New England League. A small industrial city some 30 miles south of Boston, Taunton was experiencing hard times not only with its economy but with its ragged ball club. Despite such deprivation on the ball-field and in its mills, Taunton's owners offered Matty $90 a month, certainly a generous stipend for such times. But Matty rarely saw any of it.

On occasion he managed to cajole the team's manager into giving him a few dollars to pay his rent at a local boarding house, but Matty seldom had much money to do anything else. The club refused to pay its players on any regular schedule, regardless of whether they were winning or losing. For the most part, Matty pitched well, against teams from Newport, Manchester, and Portland, among others, but invariably without much luck or success. The season ended for Matty with a mounting record of losses, as many as 14 against a couple of victories—but this is a speculative tally, for no official team records were kept. By Labor Day the team died a natural death, as Taunton lost its final three games to Fall River. If Matty literally shuffled home, his tail between his legs, his spirit somewhat diluted and with hardly a dime saved for his efforts, there was still a net gain on his ledger.

After all, he had learned, the hard way, and after too many indignities, that baseball was a game where someone always lost. And if it had to be you, so be it. If you wanted baseball for your life, you would have to learn to come back tomorrow, after defeat, and start all over again. If you couldn't react in such a way, baseball was a graveyard, a place where you didn't want to spend your time.

More important, it was at Taunton that Matty may have picked up the pitch—"the fadeaway"—that would become inextricably entwined with his name. Complementing his substantial repertoire of blazing fastball, changeup, and sweeping curve, the fadeaway's origin was almost as mystifying as the behavior of the pitch itself. But there is reason to believe that it was produced through Matty's association at Taunton with a southpaw pitcher named Williams, whose first name seems to have been lost to history. (Another Taunton right-hander, Vergil Lee Garvin, who had worked a few games for the Phillies in 1896, has also been credited with tipping off Matty to the fadeaway. But the legal brief for Williams appears just as strong.)

Williams had been using his own version of the fadeaway with Taunton—but with little success. He simply couldn't control it properly. Matty noted this. But that didn't mean he decided to reject it for his own arsenal.

Curiously, Matty himself wasn't as certain of the roots of the fadeaway as his idolators were. He seemed to recall that when he was at Keystone there was a fork-hander who threw a slow curve that behaved strangely to right-handed batters; it broke in sharply on a right-handed hitter and swerved away from a left-handed hitter. "It occurred to me," said Matty, "that this might be a worth-while pitch to work on. But I didn't take it too seriously at the time."

Whether Matty developed the fadeaway at Keystone or adapted it from the unwitting efforts of Williams, the pitch was never an easy one to throw. Such an unorthodox delivery took much out of a hurler's arm, for upon its release the wrist and thumb were wrenched inward toward the body—the palm would be face up, parallel to the ground. The action of the ball, as it spun, was kind of a reverse curve thrown by a right-hander. The ball would break away from a left-handed batter and break in precipitously on a right-handed batter.

Matty had described it as "a slow curve pitched with the same motion as a fast ball . . . but pitching it ten or twelve times in a game could be killing on the arm—so a wise pitcher would save it for the pinches."

Matty's pet pitch could be as unpredictable as a knuckleball or a spitter, both pitches in common use at the turn of the century. Within a few years the fadeaway won widespread recognition as Matty's property, just as Russ Ford's scuffed-up "emery ball," Ed Walsh's "spitter," and Eddie Plank's "crossfire" were always associated with those pitchers.

It was never reported that anyone ever spied Matty walking around in his prime, with his pitching palm turned outward. But many years later another Giants pitcher, the talented lefthander Carl Hubbell, actually did hang his arm in precisely that way. Hubbell's own version of the fadeaway, which had taken on the name of "screwball," had literally twisted his palm permanently around; such disfiguring had not happened to Matty.

3

" 'RAY, BUCKNELL!"

IN the fall of 1898 the 18-year-old Christy entered
Bucknell University, along with 71 other fresh-
men wearing their blue beanies. The school had never before seen
such a large contingent of first-year students, and Matty, as class
historian, was moved to write in *L'Agenda* that "on a sunny September morn the massive portals of old Bucknell were swung inward by an energetic Freshman class . . ."

The Susquehanna River runs alongside Bucknell through Lewisburg, but has been known to overflow angrily at flood times. A
red brick Underground Railroad building, a symbol of Lewisburg's
role during the Civil War (four Bucknell students gave their lives
for the Union cause), still stands. Gone, however, is Bucknell's
Loomis Field, where Matty made his first appearances as a college
pitcher and football player.

Bucknell was founded in 1846 on 73 acres of farmland. Its first
campus was little more than a common overgrown woodlot but
the students worked to clear out the underbrush. Eventually, they
turned it into a fine grove. At the first college commencement in
1851 seven students received their diplomas from James Buchanan,
a member of the University's Board of Curators. Buchanan, a native of Mercersburg, Pennsylvania, would become the fifteenth
President of the United States, immediately preceding Abraham
Lincoln. His presidency was characterized mainly by his timidity
on the slavery issue.

A journey from Factoryville to Lewisburg in 1898, by unheated train, could take almost half a day. (From Philadelphia to Lewisburg, by stage coach, canal boat, and train, could take almost twice that long.) But Factoryville seemed more than a world away from the stately columns, antebellum Federal architecture, and Greek Revival buildings on the growing campus.

Bucknell was already fielding competitive teams in its major sports of football, baseball, and basketball in 1898. The football team, first organized in 1883, was coached by George Jennings in Matty's freshman year, then George Hoskins took over in 1899. The team's football schedule included many colleges from the area, including Dickinson, Penn, and Penn State, but Bucknell, still a relatively small school lacking the prestige of Yale, Harvard, Columbia, or Princeton, was also reaching out to play Army, Navy, and Cornell.

Few college men had turned to professional baseball before or during Matty's years at Bucknell. Cap Anson had had a year at Notre Dame; Eddie Plank was attending Gettysburg College; Frank Chance had gone to Washington; Fred Tenney graduated from Brown; Jimmy Archer had been to St. Michael's in Montreal; and John Montgomery Ward completed Columbia Law School. But these men were rarities in the coarse, brawling world of baseball.

However, while Matty pursued his baseball career at Honesdale and Taunton, he also accepted the challenge of the classroom. He was a student who soon made a mark for himself at Bucknell, showing he could play, think, write, and attend classes. He embarked on a typical classical education at Bucknell, full of Latin and mathematics courses, tried his hand at dramatics and poetry, was active in several literary societies, including Euepia, was president of the freshman class, played bass horn in the University band, sang in the Glee Club, was a member of Phi Gamma Delta fraternity and also of Theta Delta Tau, an honorary leadership society for men.

Although athletes were expected to perform their obligations in the classroom in those times, Matty was in every way a rara avis, a conspicuous over-achiever. He even found time, while proudly wearing the Orange and Blue of Bucknell in three sports, to actively court young women. One such person, Louise Albright, who lived in Muncy, was bashful but attractive. Friends of Matty remarked how he delighted in seeing Louise blush. There was also a time when he proposed marriage to Louise while still at Bucknell. Instead of accepting Christy's offer, Louise introduced Matty to her cousin Jane Stoughton, who lived in Buffalo Valley and shared living quarters with her.

Matty appeared to have some appreciation of his own reputation and paradigmatic behavior. As class historian he once wrote "on the athletic teams and in the classroom are to be found students who are upholding the honor of the school . . . for greater honor no man could ask . . ." Such prideful, flowery language would be too much to expect from the money-driven athletes of the 1990s. But it must be recalled that Matty matured in an age when unsportsmanlike habits were sneered at as "muckerism"; his was a college generation that was brought up on Frank Merriwell, Tom Brown, and even Sir Galahad, a "heady wine," indeed, wrote author John Davies. School spirit was prevalent.

Devotion to his fellows and to the institution that he felt privileged to attend were molded deep into Matty's character. Whatever imperfections there may have been in Matty's makeup remained well hidden from his legion of admirers at Bucknell. The student paper constantly searched for adjectives to describe Matty's exploits on the athletic field. However, a classmate, Frank Stanton, who became a lawyer in Cleveland, tried to put this mesmerizing campus icon in some perspective.

"There were, indeed, a few uncomplimentary memories that I have of Matty," Stanton wrote some years after he departed Bucknell. "I choose not to enlarge on some of them. He was, after all, way above average as a student and Christian gentleman . . . However, when I played alongside him I didn't take special note of him because I never knew he would wind up as baseball's greatest pitcher . . . I found he was a bit careless in playing deep shortstop and throwing them over to first base before he was ready. Once old Professor Blackwell, our Latin professor, tried to get after him and chase him off the field. Rockwell recognized the danger Matty was running in this devotion to athletics."

Stanton also recalled that Matty was dubbed by some "the infant phenomenon," while others preferred calling him "rubber leg." Some referred to him as "YMCA," an allusion to his religious upbringing. All of these nicknames seem to represent good-natured needling on the part of his peers, although they may have also been directed at a smugness that some detected.

When Matty went out for football in his freshman year at Bucknell the game had won a reputation for being extra hazardous. There was an undue emphasis on smashing, battering plays; flying wedges; roughing the kicker with impunity; infrequent substitutions; and excessive piling-on. There were some periodic efforts to eliminate the dangers from the game, but, aside from reduction of playing time from 95 to 70 minutes (with 35-minute halves) and the addition of a third official to spot more overt violations of the rules, little had been accomplished to mitigate the savagery of the game. (It wasn't until 1906, after many colleges, including Northwestern, Columbia, Union, and Stanford, temporarily abolished football, that the forward pass was legalized, thus somewhat minimizing the brute force aspect of football. Needless to say, Matty probably would have been a superb passer, with his pin-point pitching control. Unfortunately, his college years of playing preceded these changes in technique and attitude.)

In 1898 Bucknell played nine games, beating Wyoming Seminary and Swarthmore, splitting two games with Maryland AC, losing to Navy, Buffalo, Lafayette, and Penn State, and tying Franklin & Marshall. Matty's season point totals were two touchdowns and a single field goal, drop-kicked against F & M, the first of his career.

The next year Matty truly blossomed as runner, punter, and kicker. Paced by his seven touchdowns and six field goals, Bucknell ended up winning five games, including victories over Lehigh and Susquehanna. His 65-yard run through the entire Susquehanna team was his best piece of ball-carrying.

Penn had lost only to Harvard in 1899, having amassed large point totals against almost everyone. In three previous years Penn dropped only one game, while holding Bucknell to zero. With the Penn game approaching, Bucknell's Coach Hoskins, not only eager to break the monotony of continual defeat but also determined to stimulate scoring, offered a raincoat as prize to the first player who could score against The Big Red. The second man to score would get a pair of shoes.

By his own admission, Matty played the game of his life against Penn. Although Penn won, 47–10, at the half they led only 11–10. The ten Bucknell points were two "pretty" field goals kicked by Matty. So, while adding to his limited wardrobe, Matty also proved another point: he was at his best when the chips were down.

What happened to Bucknell in the second half was amusingly described by Matty, who wrote of the event: "The ten points at the half was as good as defeat in Penn's eyes. So, at intermission their coaches got busy, and with the use of much persuasion and abuse of the English language, so wrought upon the players that we nearly got killed in the second half . . . Penn that year had two tackles who were as heavy and tough as I've ever seen. I played fullback and it was part of my job to back up the line. I did this to the best of my ability but I first had one, then the other, of these huskies butting full tilt into me, until I thought my shoulders would be pried loose from my backbone. Football isn't exactly a parlor game these days . . . it's great exercise. But before the second half was over, I thought I had amply earned the raincoat and shoes."

As a result of Matty's drop-kicking against Penn and a 40-yarder against Lehigh that beat the Engineers 5–0, he won instant recognition from Walter Camp. The arbiter of All-America selections, Camp, a former half back at Yale in 1876—and something of a drop-kicking expert himself—insisted Christy was the best drop-kicker he'd ever seen. Two interested observers of Matty's field goals against Penn were Connie Mack and Ed Barrow. The latter was then in charge of the food and program concessions at Franklin Field, where Penn played its games. In later years he became an astute judge of baseball talent as general manager of the Yankees.

But transcending Matty's performance against Penn, and far more of an incentive than shoes and a raincoat, was the presence in the stands that day of John Smith, the manager of the Norfolk baseball club in the Virginia League.

Smith, a part-time pitcher going under the quaint name of "Phenom," had hurled in the New England League, where Matty had spent a summer. Smith was thus familiar with Christy's nondescript record at that watering spot. Nevertheless, since his Norfolk team was badly in need of pitching help, he approached Matty before the Penn game. He wanted to know if Matty would be interested in joining Norfolk for the summer of 1900. Matty told him that his mind was more occupied at that moment with the muscular Penn team. "Talk to me after the game," he said to Phenom. When the game was over, Phenom kept the date with Matty. "You played quite a game against that bunch," he said, "a mighty good game. While I sat there watching you, I thought it over and I've decided to offer you $90 a month, instead of $80."

What possible connection accurate drop-kicking might have had with the increase of ten dollars, Smith didn't make clear. But Matty, sorely in need of money after the debacle with Taunton, accepted Smith's proposal. A contract was signed on October 4, 1900, for Matty's services with the Norfolk club, from May through the seventh day of September. Phenom Smith was a good judge of ballplayers—but he couldn't spell. "Ninty" was spelled that way in the contract.

The Virginia League represented a higher order of competence than the New England League, so Matty knew he had his work cut out for him. Curiously, in his several years of college baseball Matty had, from time to time, suffered some horrendous beatings. Gettysburg, for example, collected 12 runs from him; Villanova once got to him for 15 runs; and in a relief appearance against a local YMCA team one afternoon Matty was reached for eight runs. There may have been some reason for this, other than the shortcomings of Matty's fielders, for Matty possessed a rather unusual attitude toward pitching. Finding himself comfortably ahead in a ball game, he would often challenge the opposition to hit his softest pitches. There was never, even at this early stage of his career, any perfectionist madness in him. Hitters were never up there to be obliterated. They were only to be induced to make out, with the help, of course, of Matty's defense. As things sometimes turned out at Bucknell, Matty may have suspected, wrongly, that his infielders and outfielders were more up to doing the job than they turned out to be.

In his first game in a Norfolk uniform Matty beat Portsmouth 6–5, despite some unexpected control difficulties. But from there on, 1900 turned out to be a transforming year at Norfolk, for he kept mowing down teams with an assortment of pitches only rarely viewed in a 20-year-old. Even without radio and television to spread the word, Virginians came from far and wide to watch this prepossessing young man work. They arrived on foot, by wagon, horseback, or railroad from Virginia Beach, Newport News, Williamsburg, and Richmond. As Matty's victories mounted, so did the admiring crowds increase. By midsummer he had reached an astonishing total of 20 victories, while losing only twice. One of his victories was a no-hitter against Hampton, in which only one man reached base on a walk. Phenom Smith decided it was so beneficial to have Matty on his side that he put him in the outfield when he wasn't pitching. In 46 games Matty batted .289, a very respectable average for a pitcher. Thus, it became only a question of time before he'd be snapped up by one of several big-league scouts scouring the area for budding heroes.

As the Norfolk team moved from place to place in its drive for the league's pennant, Matty, a rare collegian with somewhat standoffish manners, spent his time in a smoky railroad car among his teammates. The air would get so suffocatingly thick with cigar and cigarette smoke that Matty suggested that you "could plow furrows in it with a baseball bat." Under such conditions, though he had never smoked or touched liquor before, Matty took up cigars for the first time, almost in self-defense. He would smoke until it made him sick, then try to sleep it off.

Just as he had distinguished himself on Loomis Field from the moment he'd entered Bucknell, Matty continued to do well in the classroom. In his freshman year he had earned nothing less than 90 in any course that he took. His highs were 96 in German and French, 94 in Tacitus, 93 in Cicero's de Senectute, 90 in Livy, and 90 in Analytic Geometry. In his sophomore year he got 90 in Rhetoric, 93 in Horace, 96 in Analytic Chemistry, and 90 in French. By his junior year, when it is reasonable to assume that he was distracted by transient thoughts of big-league contracts and the siren lure of faraway places, he sunk to a 75 in Geology, although still managing to get 91 in Embryology and 90 in Psychology. Indeed, he was almost as gifted in the classroom as he was outside of it.

However, notwithstanding his intellectual accomplishments, after his junior year Matty decided to leave Bucknell, where his scholarship covered most of his tuition. By so doing, he became Bucknell's most famous dropout.

4

WITH THE GIANTS

MATTY'S time had been well spent under the aegis of Phenom Smith. On June 26, 1900, the owner of the Norfolk club, William M. Hannan, suitably impressed with Matty's pitching, wrote a letter to Andrew Freedman, owner of the New York Giants. "It would be worth the trip to look Mathewson over," Hannan wrote. He added that the young pitcher had the potential for greatness, and "could be secured at a very reasonable figure," considering the woeful condition of the Virginia League at that moment.

Propelled by such endorsements, Matty's world among the towns and villages of New England and Virginia was about to end, although he couldn't be certain where he would wind up in a baseball universe undergoing wrenching changes.

Under such dynamic leaders as Byron Bancroft "Ban" Johnson and Connie Mack, a new major league was well along in the development stage. In 1893 Johnson, a former Cincinnati sportswriter, had launched the Western League—but his ambitions went far beyond that. In 1896 he hired Mack, whose frame and name (McGillicuddy) were as long as a handball court, to take over the Western League's Milwaukee franchise, thus starting a relationship that would bring about the founding of the American League in 1901.

In structuring an aggressive organization to be known as the Philadelphia Athletics, Mack would conduct crafty raids of talent, while Ben Shibe, a wealthy manufacturer of baseball equipment, was prepared to put up the money to assure the building of a park that would bear his name. Mack proceeded to dip into the pool of available players from the National League and also from college campuses, a repository of personnel that hitherto had remained virtually untapped. Napoleon Lajoie jumped from the Phillies to the Athletics; Lave Cross did the same thing. Left-hander Eddie Plank was signed out of Gettysburg College. Mike Powers came over from Holy Cross to catch, and Socks Sebold joined the Athletics' outfield from Cincinnati. The eccentric Rube Waddell, a southpaw with a penchant for chasing fires and young ladies, left the Cubs to become Mack's chief pitcher.

Under the circumstances, it was a certainty that Mack would cast longing eyes at Matty—and he did. Matty already had word from Andrew Freedman that the Giants wanted him. Cincinnati was also eager to acquire his services. In the situation, Norfolk's front office made clear to Matty that they'd be willing to let him make his own choice.

For a raw young man out of Factoryville, it wasn't an easy decision to make. He had to weigh the fact that Mack had assembled a formidable pitching staff, which might be hard for him to break into, against the reality of going to a restless, bustling New York, with its swells and toughs, and its newfound jaunty, raffish image. New York hardly seemed a likely place for such a reserved person. However, the untried pitcher finally made up his mind: he would cast his lot at the Polo Grounds, home of the Giants since 1891. "I thought I'd have a better chance of getting a good workout with the inferior pitching staff of the New York team," is how Matty rationalized his decision.

Freedman's reputation as a sleazy Tammany Hall manipulator might have been enough to deter a less intelligent young man. In many circles Freedman, a real estate speculator and bondsman, was regarded as someone to avoid in any business dealings. He was known to have a crazy streak of autocracy, which encouraged him to say things like, "The German Army, the Catholic Church and Standard Oil of New Jersey are the only great organizations left in the world." Criticism followed him wherever he trod. A bizarre figure, reputed to be overbearing, ill-tempered, and capricious, Freedman in 1895 had bought controlling interest of the Giants from John Day. The team was in turmoil ever since. Managerial changes under Freedman occurred more swiftly than shifts among French cabinet ministers—there were 15 in six years. Cap Anson lasted 22 games as manager in 1898, and Amos Rusie, possibly the possessor of the most overpowering fastball in the game, argued bitterly with Freedman over $200, then sat out a whole season in protest.

The reaction to Freedman also contained a sharp undercurrent of anti-Semitism, to which he invariably was quick to react, often with shouts and fisticuffs. (Even among Jews he was deprecated as a "gonif," or cheap thief.) But those were times when racial insults went hand in glove with rowdyism, each being accepted as routine concomitants of the game. Few were prepared to argue Freedman's case, even if they had the desire to do so.

Freedman agreed to pay Norfolk $1500 for Matty's contract. Within a few days Matty reported to the Polo Grounds, a structure in the north Harlem section of Manhattan, on Eighth Avenue between 157th and 159th streets. The park, planted beneath the lee of Coogan's Bluff, resembled a vast horseshoe. It was probably the only park in the world that a fan entered by walking downhill. In the years to come, with the help of the new pitcher in town, the Polo Grounds would become the site of some of baseball's most memorable and controversial episodes. Next to Yankee Stadium, which would spring up across the Harlem River in 1923, the Polo Grounds rates consideration as baseball's most hallowed structure.

When Matty arrived in New York on a lovely July afternoon in 1900, he joined a team of less than modest abilities. The personnel of the club reminded one of the statement the Duke of Wellington uttered in 1815 about his troops at Waterloo: "They may not frighten the enemy. But, gad, sir, they frighten me." The Giants, in 1898, had been "good" enough to finish tenth in a twelve-club league.

Prior to Matty's arrival Freedman had played his usual game of musical chairs with his managers. Buck Ewing, the catcher, was in charge of the club for 62 games, then was fired. He was replaced with shortstop George Davis, who had been Freedman's first pilot with the Giants in 1895. A man of integrity, Davis could also hit, batting over .300 in nine straight seasons with the Giants. However, he didn't seem to have enough sense to avoid the managerial job with the Giants.

Among Davis's janissaries on the Giants were: Piano Legs Charlie Hickman, holder of the all-time record for errors by a third baseman, with 91 in 1900; Dirty Jack Doyle, a first baseman who played several positions, none of them too well; Kid Gleason, at second base, in the future known mainly as the ill-treated manager of the Chicago Black Sox of 1919; Win Mercer, a 140-pound pitcher, who ended his life by taking poison a few years later; Doughnut Bill Carrick, a right-handed loser of 26 games in 1899 and 22 in 1900; George Van Haltren, as graceful an outfielder as you could find on such a team; and Frank Bowerman, the first major-league catcher to receive Matty's pitches.

In view of how Freedman had mishandled his club in the past it was a minor miracle that he'd been attracted to Matty. But Davis's first look at Matty convinced him that Freedman hadn't made another of his egregious mistakes. The switch-hitting Davis took batting practice against Matty, requesting that Matty throw his best pitches at him. The pitcher threw with ease and balance, driving straight at the plate with power, and finishing bent forward, on his toes, his feet spread apart, set to make a fielding play. Davis was quick to observe this youthful finesse. When Matty unleashed his fastball, Davis approved of it. But he wasn't so accepting of Matty's roundhouse curve, which failed to fool the manager.

"Anything else you throw?" asked Davis.

"I have something I call my 'freak ball,' " said Matty, with a touch of modesty.

"Let's see it, then," said Davis, taking a toehold, this time from the right side of the plate.

Matty threw half a dozen or so of the "freak ball" pitches. Each time Davis, even with his good batting eye, had trouble making solid contact.

"That's a good pitch, son," said Davis, who was ten years older than Matty. "Keep throwing it and learn to control it. It sort of fades away." To Davis's credit, he'd awarded a name to a pitch destined to be the most wickedly successful in history.

Matty threw his first official pitch for the Giants on July 18, coming into a game that was already lost, against Brooklyn. He faced a cast of mighty hitters such as Hughey Jennings, Fielder Jones, Wee Willie Keeler, Bill Dahlen, and Jimmy Sheckard, and fared poorly, yielding a batch of runs. In still another appearance he faced John McGraw, at third base that day for St. Louis (after coming over from Baltimore). It was the first social encounter between the two men—but it wouldn't be the last. In his first two appearances for the Giants the newspapers recorded his name as "Matthews." It was not until his third game, in relief, that his name appeared as Mathewson.

Used infrequently in the final weeks of the season, Matty didn't seem prepared for the big time. He worked in five games, lost three, with no victories, and gave up 35 hits in 30 innings. Worse yet, he distributed 14 walks to the opposition, proof that he hadn't gotten his pitches under control.

Such a performance did little to mellow Freedman, who lost precious little time returning Matty to Norfolk. On the surface Freedman appeared not to care in the least what happened to his pitcher. But things are seldom what they seem. Though Freedman had permitted Matty, in despair, to drift away, he also instructed Cincinnati to put in a bid for him. Without putting Matty on notice about their plans, Cincinnati did exactly that, offering $100 to draft the pitcher.

Convinced he was a failure, Matty was prepared to return to Bucknell, the ministry, forestry, or anything else his parents may have adjudged would be best for him under the circumstances. Instead, once again the long, thin fingers of Mack, still on the prowl for players, reached out for Matty, offering him $1500 to sign with the Athletics. Fond of college ballplayers, Mack was intent on corraling still one more of the breed. In such a dog-eat-dog environment there were few ethical requirements that had been codified concerning jumping ballplayers and scheming owners; no established Marquis of Queensbury rules had ever been invoked.

Owing money for books and other items at Bucknell, and now speculating about finishing his education, Matty screwed up his courage and asked Mack for an extra fifty dollars. At the same time, the plot had thickened, for in as much time as it would take to yell "Cincinnati," the Reds had traded Matty back to the Giants for Amos Rusie, the so-called Hoosier Thunderbolt.

Believing he was still the property of the Athletics, notwithstanding the machinations in the back room between the Giants and the Reds, Matty was called on the carpet by Freedman. The Giants' owner demanded that Matty come at once to New York to explain why he was traitorously selling out to the American League, which he insisted wouldn't last longer than a few months. Every player who dared to sign on with the American League, railed Freedman, would be blacklisted—no small threat to young men like Matty. Furthermore, Matty was brusquely informed, he was again the property of the Giants. If he didn't put on his uniform in New York, he wouldn't play for anybody else was the unsubtle warning. Freedman, a litigious man, even threatened Matty with a lawsuit.

"I didn't want to go back on my word with Mr. Mack," Matty explained years later, "and I told Mr. Freedman that I had gotten a fifty-dollar advance from the Athletics. But he wouldn't hear of that. I asked Mr. Freedman if he'd return the money to Mr. Mack and he said he would. But he never did. It ended up that I refunded the money myself, after I received enough salary from the Giants."

What Matty had failed to comprehend were the backroom shenanigans transpiring between Freedman and John T. Brush, the owner of the Cincinnati Reds. Brush, one of the organizers of the original Indianapolis club in the National League and also owner of a large Indianapolis department store, had been secretly arranging to buy the Giants from Freedman. (As long ago as 1888 he had sponsored a "classification rule" for players during a period of great turmoil over player salaries. The rule graded players A, B, C, D, and E, fixing salaries accordingly from $1500 to $2500. Needless to say, such a system caused great player resentment.) With such a deal with the Giants in the offing, he didn't want any trouble waiting for him in New York from a recalcitrant Amos Rusie.

The big farmer had won over thirty games on three occasions for the Giants, before the pitcher's mound was moved back to a distance of 60 feet, six inches from home plate. But due to skirmishes over pay with Freedman, Rusie hadn't pitched for the Giants for two years. With Rusie moving to Cincinnati, Brush knew that he wouldn't be forced to put up with the pitcher's balkiness in New York. It's hard to believe that Brush envisioned the future splendors of Matty on the mound. If he had, his would have been the most sensitive snout among all of baseball's bird dogs. Returning to the Giants, as he did, Matty was the unwitting participant in a squeeze play conducted between two scoundrels. Such corrupt negotiations were the price to be paid for baseball's version of uninhibited capitalism, operating at its most devious level.

It turned out that New York got much the better of the bargain, although few could have suspected it at the time. Rusie simply was a burnt-out case; he'd thrown one too many fast balls. He failed to win a single game for Cincinnati in 1901, thus bringing his career to an aching end.

Meanwhile, by midsummer Matty had shown he could work his way through most baseball lineups with consummate ease. The college kid, only 21, got his first National League victory on April 26, against Brooklyn, in a 5–3 win over Bill Donovan. Some 10,000 fans sat in a chilly Polo Grounds, probably the largest assemblage Matty had ever pitched in front of. The Brooklyn club, much the same one that had thrashed Matty handily the previous summer, couldn't do much with him, a sure harbinger for the rest of the league.

Appearing in regular turn from then on, Matty won his first

eight games, half of them without giving up a run. He had three shutouts in a row. When he went for his ninth consecutive win he was edged out by St. Louis, 1–0. But he redeemed himself against St. Louis not too many days later when on July 15 he pitched a 5–0 no-hitter against the Cardinals in the home bailiwick of the St. Louis team, before 5000 fans. At the end of the game the fans were rooting for him to complete the job. "Thousands surveyed Mathewson as he walked to the bench and gathered his possessions and hundreds gave him an extra cheer, with a rousing 'tiger' added as he climbed into the bus," said the St. Louis newspapers. The game, recognized as the "first no-hit game of the modern era," was a delight to watch. Invariably the first pitch was a strike, usually followed by a second. The rhythm and motion had become almost balletic, the high kick was hypnotic, as Matty swept through the St. Louis lineup. Willie Sudhoff, the tiny Cardinal lefty, never had a chance that afternoon. The Giants made one error, by George Van Haltren, who let a ball drop off his glove in center field, in the bottom of the eighth inning. Showing no discomfiture, Matty retired the next two batters easily. Back in the dugout he reassuringly patted Van Haltren on the back, the type of sportsmanlike gesture that would soon win Matty his reputation as a "grand guy" and "wonderful man," words that actually came out of the mouths of his own teammates. How rare it was to encounter a man playing this game who reacted in such a way to miscues by men playing behind him.

By the end of 1901 Matty had won 20 games and lost 17, as he completed 36 of his 38 starts. The latter statistic would be unheard-of today, when there are so many middle inning specialists and late-inning relievers on a team's roster. But in 1901 many pitchers managed to finish what they started, even if they were being bumped around a bit. Nevertheless, Matty's total of complete games that season was the third best in the National League. He had an earned run average of 1.99, while distributing an average of two walks a game. Considering how bad the seventh-place Giants were, as they lost 85 games, while winning only 52, Matty stood out to such an extent that he actually acknowledged that he "had an unusually good record; in all, I made quite a reputation as a young pitcher of promise."

Though some of Matty's teammates exhibited resentment toward this college man who was, perhaps, too aristocratic for their coarse tastes, others suggested to him that he was entitled to ask Freedman for more than the $1500 a year he was getting. There could have been self-interest here, for if Matty's salary were raised they may have figured a chain reaction would set in which would benefit all of them. However, Freedman's past record revealed no such flaw of ownerly compassion. (It's interesting to note, however, that when the bachelor Freedman died in 1915, he left his entire estate to charity, with part of his fortune being used to build a home for indigent millionaires!)

In support of their plea, Matty's teammates pointed to the fact that more fans than ever were coming out to see the team on those days that Matty was scheduled to pitch. They told him that for the first time in years the team was making money, although it is clear not one of them had access to Freedman's bookkeeping.

"My salary of $1500 seemed large to me," said Matty, "but they insisted that I shake down Freedman for a good increase."

Finally, Matty came to the reluctant conclusion that he was being badly treated by Freedman. Agreeing to consult Freedman on the matter, he realized the owner was not a likely candidate to yield under such pressure. Previously, when Freedman had been badgered by other owners to get out of baseball, he had refused to be intimidated by them. So it seemed unlikely that an individual player like Matty could do the trick. However, when Matty spoke up in Freedman's office, he was astoundingly rewarded with two new suits of clothes, "which I needed and which was a substantial item, from my point of view." In addition, Freedman promised Matty a $500 bonus. When a future contract came under discussion, Matty was primed to ask for $5000, the sum that other players had suggested that he ask for.

"When I opened my mouth to say $5000, the words just refused to come," said Matty. "I felt in my soul that no such a sum of money existed. Gripping my arms on the chair for support, I said in as firm a tone as I could command: $3500."

Freedman probably had visions of $5000 as a demand, for he immediately called for one of his clerks to bring him a contract form. Promptly he signed it—for $3500. With such a contract under his belt, Matty couldn't flirt any longer with the prospect of returning to Bucknell to get his degree. He was in for the duration as a baseball man, for better or worse.

During the winter of 1901 Matty's arm felt weary, a fact that he hadn't been willing to reveal to Freedman. His 336 innings pitched at the age of 21 had obviously taken their toll. "Like most young pitchers," he later explained, "I invariably used all the strength that I had, regardless of the score or the stage of the game. I was haunted by the idea that the arm would never get into shape again." (In the future, because of the lesson he'd learned, Matty would hoard his strength, rarely going all out, except when he had to, in the clinch.)

As the 1902 season approached, players, owners, and managers in both leagues became more transient than jumping beans. The bidding wars saw salaries doubled and tripled; loyalty to a team or organization was virtually non-existent. The Giants began the campaign with over a dozen new players, none of them of great distinction. One newspaperman referred to them as "the rankest apology for a first-class team ever imposed on a major league city."

As expected, and true to past form, Freedman made his move. Over the winter, having fired manager Davis, he hired Pittsburgh second baseman George Smith to take over as playing manager. Also added to the front office was Horace Fogel, whose credentials included managing the Indianapolis club into eighth place 15 years before. Fogel followed that personal achievement by becoming president of the Philadelphia franchise. Nobody, including Freedman, knew precisely what Fogel had been hired to do, although he seemed to be adept at second-guessing from the bench. The players concluded that they were being managed by both men, proving two heads could be infinitely worse than one.

Little more than a directionless rabble, the Giants kept on losing and whining. When Dummy Taylor, a deaf-mute right-hander from Oskaloosa, Kansas, jumped to Cleveland, the team was left with only one solid pitcher, Matty.

As the team sank to a dismal last, Fogel was anointed by Freedman as sole manager, with Smith staying on the roster as a player. Such chaos and near-anarchy even rubbed off on the usually unassailable Matty.

Several members of the club, now angry about Matty's salary and the fact he wasn't winning regularly (he registered a 13–18 mark during the year, despite eight shutouts), urged Fogel to get him off the pitcher's mound and into the outfield. That was tantamount to recruiting John L. Sullivan to desert the saloons and lead the choir. Heeding such wisdom, Fogel put Matty on first base, in the outfield, and at shortstop, for half a dozen games. The leaders of the "revolt" threw poorly to Matty at first, causing him to be pulled off the bag or to be sent embarrassingly into the dirt scrambling for their tosses. The experiment reaped the expected result. It failed, and Matty was returned to the pitcher's box where he belonged. The only thing that can be remarked about Fogel's misuse of Matty was that, as usual, Matty put forth his best efforts.

When the Giants returned home from a disastrous western trip of three victories and 12 losses, even the pained editorial writers took notice. It was the lowest point in the Giants' history, and the wrathful Freedman knew something had to be done. Losers of 27 out of 32 games, the club appeared capable of dropping right through the bottom of the league.

For all of his flaws, Freedman, now taken to barring critical writers from the clubhouse, always had his ears to the ground. Also he appeared to have lost his enthusiasm for baseball. In June he learned that all wasn't well with John McGraw, Baltimore's manager. An ongoing dispute between McGraw and Ban Johnson, the president of the American League, gave Freedman the notion that possibly McGraw could be pried loose from his moorings in Baltimore, where he had managed for the past three years and had gained recognition as one of baseball's original thinkers. For a decade the runty McGraw had scrapped, shouted, and schemed his way into the hearts of Baltimoreans. At the same time he had antagonized that part of baseball's world that opposed him on the field. One day he would spit in an umpire's face, the next he'd have to be dragged, kicking and screaming, off an enemy player's back. Such behavior didn't sit well with Johnson, who constantly moralized about "clean baseball" and its merits.

Freedman encouraged Brush, who held stock in the Giants for many years (even while he owned the Reds, in a blatant conflict of interest that didn't seem to bother anybody), to set up a secret meeting with McGraw in Indianapolis. The fact that Brush also shared an intense distaste for Johnson, going back to the time the latter had written caustically about him when he was a sportswriter for Cincinnati's *Commercial Gazette,* added to the mutuality of interest between Freedman and himself.

Brush went along with the plan, even insisting that McGraw arrive in the city by train at dawn so that no prying eyes of the press would be around to report on the event. A deal was settled in several hours of conversation, and McGraw returned at once to Baltimore.

The next move was up to Freedman, and he seized the moment. He sent his club secretary to Baltimore to invite McGraw to New York for another conference. McGraw wasted little time in accepting the invitation. When the two men met, Freedman was prepared to offer McGraw almost everything except suzerainty over the Polo Grounds itself.

"I want you as the manager," said Freedman, "and you'll have absolute control." Freedman garnished the offer by telling McGraw he could also own the concessions. Since McGraw was an old pal of Harry Stevens, who had control of the Giants' concessions for many years, he told Freedman he didn't want to cut into Stevens's livelihood.

Okay, countered Freedman, then it'll only be the managership of the Giants. But he threw in another lagniappe, by averring that he was soon going to sell the club to Brush. That served to convince McGraw to make the move, even though one further detail remained to be ironed out—the matter of McGraw's contract with the Baltimore club.

The Orioles owed McGraw some $7000, money that McGraw had advanced to pay player salaries at a time when the once-mighty Baltimore franchise was floundering. Now it was McGraw's ploy to ask for his money back, knowing full well that the Baltimore exchequer was drier than the Sahara. Since Baltimore was incapable of paying him, McGraw then requested to be released from his contract. The club granted his request.

McGraw had owned a half-interest in the popular Diamond Cafe in Baltimore; his old Oriole teammate, Wilbert Robinson, owned the other half. He sold off his interest to Robinson. While Johnson denounced McGraw as a traitor to the American League, the expatriate Oriole then engaged in a vicious disassembling of the Baltimore roster. Roger Bresnahan, commonly conceded to be the premier catcher in baseball; Joe McGinnity, who would come to be known as an Iron Man pitcher; Dan McGann, a first baseman who was scheduled to relieve Matty of any further responsibility as an infielder; and Steve Brodie, an outfielder, were all persuaded to pick up their gloves and leave Baltimore. "This was the most successful raid on the city of Baltimore since the War of 1812," wrote author Noel Hynd of McGraw's guerilla tactics.

The stage was set for McGraw to parade into New York in triumph, where he would sign a four-year contract to manage the Giants at $11,000 a year, certainly a princely sum for those times. (The average player salary in 1900 was scarcely more than $2500, with stars receiving about $5000). McGraw also promised to be a player as well as manager, a program that he had followed in Baltimore.

Proudly displaying his contract, McGraw issued an uncompromising public insult to Ban Johnson and the Baltimore owners. For the benefit of excited New Yorkers he added that though the Giants "may be out of it this year, they are going to be a club to watch in the future."

When McGraw took charge of the Giants on July 17, they were over 30 games behind the front-running Pittsburgh Pirates and had already dropped 50 games. The new regime was pressed to act fast— and that's just what McGraw did. He asked Freedman for a list of all the Giant players. There were 23 names on it. Within minutes McGraw had rudely scratched off nine names with his pencil. "These guys can be released," said McGraw. Freedman let out a howl. He reminded McGraw that these players had cost him $14,000. But McGraw was unrelenting. "If you keep them, it'll cost you more," he growled. The nine players disappeared from view in short order.

The second act on the McGraw agenda was to immediately reinstate Christopher Mathewson to his rightful place on the pitcher's mound. Fogel's experiment, mocked McGraw, was "sheer insanity . . . any man who did that should be locked up." Fogel didn't go to prison, but he suffered his release within days. John J. McGraw was indeed in "absolute control" of the Giants.

Much despised as he was, Freedman, by coaxing McGraw to New York, had brought New Yorkers, at long last, a brand of baseball they thought they deserved.

5

MATTY AND
LITTLE NAPOLEON

THE near-paranoid John Joseph McGraw, as nasty in victory as in defeat, marched across a decade of Baltimore glories, like an aggrieved bantam cock. Now, at last, he had come to New York with a demonic desire to win.

McGraw was born in poverty on April 7, 1873, in the little Finger Lake town of Truxton, New York, fifteen miles from Syracuse. His father, John, a native of Ireland and a railroad maintenance man, had fought in the Civil War. When McGraw was 12 years old his mother, sister, two brothers, and a 13-year-old stepsister all died in a diphtheria epidemic. It was a bewildering succession of events that numbed the head of the family and had a harsh impact on the youthful John. It isn't hard to imagine how these deaths, so closely connected to him, contributed to the development of McGraw's character and complex personality.

Adding to father John's concerns was the fact that his scrawny son cared more about playing baseball than he did about the Irish national game of hurling. Yet the only way out of the hard-scrabble Cattaraugus County farm country was baseball—and the young McGraw knew that. By the time he was 16, McGraw had taught himself to swing with a shortened grip, giving him surprising accuracy from the left side of the plate. He also showed increasing evidence of his pugnacity: he never ducked a brawl, regardless of how large the enemy or perceived enemy happened to be. "From the start McGraw attracted trouble the way tall buildings attract lightning," wrote Tom Meany.

In 1890 McGraw got his first job in professional baseball with Olean in the New York-Pennsylvania League as a third baseman. He had started out as a pitcher but his skills at the plate caused his removal to the infield. The next year he played at Wellsville, New York, getting on base so frequently that he appeared to be permanently stationed there. With the Wellsville club he joined a barnstorming trip to Havana, Cuba, where the fans took to his bellicosity and aggressiveness. They nicknamed him, oddly, "Yellow Monkey," which didn't please him very much. But for the rest of his life he had a sincere affection for the Cuban people, though they existed in a world of tropical foliage and brilliant sun, so foreign to his own rural upbringing.

McGraw's next venue was in Ocala, Florida, where he played for board, shaving, and washing expenses, plus one cigar a week. In Cedar Rapids, Iowa, the following year, he found the Illinois-Iowa League to be a hotbed of baseball interest. As Cedar Rapids' regular shortstop, he attracted attention all the way across the country to Baltimore. The Baltimore manager, Bill Barnie, a former stockbroker, had heard about the exploits of the teenage 120-pounder from a Cedar Rapids friend. He pressed McGraw to come east to join the Orioles. McGraw hopped the first train for Baltimore, where his combative style of play characterized the Orioles club for the next ten years. In this period McGraw also assumed the captaincy of the Orioles, further putting his stamp on the ball club.

By 1892 McGraw was earning $200 a month, and within two years, working under the aegis of Ned Hanlon, one of the highest paid player-managers in the game, he was judged to be the best bunter in baseball. Hanlon promoted a brand of "inside baseball" that featured such new concepts as the hit-and-run, pinch-hitters, relief pitchers, and "hitting 'em where they ain't," which McGraw took to eagerly, ultimately adopting and enhancing these strategies as the years rolled by.

Considered the fastest, most daring team around, the Orioles won their first title in 1894, setting off the wildest celebration in the town's history. "The entire city was an open house," wrote Arthur Mann. The next two years Baltimore won again, dominating all comers with their trickiness, belligerence, and total dedication to winning. Along with Captain McGraw there were other early baseball greats on the team, including the rotund Wilbert Robinson, McGraw's best friend and as passive as McGraw was hyperactive. The others were Wee Willie Keeler, Hughey Jennings, Steve Brodie, and Dan Brouthers. Brodie was immensely durable—something of an early-day Lou Gehrig—while the mustachioed Brouthers led the league five times in hitting. Keeler was the man who "hit 'em where they ain't," and he was, indeed, Wee, at 5'4" and only 140 pounds. Adept at working the hit-and-run with McGraw, Keeler was a man, like Robinson, who confronted the world with more cheeriness than McGraw.

Led by McGraw, the Orioles even introduced an element of terror by filing their spikes before each game, in full view of the visiting club's quarters. The tactic was meant to fill the foe with fear—and loathing, with an ultimate aim of intimidation. Ty Cobb later adopted the identical strategy in his program to terrorize defending infielders.

In 1899 McGraw's wife, Minnie, became desperately ill in Baltimore. When her appendix ruptured, she died; they had been married only two years. Added to the previous tragedies in his family, this death of a loved one further scarred McGraw's psyche.

With his attachment to Baltimore, McGraw figured he'd spend the rest of his playing life in that city. But one morning he woke up to find that Baltimore's bosses had traded him to St. Louis, along with Wilbert Robinson. This second shock, which started off 1900, occurred just a few months after Minnie's death and materialized because the Baltimore franchise had been dumped out of the National League due to the interminable baseball wars of the time.

McGraw was depressed going to St. Louis but not so depressed that he didn't become an enthusiastic bettor at St. Louis' race tracks. Playing with little esprit, he still managed to bat .344, a considerably better average than he maintained at the tracks.

With Ban Johnson putting together a new American League in 1901, once again Baltimore popped up as a key franchise. And there was John McGraw back in Baltimore town. He hadn't thought of his St. Louis contract as binding in any way and by his actions anticipated the future battles over baseball's supposedly sacrosanct reserve clause. Not only was McGraw an Oriole again but, mirabile dictu, he was also the manager and chief stockholder of the club. Accused of many crimes and misdemeanors in his career, McGraw could never be accused of lacking resiliency.

Nor was McGraw a man who, despite his rancid tongue, lacked a special appeal, for the ladies—refined ones, at that. For some months he had been courting Blanche Sindall, the comely daughter of a Baltimore contractor. Blanche's father had declared the ballplayer to be a "man of indestructible confidence," thus lending wholehearted approval to the union. On January 8, 1902, before a supportive crowd of Oriole players and Oriole fans, John and Blanche were married at St. Ann's Roman Catholic Church in Baltimore. Hundreds of the curious besieged the church, unaware that within half a dozen months this local titan and his new bride would be setting up quarters in New York, O. Henry's "Baghdad on the Subway."

With his ascension in July 1902 to his role as manager of the Giants, McGraw (already dubbed "Little Napoleon" by admirers and detractors, in what amounted to a whopping redundancy) was in position to become the dominant figure in the baseball world—with the help, of course, of a pitcher named Mathewson.

There was absolutely nothing in the background or temperament of either McGraw or Matty to telegraph the fact that over the next 23 years, following Matty's first mound appearance and victory under McGraw—a 2–0, five-hit shutout on July 24—their implausible relationship would blossom. Despite their differences, Matty was the single ballplayer who defied McGraw's acerbic observation that only "one percent of players are leaders, the other ninety per cent are followers of women."

It is difficult to account for the firm ties that developed between this early twentieth-century odd couple—the well-educated man of equable disposition, the near-saintly pitcher with supposedly spiritual dimensions, on the brink of canonization in the minds of fans, press, and players alike, teaming up with his mentor McGraw, the vitriolic, angry, pot-bellied (in his later years), short-armed figure always on the verge of an auto-da-fé by a hostile outside world.

McGraw's wife, Blanche, once said about her husband John that "life without baseball had little meaning for him . . . it was his meat, drink, dream, his blood and breath, his very reason for existence."

Matty, on the other hand, was certainly not that one-dimensional. He was a man of eclectic interests and tastes, who read books, played checkers, chess, and bridge at a championship level, and was capable of writing colorful, descriptive, declarative sentences. Yet he did share with McGraw a tremendous love of baseball and a burning desire to win.

Was it the fact that from the first summer of their association McGraw's shrewd instincts told him that Matty was going to be the key to the team's success? Thus, he had to nourish and cultivate their relationship. The mind and character of Matty fascinated McGraw, who under ordinary circumstances might have been expected to be repelled by it. Did McGraw, who never had a son, think of himself as a surrogate father to Christy?

Was it possible that Matty, who was sometimes unfairly portrayed as a prig, enjoyed the rough edges and unvarnished enthusiasm of McGraw? "McGraw leaps in the air, kicks his heels together, claps his mitt, shouts at the umpire, runs in and pats the next batter on the back, and says something to the pitcher . . . the whole atmosphere inside the park is changed in a minute . . . the little actor on the third base coaching line is the cause of the change," is how Matty described the catalytic role that McGraw played on a baseball diamond. (The Matty-McGraw alliance could never have evolved had Matty's contract, signed in the off-season of 1902 with the St. Louis Browns, not been reassigned at a Cincinnati peace pact in January 1903 between the two squabbling leagues. Many stars, including Lajoie, Keeler, Ed Delahanty, Norman Elberfeld, and Sam Crawford, feeling the American League was a better roosting place to make money, signed with American League clubs, as did Matty. Still with a tail-end club in 1902, Matty was also searching for greener fields. "One can imagine the change in the fortunes of John McGraw, the Giants, the Browns and Mathewson if he'd been awarded to the Browns, instead of being returned to New York," wrote Fred Lieb.)

This mutual admiration between the two men was subsequently reinforced by a warm and intimate relationship between Blanche McGraw and Jane Mathewson, who married Christy in Lewisburg on March 4, 1903, right before the Giants set up their spring training camp in Savannah, Georgia.

In the winter of his third year at Bucknell Matty had started to court Jane Stoughton, daughter of Mr. and Mrs. Frank C. Stoughton of Lewisburg. He had met her at college and fraternity receptions and enjoyed dancing and talking to her. Jane was a lively, intelligent young woman, who dressed circumspectly, as a Sunday school teacher should. She had gray eyes and dark brown hair, and at the time she started to date Matty had only a modest interest in sports and baseball. Shortly before Matty monopolized her attention she had been engaged to a former student at Bucknell, who was a fraternity brother of Matty.

In Lewisburg Jane was regarded as an extremely "good catch," for her family was "society." In reporting on Matty's marriage the local newspaper noted that "Matty's calls upon Miss Stoughton, even in 1900 and 1901, were not frequent enough to cause any comment and it was not until he left college in March of 1901 to play baseball with the Norfolk, Virginia team that the busybodies of the small town regarded his intentions as serious. . . . After Mathewson joined the New York team in 1901 his visits became more frequent and last summer it was generally known that he and Miss Stoughton were engaged . . . the wedding will be one of the most fashionable of the season and will be attended by 100 guests. Rev. W. C. Thomas, pastor of the First Presbyterian Church, of which both Mr. Mathewson and his bride are members, will perform the ceremony."

Matty, still a Baptist before marrying Jane, had only recently become a member of the Presbyterian Church, due to a solemn compact he had made with his wife-to-be. She had promised him that, if he consented to join her church, she would abandon the Democrats and become a Republican. Who made the greater sacrifice is not certain, for Matty was not the most political of persons. Yet in his neck of the woods many of his family and friends either were admirers of the progressive Republican Teddy Roosevelt, or preferred William Howard Taft, a more conservative Republican.

The newly married couple spent their honeymoon at spring training, unusual in itself, for many married players fancied the spring period as an escape valve from their wives. However, one of the wives who did come to Savannah was Blanche McGraw.

In a few weeks the two women, the strait-laced but charming Jane, and Blanche, her more worldly, outgoing companion, became close friends. They shopped together at the stores, drank tea late in the afternoon, while their men were sweating under the Georgia sun at Forsyth Park, and took long walks down Bull Street. Blanche was quick to tell John how fond she was of Jane and, since she had previously spent little time in Christy's company, she exhibited great curiosity about the big pitcher. "What kind of a man is he?" she asked John about Mathewson.

McGraw's response, strictly in a baseball framework, spoke worlds about his own values. "Christy looks like a pitcher with both his head and his arm," he said. "You will never have to tell him anything a second time."

John then reflected on the prodigious memory that his young disciple possessed. Christy had near-photographic recall, he said, and played most social games by remembering numbers. In checkers and chess, which Matty could play blind-folded, against half a dozen opponents at a time, or in cards, where he also was able to recall all of the cards that had been played, Matty was almost invincible. Such a retentive mind was also of invaluable use on the diamond, as McGraw, the thinking man's manager, well knew. Never before had McGraw come across an athlete capable of remembering the precise details and chronology of each ball game, including all of the pitches he'd thrown and to whom he'd thrown them. Before long Matty had charted the weaknesses and strengths of all National League batters. He didn't take notes, either, for all of it was nestled in his mind. Between the two men they were able to reconstruct a ball game, pitch by pitch. If you asked Matty what pitch he had thrown in a crucial situation in a particular game he could recall it without a moment's hesitation.

As close as he turned out to be with Matty, McGraw always made a determined effort to be impartial in doling out punishment to players when the situation demanded it. Matty turned out to be no exception to the autocratic rule of Little Napoleon.

Some years after McGraw took command of the Giants, he fined Matty $500, a truly large sum in those days, for playing high-stakes poker with other members of the team. As in everything else he did, Matty played poker with patience and skill, invariably coming out a winner. McGraw admired Matty's persistence at the card table, but he felt it was bad judgment on Matty's part to play a card game against teammates he was bound to beat.

"I'd fine anybody else 25 or 50 dollars," McGraw explained. "But Matty should know better, so the fine is 500."

Matty's own post-mortem of the event showed an understanding of his manager, even if he didn't fully appreciate what McGraw had done. "You may wonder how a man who meant so much to me—and I to him—could do such a thing," he said. "The fact is he fined me 500 and made it stick. I never got it back, either."

If McGraw could be an unflinching martinet, Matty was aware of another side of him. There were innumerable occasions when McGraw bestowed small amounts of cash—tens and twenties—on players who had performed well in a game. The money was usually dropped into the mail or surreptitiously slipped into a player's locker.

In such situations McGraw played no favorites. The gratuity was designed to improve team morale. Generally, it seemed to work like a charm, even if some players realized that the money-dispensing went along with the frequent tongue-lashings and bitter invective, an activity that McGraw had made into an angry art.

"The club *is* McGraw," Matty repeatedly said about his manager. "I have seen him go onto ball fields where he is as welcome as a man with smallpox and I have seen him take all sorts of personal chances. He just doesn't know what fear is."

So as sulphurous as McGraw was, Matty also had an appreciation of what stern stuff the man was made. Whether Matty approved, without reservation, of the bullying tactics often employed by McGraw or the marginally legal devices his manager might pull out of his hat has never been clear. For example, McGraw would think nothing of trying to impede a runner's progress from third base, where McGraw was playing or coaching, by hooking his fingers in the runner's belt in order to delay the player's start for home. It was said McGraw often got away with such strategy, until the day a base-runner unbuckled his belt before heading for home. The belt was left dangling in the embarrassed McGraw's chubby fingers. A good part of the baseball world knew what "the snarling little bastard" had been up to. But did Matty approve of such unsportsmanlike behavior?

Since McGraw literally ran a ball game, from first pitch to last, as Matty often pointed out, there were occasionally light moments that could break through the tensions that McGraw himself created. "His fingers were always on the pulse of the game," said Matty. But sometimes it was McGraw's nose that got in the way. One day McGraw was signaling batters to hit away by blowing his nose into a handkerchief. Since he was nursing a bad cold, McGraw kept blowing into his hanky, as batters kept chopping at the ball, in obedience to McGraw's signal. When McGraw chose to shift to a bunting game, he couldn't get his batters to bunt. He had forgotten, pointed out Matty, that by constantly blowing his nose, he was giving the wrong signal.

McGraw was probably one of the first managers to employ psychological intimidation—and see it work. In a post-season series with the Yankees, the Giants found themselves in a ninth-inning tie. When the New Yorkers loaded the bases, the Yankee pitcher, Russ Ford, seemed to be wabbling.

"Anything might push him over," wrote Matty. "So McGraw stopped the game for a moment and whispered into the ear of Al Bridwell, the Giants' next batter. 'How many quail did you say you shot when you were hunting last fall,' asked McGraw. Foolish words. But enough to make Ford wonder what McGraw was saying, what trick he was up to. Was he telling the batter to get hit? Yes, he must be. Then Ford did just that—he hit the batter and lost the game."

Admiration for McGraw's clever ploy emerges from every word

of Matty's narrative. Aware of what might be accomplished in such a mental game, Matty decided he wasn't very good at it. "I find talking to batters to disconcert them, disconcerts me almost as much as it disconcerts the batter. Repartee is not my line, anyway," he acknowledged.

6

IN MATTY'S TIME

THE first home that the McGraws rented in New York was in the Victoria Hotel, at 27th Street and Broadway, only two blocks from the Giants' office and a thirty-minute ride on the Sixth Avenue El from Coogan's Bluff. The area was pock-marked with theatres, where melodramas and light comedies were performed by a new breed of matinee idols. The McGraws liked the night life, after the long, sunny afternoons at the Polo Grounds, and John developed friendships with many of the stage artists of the period.

Will Rogers, the Oklahoma cowboy philosopher, became a pal, as did the patriotic song-and-dance man George M. Cohan, who rarely missed a game managed by McGraw. Comic Eddie Foy and the popular team of Weber and Fields were frequent visitors to the Polo Grounds; so was actor Willie Collier. When James J. Corbett, the heavyweight conqueror of John L. Sullivan, tried to be a serious stage actor, McGraw applauded his efforts. John couldn't get enough of De Wolf Hopper's recitations of "Casey at the Bat," and when Florenz Ziegfeld later produced his first Follies the McGraws were always on hand in the best seats, watching W. C. Fields or Will Rogers surrounded by beautiful young women.

However, McGraw wasn't too selective about all of his friends or tastes. The gambler and pool-hall hustler, Arnold Rothstein, later to be implicated in the Black Sox Scandal of 1919, was a "silent partner" in several pool-hall ventures of McGraw. Rothstein, a salesman who had turned to poker and pool, lived in the shadows, hardly a suitable companion for McGraw—or for anyone else involved in baseball. But McGraw, who loved gambling, race tracks, and all pitchers over 5'10", refused to inoculate himself against such associates. He had few scruples that would keep him away from gamblers like Rothstein. Doing questionable business with Rothstein, while maintaining such a close relationship with a man like Matty, added considerably to McGraw's enigmatic portrait.

Soon after spring training of 1903 the Mathewsons moved with the McGraws into a new, furnished ground-floor, seven-room apartment, at 85th Street and Columbus Avenue, one block from Central Park. The rent, fifty dollars a month, and expenses for food and gas, were divided between the couples. It was a sign of increased respect for ballplayers that Matty was given a lease in such a respectable dwelling. Such a living arrangement between Matty and his manager was almost unheard-of in baseball—and is, to this day. It spoke volumes about the compatibility between the two men and their wives.

"We led normal lives, fed the men well and left them alone to talk their baseball. Their happiness was our cause," wrote Mrs. McGraw in her memoirs.

Although only thirty years old, McGraw was beset by a number of injuries that threatened to cut short his active playing career. In 1902 he had participated in only half of his team's remaining games because of a weak left knee. During spring training of 1903 the knee continued to bother him when he tried to slide or pivot. It made him wonder whether he was going to be reduced only to managing.

His fears were reinforced during a pre-game batting practice session at the start of the 1903 season when his nose was struck hard by a ball thrown in from the outfield by Dummy Taylor, long one of McGraw's favorite projects. When the nose hemorrhaged, McGraw was forced to go to an emergency medical room, even as Dummy agonized over the mishap. McGraw had been one of the few men able to communicate successfully with the deaf-mute pitcher.

McGraw returned to the Polo Grounds before the game the next day, against the advice of his doctor, then traveled to Philadelphia, where the Giants were scheduled to play the Phillies. Mrs. McGraw had learned that the blow had severed a cartilage in John's nose, rupturing an artery, so she deemed it advisable that she go along with her husband to Philadelphia.

"No, stay here in New York. I'll be all right," said John. But Blanche was adamant about accompanying him on his journey.

If Blanche were to be in Philadelphia with him, McGraw realized that would leave Jane Mathewson all alone in their ground-floor apartment. In such circumstances, Jane had always been apprehensive about being without Matty. Despite his pain and discomfort, McGraw ruled—and it was always *rule*, with him—that Matty remain behind in the apartment with Jane, even if it meant that he'd miss a pitching turn in Philadelphia. Morale of his players was uppermost in McGraw's mind. He knew well that Matty would be bound to worry about Jane, all alone in the apartment. So there was no alternative to his decision.

McGraw, truly a master at understanding other men, never could master his own behavior quite as well. "The obelisk of splendor," as Donald Honig described Matty, had to be dealt with tenderly but firmly, if McGraw was to reap the untold dividends of his pitching arm.

Many men like Matty and McGraw thought of New York in 1903 as a harsh, rough place. McGraw's unruly presence made it rougher. His own name sparked images of rotten eggs, foul oaths, and players bent on mayhem. "The Giants of the McGraw era," wrote Harry Golden, "represented New York of the brass cuspidor, that old New York that was still a man's world before the advent of the League of Women's Voters. Those were the days of swinging doors, of sawdust on the barroom floor"—and, Golden might have added, swinging fists.

(Larry Doyle, a handsome, strapping kid from the Three-I League, came to play second base for McGraw in 1904. In awe of his new environment, Doyle uttered the immortal phrase that "it's great to be young and to be a Giant." This was unchallenged Holy Writ before World War I. In the 1920s Waite Hoyt, an equally handsome right-hander for the Yankees, also volunteered that "it's great to be young and to be a Yankee." Even if Waite had stolen Larry's lines, both men were speaking the truth, for those were the years when New York baseball dominated the universe. To be a satellite of McGraw's kingdom or to grow up with Babe Ruth & Company later on was to be part of the greatest baseball show on earth.)

But New York was more than a place where ball clubs and vice grew, where drunks battled and Tammany Hall reigned over civic and business affairs with breathtaking insolence. It was also restaurants and private ballrooms such as Delmonico's, Rector's, Jack's, Churchill's, Dinty Moore's, and the Waldorf Bar, where self-styled society created its fun while most New Yorkers ate at home. It was the Madison Square Garden roof, designed by the famed architect Stanford White, who was murdered there one night by a jealous man named Harry Thaw. Such watering spots, which soon became favorites of McGraw and Matty, were a symbol of the pulsating metropolis that outsiders chose to call the "terrible town."

For those who damned New York as a dangerous, libertine mecca, the existence of over 20,000 prostitutes doing steady business was ample proof. "It costs a dollar and I've got the room," was the universal come-on of the time.

There were dives in Greenwich Village and fancy eating places and shops along Fifth Avenue. In Hell's Kitchen you might get your head bashed in by a member of the Stovepipe Gang. But you could also dance the night away at the Tivoli, doing the "Turkey Trot," "Grizzly Bear" or "Bunny Hug." Broadway was a wonderful artery on which to promenade. Everyone was invited, and if you walked far enough, uptown to the north, you could wind up at the Polo Grounds.

As prosperity spread throughout the nation, New York was experiencing a building boom. Although the city had no high-rise apartment houses, the Woolworth Building, with its white-shafted spires, was in the planning stages to become the tallest skyscraper in the world.

In 1896 an Ohio Republican, William McKinley, had just been re-elected President over Democrat William Jennings Bryan, the populist orator. McKinley's enticing program stressed a "full dinner pail" for all Americans. The Spanish-American War was a brief adventure, now all but forgotten, while unrest in the Philippines, with its guerilla insurrection under Emilio Aguinaldo, had been crushed. China's Boxer Rebellion was only mistily perceived, if at all, by most Americans, who preferred reading the latest Sherlock Holmes tale by Sir Arthur Conan Doyle.

The working class in bustling New York began toiling in the early hours of the morning and generally sweated until 9 p.m. Nearly 7 percent of New York's population was illiterate, and 175,000 people couldn't speak a word of English. Most of the immigrant flow came from Germany, 20 percent from Ireland, (the swollen number of immigrants from these two countries was dramatically reflected by the large cadre of German and Irish players coming into baseball), 12 percent from Russia, 11 percent from Italy and 5 percent from England and Australia. Only 65,000 blacks resided in the city.

The Lower East Side teemed with more than 700,000 Jews, who

had fled to America from Russian pogroms and the structural anti-Semitism of other lands. When the first Columbus Day Parade got under way in 1900 many of the 150,000 Italians in New York joined the march up Fifth Avenue.

Horse-drawn vehicles moved along at less than 12 miles an hour, elevated trains screeched their way through Manhattan, and the first New York subway was noisily under construction, providing work for thousands of immigrants. Many worked for 20 cents an hour in a ten-hour-day underground. Central Park refused entry to cars but in the rest of the city a nine-mile-an-hour speed limit was imposed. Automobiles were still regarded as expensive instruments of the rich.

Pushcarts crowded Second Avenue, as well as the Lower East Side. In chic residential areas blacksmiths pounded away in their shops. "One could often hear white horseshoes being plunged into a bucket of water," wrote critic Stanley Kaufmann.

Under the warming rays of the summer sun, children gleefully rode on carousels that visited their block. Drivers operated the carousels by hand; passengers, at a penny a ride, squealed with delight as the carousel rode 'round and 'round. Old men walked through backyards, with giveaway garments on their backs, crying out to eager potential buyers, "I cash clothes, I cash clothes!" Ponies that could never have run at any racetrack clopped their way through neighborhoods so that children could have their pictures taken on the backs of the spavined animals. Italian organ-grinders, assisted by tiny monkeys, played tunes for street crowds, as people craned their necks out of windows.

Newspaper extras, shouted in the almost indecipherable phrases of street hawkers, brought the latest crime and world news to people. Most of New York's banks, retail stores, and offices opened for half a day on Saturdays, and on Fifth Avenue the omnibus, fed by gasoline, provided a wonderful perspective for passengers sitting on the upper deck.

Radio was mainly employed by ships on the high seas, while the long-distance telephone was a miracle that few had access to, including the very rich. No airplanes buzzed the skies over New York, for such machines performed almost exclusively at country fairs and parade grounds.

Away from the glittering residences and private brownstones, 1,500,000 New Yorkers lived in slums that bred disease and crime. At restaurants that weren't meant to serve a "high class" clientele, a regular dinner cost 15 cents. A five-cent stein of beer in a nearby saloon also entitled anyone to a hard-boiled egg, a chunk of salami, a salty pickle or a slice of tomato. Sundaes, served up in gaudy ice-cream parlors lit by Tiffany lamps, were more popular than any other delectation.

In the winter men planted derbies on their heads, in summer they substituted straw hats. At night, if women went formal, they partially exposed their bosoms, much in the manner of the chesty singer and actress Lillian Russell. During the day the ladies wore shirtwaists, with long skirts and uncomfortable high collars. Even in sweltering weather it wasn't proper for men to remove their vests—but jackets could come off in offices. Many men grew handlebar mustaches, à la John L. Sullivan.

Robert Moses, the planner who would one day shape New York to his own specifications, was of bar mitzvah age as the century turned, while Babe Ruth, who would soon shape baseball to *his* specifications, was only five years old. Franklin D. Roosevelt, at 18, was a humdrum student at Harvard. Jimmy Walker, later a hell-raising, song-writing mayor of New York, was 19 and refereeing prizefights at a Hudson Street bar. His reformer counterpart, Fiorello LaGuardia, was an 18-year-old clerk.

The loudest evangelistic noise in the country was being emitted by Billy Sunday, a former outfielder for the Chicago White Stockings and Pittsburgh Pirates. As a player Sunday attributed all of his base hits and catches to the Lord. He was born in an Iowa log cabin and was the son of a soldier in the Union Army.

By the time Matty reached the big leagues, Sunday's playing career was over. But Sunday went on to spearhead the Prohibitionist movement and preach, until he was hoarse, against the pernicious evil of Sunday baseball—an issue on which Matty agreed with him. (It was ironic that Sunday's name was not an invention, considering his crusade.) There were others who went along with the Sunday baseball decree. One of them, Carl Mays, the sour-tempered submarining pitcher, was the son of a Methodist minister. Mays later won reverse fame by killing Cleveland's Ray Chapman with a pitched ball.

"I promised my parents that I would never pitch on Sunday," said Matty, even after he won fame with the Giants. He never violated that promise, but, in time, as the needs of commerce intervened, Matty became less rigid about his position. He was not out to inflict his self-righteousness on others.

"At the outset of my career I honestly believed that playing

Sunday baseball was wrong," he said. "In the years that have passed I have naturally changed my views on many matters. New York has a much wider horizon than Factoryville. There is much to be said in favor of allowing the laboring man his only opportunity to go to a baseball game on Sunday. My main argument now will be on behalf of the player that he would be allowed one day in seven to call his own. This is another matter that every man must decide for himself."

With or without Mathewson on Sunday, the Polo Grounds became the place to be in New York. Almost from the moment McGraw made his first appearance in his baggy trousers with the black pinstripes, the baseball worshippers flocked to the quaint ball park next to the shimmering Harlem River.

From 1883, when the Giants were the eighteenth club sanctioned for play in the National League, the team had shifted its home base from Staten Island to Jersey City, then to Brooklyn. However, most of the time the club played on a field adjoining the northeast corner of Central Park, on 110th Street, off Fifth Avenue. Polo actually was played there at that time, mainly by the social clubs of the New York *Herald's* multimillionaire James Gordon Bennett. As the horses romped, rich, proud gentlemen decked out in striped trousers watched the exotic activity from under their silk hats.

When the plotters at City Hall decided to kick the Giants out of their Fifth Avenue home because, they said, a traffic circle at that corner was a necessity, John B. Day, then the Giants' owner, leased a grassy meadow uptown at 155th Street. At the time this site was called Coogan's Hollow, named after James Coogan, a prominent merchant who became Manhattan's first borough president in 1899.

In April 1891 the Giants played for the first time at their Coogan's Hollow location, and, though polo was never played there, the original name of the Polo Grounds stuck. Nobody ever lobbied to change it.

As first constructed the Polo Grounds was a four-story ball park, with wood, concrete, and steel grandstands painted green. Home plate was directly under the cliff of Coogan's Bluff. The playing field itself was almost two hundred yards long, featuring a cruel expanse in center field that was mischievously designed to foil the efforts of those hitters not inclined to pull the ball toward the beckoning right-field stands (257 feet away and 10 feet, 7¾ inches high), or to left-field (279 feet away and 16 feet, 10 inches high). Such asymmetrical dimensions, an absurdity to some, glorious to others, might frustrate even the finest of batsmen.

There were tiny bleachers on the left and right side of the center-field area, but, for these most fervent of Giant fans, there was no individual seating. It was first come, first served. Those who couldn't raise the price of a bleacher seat were welcome to climb to the top of Coogan's Bluff, where it was possible to get a clear view of second base and not much else, while perched on rocks, dirt, and grass.

The upper left-field deck hung over the lower deck by some 30 feet, an unusual projection and one that would play a singular role in the subsequent history of the team half a century later, when Bobby Thomson hit his famous home run.

When first built the park had about 16,000 seats, not counting the views of those who saw the proceedings from their horse-and-carriages stationed behind ropes in center field. In a few years seating capacity was enlarged to 23,000, mainly by adding single-deck bleachers in the outfield.

If one were up in a balloon looking down at the Polo Grounds, as it sat on the west bank of the Harlem, the park had more the appearance of an enormous outdoor green bathtub than a ballfield. Certainly it looked a good deal less like a ball park than Yankee Stadium, which, in 1923, became its rival in the Bronx, on the right bank of the Harlem.

7

THE RISE OF
THE GIANTS

I N 1903 Matty won 30 games for the Giants, almost three times as many games as participated in by McGraw during the year. Matty became the second major-league pitcher—Cy Young did it first for the Red Sox in 1901—to win 30 or more games. Included among the 30 wins were eight straight victories over Pittsburgh, the team that won the National League pennant in 1903, with a lineup that included the great Honus Wagner at shortstop.

In accomplishing his feat Matty pitched 367 innings and walked 100 batters. The latter figure, good for most pitchers, but not that good for a Christy Mathewson, was the last time he'd ever yield anything close to that number. For it had become clear that among all of his skills on the mound, precision control was Matty's chief asset, aside from the inscrutable fadeaway.

Curiously, even as a 30-game winner, Matty was still not yet the dominant pitcher on the club. That distinction fell to Joseph Jerome "Iron Man" McGinnity, who had come by his nickname even before he pitched two double-headers in the uniform of the Baltimore Orioles, winning one and splitting the other. Having worked in an iron foundry where he grew up in Rock Island, Illinois, McGinnity was tagged Iron Man early in his life.

Weighing over 210 pounds, McGinnity loved to pitch, whether in starting roles or relief. McGraw lost no time prying McGinnity loose from the Orioles. In August 1903, McGinnity pitched both ends of double-headers on three occasions, winning all six games. When he licked the Phillies twice on the last day of August, the *New York Times* reported that he did "the double job in three hours and three minutes and at the end showed no signs of fatigue—in fact he seemed fresh enough for a third contest if that were necessary."

If anything, McGinnity, with his 31-20 record in 1903, was more durable than Matty, as he hurled 434 innings, a record that remains to this day. (Matty worked almost as often as McGinnity, but on one occasion during the year he protested to McGraw when called on to pitch with only two days' rest. Bowerman, his catcher, supported him in his polite revolt—and McGraw gave in to him.) Ten years older than Matty, McGinnity was in every way McGraw's kind of pitcher: tall, husky, willing, a workhorse. In the off-season he ran a saloon, which didn't lose him many points with his manager, for McGraw didn't mind his players hanging around beer gardens, as long as it was confined to the winter months.

Of the 139 games that the Giants played in 1903, Matty and McGinnity appeared in 100, winning 61 of them, a higher total by 13 than the team had won the previous year. Their pitching, along with a more respectable lineup, including catcher Roger Bresnahan, George Browne, an infielder purchased from Philadelphia, and a bargain-basement second baseman Billy Gilbert, who had been released outright by Baltimore, rocketed the Giants into second place behind the Pirates. The fact, too, that Andrew Freedman, having sold the team to John T. Brush, was no longer a presence in the front office also made the fans and players happier. This became evident as the season progressed, for crowds flocked to the Polo Grounds—sometimes as many as 30,000—to see McGraw's revivified crew. On the road, too, the message of McGraw, Matty & Company was getting through, as the club became a compelling gate attraction. In no time at all, as the Giants started to win, and as McGraw fumed and argued on the field, fans on foreign territory came to boo and hiss the New York villains. Inevitably, as the years went by, the Giants became the team to hate. Matty himself, however, was rarely the focus of such dislike.

Matty and McGinnity were on the mound so often that many believed they were the only pitchers that McGraw had. That wasn't true, for the Giants also had the creditable Dummy Taylor, Jack Cronin, and Roscoe Miller, even if those gentlemen contributed little to the total picture. When fans arrived at the ball park they expected to see either Matty or McGinnity on the mound. This one-two punch frustrated foes and delighted Giant rooters. Mc-Ginnity's presence also became doubly important to Matty, for as much as he already knew about the art of pitching due to his own work habits and intelligence, there were always other ideas to be studied and adopted. Matty noticed, for example, how the Iron Man was a master at conserving his strength during the course of a contest. Knowing he would never be able to survive the rugged schedule that he maintained, McGinnity shrewdly paced himself. He always appeared to have something in reserve when a crucial inning approached or a key out had to be obtained. Matty appreciated such strategy and soon made it his own.

As Matty's popularity grew along with his string of victories, a nickname was bestowed on him. He'd been known as Husk in his youth. Until now he was just Matty—but soon they began to call him "Big Six," a name that had considerably more stature than Doc, Pop, Rube, Muggsy, Wild Bill, or Babe. Those nicknames were popular at the time, but somehow lacked the dignity that came with the more arcane sobriquet of Big Six.

The origin of Big Six has long been in question, although various theories, fanciful and otherwise, have been advanced. Only one thing is certain: it had nothing to do with his number, for in Matty's day ballplayers didn't have names or numbers inscribed on the backs of their shirts. That leaves us with several notions about its derivation, one in particular having to do with Matty's size. Ballplayers who were six feet or over, in the early 1900's, were a rarity. Matty in the minds of many was a huge guy. "Hey, he's a big six, isn't he, the biggest six you ever saw," said one sportswriter of the time. Thus "Big Six."

But another sportswriter named Samuel Newhall Crane, who came out of Springfield, Massachusetts, to work for the Hearst papers, is generally given more credit in the matter. Sam Crane had an unsuccessful career from 1880 to 1890 as a player with the Giants, Detroit, and St. Louis. Finishing up with a lifetime batting average of .203, it appeared that he might have been batting against Matty most of the time. Crane noted that in New York there was an antique horse-drawn engine called Big Six, used by the volunteer fire department, that was effective in dousing out fires. Some said it could pump more water than Niagara Falls. Since Crane often had dubbed Matty as a "great flame-thrower," he carried the metaphor a step further by naming him the "Big Six of all pitchers."

However, even as Crane often received credit as a name-thrower, still another theory suggested that Matty was named after a "peerless car" made by the Matheson Motor Company in Wilkes Barre. The car went by the name of "Big Six." What has never been too clear is whether the car was named after Matty, or Matty after the car.

With Big Six and McGinnity working at full throttle, McGraw sensed that all that he had to do to make the Giants a winner in 1904 was to plug up a few glaring holes in the infield and outfield. He acquired Harry "Moose" McCormick, an outfielder, from Philadelphia, bought a third baseman, Art Devlin, like Matty a former collegian, and gambled by acquiring "Turkey Mike" Donlin, an outfielder with a penchant for nightlife that caused his owner, Garry Herrmann of Cincinnati, to despair of him, even as Donlin batted .356. Thirty-three-year-old shortstop Bill Dahlen arrived in another trade from Brooklyn, and Hooks Wiltse, a left-hander without a single inning of big-league experience, also was signed by the adventurous McGraw.

Having a roster complete to his satisfaction, McGraw, accompanied by his wife, Christy, and Jane Mathewson, plus a handful of other Giants, set sail on *The City of Memphis* for the coastal voyage down to Savannah, again the spring training headquarters for his team. After only a week in Savannah McGraw transferred his team to Birmingham, Alabama, an industrial city full of dark clouds, where the local athletic club had invited the New Yorkers to use the facilities.

Birmingham was noted, among other things, for a large and available community of prostitutes, causing Matty to remark that "any man who would cheat on his wife, would also cheat in baseball . . . would such cheaters also betray their country?" Such moralizing oozing from another man probably would have whipped half the club into gales of laughter. But Matty had earned too much respect from his teammates, even if they managed to reject his sermonizing.

During that spring training, McGraw hired a black friend and admirer, Andrew "Rube" Foster, as a secret unofficial pitching coach for Matty. McGraw once wanted to sign Foster, a capable pitcher, for the Giants, but the suffocatingly bigoted mores of the time precluded such action. What Foster, only a few years older than Matty, could have imparted to him in the way of pitching knowledge is questionable—but several black historians have written that there was such a relationship. Foster in later years became a prominent executive in the Negro League.

Returning to New York in April, McGraw at once announced

that he had "the best team I've ever led in a pennant race." The club, behind Big Six, then lost precious little time persuading the fans that McGraw was correct. On the April 15 opening day in Brooklyn's Washington Park, over 16,000 people, a record for that park, jammed the stands, despite the fact that snow had been pelting down since early morning. Matty got off to a two-run lead, then augmented it with his own run-scoring single. At the end he was a 3-1 victor, the first of 33 triumphs he'd register during 1904. Again combining with the indefatigable McGinnity, Matty added considerably to his reputation, even as the Iron Man won two more than he did.

With such overwhelming pitching and a veteran club of 17 players, the Giants were in first place almost from the opening gun. They had an 18-game winning streak during June and July, winning 53 of their first 71 games. By September they opened up a 15-game lead, a remarkable turnaround for a team without a single .300 hitter and a club that had been at the bottom of the league in 1902.

By season's end the Giants captured 106 games, with Matty and McGinnity responsible for over half that amount. McGraw was the eternal goad that everyone expected he would be—abusing umpires, chastising foes, directing each play from the bench or the coaching lines (though he did usually permit Matty to call his own pitches), and keeping the fans in a perpetual state of half-controlled dementia.

However, there was an episode in 1904 when one of Matty's self-prescribed pitches hurt the Giants. It caused McGraw to object, despite their cordial relationship, to what Matty had done.

In an early-season game Chicago's center-fielder, Jimmy Slagle, a notoriously weak hitter, connected for a home run off Matty. The blow stunned the pitcher, as well as his manager. The next day when McGraw got Matty alone he asked what pitch he'd thrown to Slagle.

"A fast ball," said Matty.

"Don't you know that Slagle murders fast balls?" asked McGraw.

"No, I didn't know," acknowledged Matty.

"Don't ever throw one of those things to him again," said McGraw.

Presumably Matty never did.

When it was all over Matty was 33-12, with an earned run average of 2.03. He walked only 78 men, much better than his 100 bases on balls in 1903. However, McGinnity was still the dominant pitcher of the club, appearing in 408 innings and hurling nine shut-outs. However, it was the last time he'd ever show the way to Big Six. As well, it marked the first time that McGinnity confessed to McGraw that his arm felt tired. Coming from this unshirking pitcher, such a complaint had to be taken seriously.

Another supercharged episode, in a year full of conquest for the Giants, was the seething hostility that cascaded from McGraw and his club toward the Pittsburgh team. Several accusatory stories appeared in the Pittsburgh press concerning the Giant manager. "McGraw is loud-mouthed," ran one newspaper article, "and the expressions he uses to occupants of the grandstand are not all within the bounds of propriety . . . it's a shame that patrons of the game should be subjected to such talk." What was truly surprising was the scurrilous assault on Matty's character. He was referred to as "Sis," possibly because of his tenor voice. In addition, he was accused of using foul and vituperative language. The latter charge was certainly not impossible. But Matty's fellow players could have testified that he rarely used profanity—at least he hadn't been caught at it very often.

McGraw threatened to sue, for there was a clause in his three-year contract against foul language and rowdyism. But it wasn't certain who he would sue, for he had loudly blamed Barney Dreyfuss, the Pirates' owner, for putting the Pittsburgh writer up to it. Would he sue Dreyfuss or the journalist? The problem was resolved when McGraw decided not to proceed with any litigation.

"I'll handle it myself," he said. "The newspaper itself isn't to blame but some writer behind it, or some other person."

The McGravian implication was that he'd take it out on Dreyfuss and the Pirates on the diamond, where such battles could be joined. In the next few tumultous years, as the Giants reduced the Pirates to also-rans, he did exactly that.

The matter, which could have been serious, had been so exaggerated by the writer—including the uncalled-for attack on Mathewson—that McGraw's possible suspension or an abrogation of his contract by Brush was never considered.

When Boston wound up as the winner of the American League pennant that year, after having beaten the Pirates five games to three in the World Series of 1903, there were great expectations about a forthcoming Red Sox–Giants series.

Unfortunately, the intense hatred against the American League's Ban Johnson, on the part of both McGraw and Brush, destroyed any chances of such a World Series meeting in 1904. There was a suspicion that McGraw and his owner nursed fears that the Red Sox might do to the Giants what they had done to Pittsburgh in 1903. In addition, McGraw insisted that the Red Sox didn't belong in the same World Series ball park with his minions.

"That's a minor league; why should we play them?" he asked. "The Giants would totally outclass them."

Such McGraw protests were flawed because normally he would have been pleased to knock the brains out of any other ball club. If the Red Sox were as mediocre as he said they were, all the Giants had to do to prove their case was to show up. Such a World Series could also have provided a perfect showcase for those two sturdy right-handers, Matty and McGinnity.

The fans wanted the games to go on; the press set up a din for it; and the players, desiring to earn the extra Series cash, heartily petitioned for it. Relenting somewhat, McGraw took the matter up with Brush. But he discovered that his owner was "like a stone wall."

The players knew that the resuscitated Giants, drawing over half a million to the Polo Grounds in 1904, had put a bundle of money in Brush's pockets. They wanted some of it back for themselves. But Brush's resistance was based primarily on the fact that Johnson had put the Highlanders (later to become the Yankees) into New York as part of the American League. Thus, Brush had himself a new, stiff competitor. The Highlanders, ending up second behind Boston that year, were already threatening to lure customers away from the Polo Grounds.

Thus, the World Series of 1904 was never played. It was the last time in the game's modern history that an owner of a pennant-winning club could unilaterally kill off the World Series. It wouldn't happen again. Thereafter, the Series was played every year on schedule, becoming the ultimate theatrical moment of every baseball season. No autocrat like Brush, no despot like McGraw would be able to do a thing about it. Baseball's National Commission brought a modified peace to the game, outlawing such behavior in the post-season of 1904.

In order to pick up the extra pocket money that they had lost, some of the Giants, including Matty, played a barnstorming schedule of exhibitions against a number of corporate and industrial teams. One such occasion pitted Matty against a club representing the Ingersoll-Sergeant Drill Company, in Easton, Pennsylvania. It was like returning to his home roots, and, though Matty overwhelmed the Drill Company team, the fans who turned out at the field near Northampton and 12th Street were impressed that such an icon would come to visit them.

All of this turmoil meant that Big Six had to wait until 1905 to pitch in his first World Series.

8

BIG SIX
AT HIS PEAK

IKE many men of his baseball generation, McGraw was superstitious. He regarded meeting up with hunchbacks as a good luck omen and believed that passing empty beer barrels on the way to the ball park was bound to produce dividends. (Naturally, on many occasions, he craftily *arranged* for his players to encounter such barrels enroute to the Polo Grounds.)

Matty himself once wrote that many players, some on his own club, would rub the head of "colored kids for luck." As barbaric as such a practice was, ballplayers echoed many of the racial stereotypes that convulsed the country. In such matters, Matty did not appear to be an exception. His college education failed to deprive him of such biases.

However, in most instances, Big Six was practical-minded. He believed that his brains and preparation could accomplish more than superstition. More often than not, he was right. But he had one inhibition on the field: he refused to warm up with his third baseman, as he waited for his catcher to strap on his paraphernalia. He became prejudiced against the practice when he first broke in with New York. "I threw the ball around with my third baseman, then got knocked out of the box," recalled Matty, "so I never did it again."

At the start of the 1905 season Mathewson was forced to abide by another of McGraw's superstitions. For some inexplicable reason, McGraw chose to hold Matty out of opening games. There was little Matty could do about it, for in this case the manager could call on McGinnity, who had won more games over the past two years than had Big Six. So Matty wasn't on the mound when a crowd of 25,000 gathered at the Polo Grounds in mid-April to watch the opening game against Boston. Brush went all out, with a parade of 16 automobiles carrying the players of both teams from the Polo Grounds down to Washington Square and back. The Giants hoisted their 1904 pennant, somewhat tainted by their failure to play the World Series, and a United States Coast Guard patrol boat, stationed in the Harlem River for the occasion, fired off a 21-gun salute. The esteemed "white hope," Jim Jeffries, still the heavyweight champ, also was on hand to celebrate the event.

Suitably, the Giants romped to victory, 10-1. The season had started just as McGraw felt it would, for before the campaign began he brayed that this was probably the best ball club he'd ever managed. At least it lived up to one requirement of McGraw's: it was smart, without any "slow-thinking players on the roster."

If the crowds at home were behind McGraw's scrappers 100 percent, on the road the Giants, with their reputation as bullies and rowdies, caused enemy fans to be constantly on the edge of physical retaliation.

McGraw had chosen in 1905 to adopt the full array of intimidating tactics that the Orioles initiated in his days with Baltimore. With few exceptions his Giants gleefully echoed his ruthless style of play. There was hardly a pleasant summer afternoon at the ball park that wasn't rudely interrupted with fist-fights, threats against umpires, and a torrent of verbal abuse.

If McGraw could have invented an alibi for stretching the boundary lines of fair play, it was because he believed the destiny of each game was in his own hands. Therefore, it was legitimate to use any measures to win. With such a guiding scripture from the bench, the gentlemen on the club often wound up on the same side as the rowdies.

A week after the start of the season, Matty thrust himself into the middle of an ugly brawl, "just to show that his association with the old Baltimore crowd had also made a hoodlum out of him," taunted one Philadelphia reporter. It was one of the few instances of Matty's derelict behavior. But it did point up that he was capable of losing his temper and that he was tougher than his widely accepted image.

The incident evolved when Dan McGann of the Giants tried to score against the Phillies, as catcher Fred Abbott protected home plate. As Abbott tagged out McGann, the latter emerged from the cloud of dust fighting mad. Umpire George Bausewine terminated the exchange by throwing McGann out of the game, bringing the red-faced McGraw storming out of the dugout, protesting the umpire's edict. The Philadelphia crowd of 20,000 screamed bloody vengeance at the hated manager. They demanded that he, too, be thrown out of the game, if not off the earth. In the spirit of the occasion, in full view of the spectators, Matty threw a punch that leveled a lemonade boy who had run on the field during the tumult.

"This brutal blow," as a Philadelphia writer described it, was presumably struck because of a remark that the boy had uttered about one of the Giant players. The boy's lip was split, and several of his teeth were loosened. When the game finally continued the Giants won, 10-2, further enraging the Philadelphia constituency. Mobbed in their carriage by several thousand people after the game, the Giant players were targets of a variety of lethal objects, including rocks and bricks. It was some time before the local gendarmes managed to get the affair under control.

In May, against their now bitter rivals, the Pirates, McGraw set off another brawl of majestic proportions by baiting a Pirate pitcher, Mike Lynch, as Lynch ambled by him at the third-base coaching box. So incensed was Pittsburgh manager Fred Clarke at McGraw's incendiary words that he offered on the spot to fight him. As both clubs prepared for the donnybrook the umpire tried to tamp down the situation by tossing McGraw out of the game. Later Matty also got the thumb from umpire Jimmy Johnston after he ran close to the Pirates bench and struck an orthodox fighting posture, much like a *Police Gazette* photo. Supporting the hometown Giants, the crowd wailed in protest, as Matty was forced to leave the premises, along with McGraw's assistant Noisy Bill Clarke, a former Baltimore player.

One might ponder why McGraw found it necessary to stimulate controversy wherever he walked. After all, with Matty, backed up by a quick-witted, first-rate club, there didn't seem that much need for such distractions. But some believed that McGraw's quick temper, often following moments of radiant sweetness, was "carefully plotted and perfectly timed, particularly true where the Pirates were concerned," wrote Frank Graham, who had trailed McGraw around for years as a New York sports columnist.

Since McGraw regarded the Pirates as his most potent foe, he chose to make life miserable for them by keeping them off-balance. Facing this provocation, Fred Clarke had a hard time maintaining his equilibrium and was thus a vulnerable target. On the other hand, the stoic Dutchman Honus Wagner stood up under the barrage nobly; McGraw was like a fly speck on his itchy shirt. Barney Dreyfuss was not as equable as Wagner. He could scarcely contain himself, as McGraw filled the air with insults and mocked his thick accent.

While McGraw strutted around like a petulant peacock, defying the world, Matty continued to rack up victories, as the Giants pulled away from the field. On June 13, in a mound duel with Mordecai "Three-Fingered" Brown—one of many with Brown that Matty would engage in during his career—Matty pitched his second no-hitter. This game marked another milestone for him, as he became the first to pitch two no-hitters in the modern era. The 1-0 performance was particularly impressive, coming as it did against the Cubs, at their home field in Chicago, with their storied infield of Joe Tinker, Johnny Evers, and Frank Chance, as well as their all-time catcher, Johnny Kling. In observing Matty, Brown had once said of him: "I can see him making his lordly entrance onto the field. He'd always wait until about ten minutes before game time, then he'd come from the clubhouse across the field in a long linen duster like auto drivers wore and at every step the crowd would yell louder and louder."

The *New York Times* exulted in Matty's work that day: "He did wonders with the ball, stopping Frank Selee's breezy players to a standstill. Neither run nor hit nor base on balls did he allow and if his support would have been perfect (there were two Giant errors) he would have tied Cy Young's record of not permitting an opponent to reach first base . . . Chicago's recent successes, combined with the possibility of a row, attracted a big weekly crowd of 9,000, in spite of the weather, which promised to stop the game before it had gone far . . . The spectators were obliged to see their idols look like animated automats of putty, so completely did Mathewson have them faded . . . just twenty-eight men, one more than the necessary three an inning, faced Matty during the game . . . only once did the Chicagoans even make a noise like a base hit, that was when Evers hit a line drive straight into Mike Donlin's hands in the third inning."

The no-hitter was typical of Matty's productivity in 1905. He won 31 out of 39 decisions, the best percentage of his career, and led the league with an ERA of 1.27. McGinnity's record was "down" to 21 victories, but McGraw had been forewarned that his big pitcher suffered from arm fatigue. Red Ames also won 22 games, while Dummy Taylor and Hooks Wiltse each chipped in with 15 victories. The Giants' stolen bases accumulation of 291 reflected Mc-Graw's brand of baseball. Yet another story was their meager output of 39 home runs, still high enough to lead the National League and evidence that the ball, with its hard rubber core, was heavy as well as dead.

It was ideal for Matty to pitch with such a ball, for there was no sense throwing your arm out against every batter when it was unlikely they would crush one out of the park. Base-hits could be tolerated, as long as the proper strategic pitch could be unleashed in a pinch. Even if the tiny, crudely made gloves that players wore permitted more base-runners than a pitcher liked, skilled hurlers like Matty were at their best when they were threatened.

Matty worked 339 innings in 1905 striking out 206 batters and walking only 64, about one every five and a half innings. Typically, few hitters facing Matty were ever rewarded by disputing the strike zone with him.

The most trouble Matty experienced all year occurred not on the pitching mound but on a country road in Westchester County. Christy and Jane often enjoyed riding in their new car, an elegant $1400 Cadillac featuring several polished brass kerosene lamps and black leather upholstery. One day the McGraws accepted Matty's invitation to join them, after being reassured that a chauffeur would be behind the wheel. (McGraw trusted Matty's control as a pitcher but not as a driver.)

As luck would have it, the chauffeur lost control of the big touring car, causing the machine to plunge off the dirt road and into a nearby sand bank. In describing the incident, Mrs. McGraw said "they all held their breaths, until Jane waved from a cramped position in the front seat, informing all parties that she was all right." Pregnant at the time, Jane could have been seriously hurt. The next day she reported that all was well, much to the relief of all the parties—and certainly to prospective father Christy.

Now it remained for the runaway Giants to sew things up in the National League, which they did by knocking the Pirates out of contention in September. They clinched it by beating the Cardinals in St. Louis on the first day of October. At the end the Pirates, hazed all summer by McGraw, trailed the Giants by nine games, as the Giants captured 105 wins against 48 defeats.

For the second straight year the Giants had won the flag. This time, they did not walk off in a pique over the prospect of having to play an American League team in the World Series, in this case Connie Mack's Philadelphia Athletics. For one thing the Giants were eager to prove they were the best ball club in existence. For another, all the players wanted the extra Series money that they had missed in 1904. Last, but not less important, Brush himself wanted to add to his exchequer after an already profitable season. He was smart enough to appreciate that his Giants were now the most dynamic sports attraction in New York, possibly the country, and that the forthcoming World Series would underscore the enormous popularity that the game was experiencing. He was confident that Matty and the Giants would humble a team from a league at which McGraw continued to scoff. "Just bushers, a bunch of white elephants," sniffed McGraw. Now his team would have to certify that on the field.

This World Series would be the first to be played under Brush's rules governing such classics. Administered by a three-man commission consisting of August Herrmann, president of the Cincinnati Reds, Harry Pulliam, president of the National League (a man constantly denounced by McGraw as "Dreyfuss' employee"), and Ban Johnson, president of the American League (still equally despised by McGraw), the Series would be won in a best four-out-of-seven format. Players on both clubs would share 60 percent of the total proceeds of only the first four games, presumably to avoid any disposition on the part of the athletes not to go all out in each game. The winning team would receive 75 percent, with 25 percent going to the losers.

The fans looked forward eagerly to a clash between the Giants and the Athletics, even if the Athletics slumped badly in the latter part of the season as they staggered to the American League pennant. They won only 92 games, 13 less than the Giants, and had also played four games fewer than the runner-up White Sox, However, Johnson declared them as champions of the American League.

New York and Philadelphia, two of the biggest cities in the country, were close enough geographically, if not temperamentally, for their passionate rooters to commute, as the Series migrated from one locality to another. Two men, accepted as giants of the game, McGraw and Mack, would direct the clubs, adding to the high drama. If a poll had been taken most people probably would have expressed their sentimental preference for the Athletics.

In this confrontation between the gaunt, straw-hatted, starch-collared Mack, with his reputation for reclusiveness and abhorrence of profanity, versus McGraw, regarded as nothing less than a son of a bitch by most of the baseball world, many would have come down hard on Philadelphia's side. However, there were those who insisted that Mack was mistakenly regarded as a saint. He reminded some people, instead, of a banker specializing in foreclosures, even as others emphasized his wisdom and courtliness. Certainly Mack was vastly different from McGraw, as he steered his Philadelphia team from a discreet corner of the dugout, inscrutably wig-wagging a rolled-up program in the direction of his outfielders. If McGraw needed any more negatives it was said that his players were scarcely more than marionettes and that his gnarled fingers had become calloused as he pulled all the strings.

Mack's lineup for the Series was not exactly a powerhouse, but it did include some capable players. Ossie Schreckengost, who had once changed his name to Schreck to accommodate editors and sportswriters, was a fine catcher. More than that, he took on the burden of rooming with Rube Waddell, the pitcher whose name was always preceded by the word "eccentric." Schreck was no mean oddball himself, for he had a clause inserted in his contract, at the request of Waddell, that prohibited him from eating crackers in bed. Waddell once threatened to leave the club and go into vaudeville if Mack refused to enforce the prohibition on Ossie's eating habits.

Harry Davis, at first base, had been a clerk before Mack encouraged him to sign with the A's. His eight home runs led the American League in 1905. The bow-legged Lave Cross played third base and was the team captain. Socks Seybold, an outfielder with some home-run power, had come over from Milwaukee, while another outfielder, Topsy Hartsel, added more color to a team hardly lacking in that quality.

However, it was Mack's pitching staff that propelled his team to the top. Under his wing were southpaw Eddie Plank, right-handers Chief Bender and Andy Coakley, and, of course, Waddell, as good an American League quartet as could be found. Waddell was considered the best of them, for the free-spirited pitcher from Punxsutawney, Pennsylvania, had won 26 games, with four saves during the year, as he compiled an ERA of 1.48. Unfortunately for the Athletics, Rube would not be available for the World Series.

In a "playful" tussle with Coakley in September, Waddell had supposedly injured his left arm. In his idea of a joke, Rube had crushed Coakley's straw boater over his head while the two were standing on a Providence, Rhode Island, train platform. Coakley, crafty enough years later as Columbia's coach to develop a student named Lou Gehrig, wasn't smart enough in this instance to restrain himself from wrestling with Mack's best pitcher. The result was that Waddell, often rated by Mack as the greatest pitcher he ever managed, was forced to sit out the Series.

Rube's presence was missed to such an extent by his teammates that some of them approached Giant players with a business proposition. Would the Giants care to split 50-50 on the first four games, they inquired, instead of the 75-25 split that was already designated by the baseball satraps?

Some of the players actually paired off that way, but when Coakley was paired off with Matty, Big Six did not find it the most congenial deal. Let's see how things go after the first game, Big Six suggested. Matty was shrewd at more than just checkers and chess.

Meanwhile, rumors were rampant that Rube had been bribed by gamblers to sit out the Series. In the last days of the season Mack even accused Waddell of malingering. Rube's response was that he'd been pitching in pain for almost a month.

"It'd be worse for the team if I pitched," he argued. "That would be better for the gamblers, wouldn't it, I'm no crook."

Most folks were inclined to believe Rube. Maybe he liked to dive off ferry boats or squeeze behind saloon counters to serve beer on days he was scheduled to pitch. He was a flake, yes. But that didn't make him dishonest.

The day before the Series was to start at Philadelphia's Columbia Park, the A's showed their insouciance by scheduling an exhibition game against St. John's of Brooklyn. When Waddell suddenly announced he might play right field in the exhibition, skeptics took that to mean that he'd been playing possum all along. Was Mack about to pull a fast one, despite all the talk about his wounded southpaw, and start him the following afternoon?

The next day was October 9, and over 18,000 rabid fans squeezed into a ball park that normally accommodated about 10,000, mostly bleacher seats. The ground in the outfield was roped off, along with the farther foul lines; standees paid an extra fifty cents to gain a slightly better vantage point.

Among the 18,000 were over 500 entertainers, saloon-owners, gamblers, restaurateurs, prizefighters (including Gentleman Jim Corbett), and McGraw hangers-on who made the trip from New York by special train to root for Little Napoleon's proud boys. George M. Cohan sang along with the 56-piece Giant band en route. "Tammany, swamp 'em, swamp 'em, got that wampum," was the refrain, connecting the political mahouts of the time with McGraw's team.

Columbia Park, located at 29th Street and Columbus Avenue,

was in a section of Philadelphia known as "Brewerytown." An aroma of fermented barley and hops filled the air, along with epithets against the Giants.

Seeking a psychological advantage, McGraw outfitted his club with special uniforms for the occasion—coal-black suits with sparkling white lettering, white stockings and white box-caps with black visors.

"I'll never forget the impression we created in Philadelphia," McGraw wrote, "and the thrill I got personally when the Giants trotted out from their dugout in their new uniforms. I have heard army men say that the snappiest looking outfit is usually made up of the best fighters. I can well understand that. The effect of being togged out in snappy uniforms was immediately noticeable among the players. The Athletics, in their regular season uniforms, appeared dull alongside our players."

In his new uniform Matty, the starting pitcher in the first game, looked calmly regal, a blond giant with his muscles taut and tense under the billowing knickers and top shirt.

Before the game began at three in the afternoon a squadron of photographers ran on the field, delaying the start of proceedings, in order to snap pictures of Big Six as he warmed up. Matty was getting accustomed to such attention and seemed to flourish under such pre-game pressure. The Athletics' starting pitcher, Eddie Plank, went about his pre-game preparations with nary a photographer to bother him.

Then Matty watched casually as McGraw strutted to home plate to accept a small statue of a white elephant from Lave Cross, as a rebuke to his remark about Mack having a "white elephant on his hands." Surprisingly, McGraw was gracious, as he took the statue, doffed his cap, made a small bow to the jeering fans, and returned to the Giants' dugout. (The A's already had adopted the white elephant as their symbol.)

When the game began, Plank hit Bresnahan with the first pitch, sending Giant supporters into a rage. On the other hand, Matty threw exactly four pitches in the bottom of the inning, disposing of the first three A's batters—Hartsel on one pitch, Bristol Lord on one pitch, and Harry Davis on two pitches. In the second inning it took only six pitches for Matty to retire the side. Using his big overhand curve, mixed in with an occasional fadeaway, fastball, and spitter, Big Six was in complete control. Rarely did he fall behind A's batters. The worst damage he suffered through five innings was when Seybold rocketed one off his stomach. Matty scrambled after the ball to throw Seybold out, then retired to the bench for minor first aid.

The first Mackman to reach first base was Schreck, whose short pop into center was dropped by Donlin after some confusion about who was going to take the ball—second baseman Billy Gilbert or shortstop Bill Dahlen. But Matty quickly induced his rival hurler Plank to bang into a double play. To open the fourth inning the first legitimate hit off Matty was Hartsel's liner over second base. But Hartsel advanced no further, as Matty put the clamps on the A's.

With both sides scoreless going into the fifth, Matty, a batter with more than the usual skills possessed by a pitcher, started things off by singling into centerfield. After Bresnahan forced Matty at second base, the catcher stole second and came home as Donlin grounded one through the left side of the Athletics' infield. A mighty roar went up from the 500 Giant fans in Columbia Park and in all of those taverns back in New York where, via tickers and black-boards, thousands of viewers received notice of each play little more than five seconds after it occurred.

The roar became even louder when Sandow Mertes, the left-fielder, doubled Donlin home with the second run of the inning. Having a two-run margin to work on, Matty gained confidence as he rolled along. Schreck's ground-rule double opened the sixth for the Athletics, but he could advance only as far as third base, as Big Six fanned Hartsel and retired Lord on an easy fly ball. Schreck, the cracker-eater, was the only Athletic to reach third base on Matty all day.

The Giants added a run in the ninth, helped along by a bunt from Matty's bat that advanced Gilbert to second base. Gilbert scored from there on Bresnahan's single. The final score of the game was 3-0. Matty's docket read: no walks, six strikeouts, four hits allowed (all ground-rule doubles), and, of course, no runs allowed.

The next day the Series traveled to the Polo Grounds. Charles Albert "Chief" Bender, Mack's Chippewa Indian hurler who always signed his autograph as "Charley Bender" as a way of quietly signaling the world how he felt about his nickname, duplicated Matty's 3-0 game. He gave up only four hits, beating McGinnity.

With the Series tied at one game each, it was obvious that, regardless of how the cynics felt, Waddell would not get to take his turn on the mound. Instead, Mack announced that Andy Coakley would work the third game in Philadelphia. When it rained heavily on the morning of October 11, the two clubs named McGraw and

Mack's captain, Lave Cross, to inspect the damp premises. By the time they made a tour of the field, the sun emerged. But with only 4000 fans in the stands it was mutually decided to call off the game. By agreement the third contest would still be played in Philadelphia, then the next two in New York. With the schedule reshuffled and an extra day of rest, Matty received an opportunity to start the third game. It would set up a mismatch, for by this time Matty's fadeaway was working as never before. The A's, having never been subjected to such a pitch before, were baffled and frustrated by it.

The Giants won, 9-0, as Matty's teammates clubbed Coakley for nine runs on nine hits, while taking advantage of four errors. Under the circumstances, it was remarkable that Coakley pitched all nine innings on a cold, raw afternoon. Throughout the proceedings the benumbed Philadelphia fans, 11,000 of them, looked on glumly as Matty pitched his second straight shutout. This time he loosened up a bit with his bases on balls, finally yielding *one*, even hitting one batter. But he struck out eight men. Not a single Athletic reached third base.

Matty had now won two Giant victories on shutouts, both in hostile Philadelphia territory. With the Series shifting to New York on Friday and Saturday, the newspapers reported that the momentum was now with the Giants. McGraw was prepared to pitch McGinnity on Friday in the fourth game. Normally Matty would pitch again on Sunday, giving him two full days of rest. However, there would be no Sunday game in New York, due to the prohibitive encyclical against Sunday baseball in both New York and Philadelphia. The only question that remained was whether McGraw would choose after the Friday game to come back with Matty on Saturday, after only 24 hours. When McGinnity took a sizzling 1-0 game from Plank at the Polo Grounds on Friday the thirteenth, to give the Giants a 3-1 edge in games, McGraw chose to go all out to end it the next day. He might have elected to pitch Dummy Taylor, thus providing Matty with three full days of rest if the Giants lost on Saturday. Instead, Matty was McGraw's choice. Although he hadn't worked with one day of rest as a regular habit, Matty had done it before; McGraw was certain he could do it again.

An overflow crowd of 24,817 flooded the Polo Grounds on Saturday, October 14. Many stood ten deep for hours in the roped-off portion beneath the fence, along with horse-and-buggy parties parked there. There was also a scattering of automobiles in the area, packed with passengers. Fans hung on the fence or sat precariously on the grandstand roof; some peered at the game through glasses from housetops and distant poles. These diehards were confirmed in their belief that the Giants were the best team in creation. All that remained was to codify the fact that Matty, too, was the best pitcher in the universe.

As the Giants trotted onto the field, Matty, the last to arrive (which was his studied practice), received a magnificent reception. For over a minute the crowd applauded him, yelling for him to acknowledge their tribute by doffing his cap. Instead, he walked over to McGinnity and ostentatiously removed Joe's headgear. McGinnity returned the compliment. Then Matty waved his arm at the crowd, as they implored him to "Go get 'em!"

Up against Matty was Bender. For four innings both pitchers shut out the opposition. In the fifth inning Bender suddenly lost control, walking the first two Giant batters, Mertes and Dahlen, on eight pitches. Devlin's precise bunt moved them up on the bases. Gilbert, a clutch hitter throughout this Series, flied deep to left, as both runners again advanced, with Mertes scoring the first run of the game.

The way Matty kept mowing down the Athletics, the one run loomed larger each inning. But in the eighth Bender gave up an insurance run, with a walk to Matty setting it up. (Matty batted .250 in the Series, better than his team's batting average of .209.) Bresnahan walloped one over the crowd in left field for a ground-rule double, permitting Matty to go to third base. From there Matty scored the second and final run of the game when Browne's grounder caromed off Bender's leg. It was only fitting that he should score the run that placed the game beyond the Athletics' reach, for he had been more dominant than any pitcher ever had or ever would be.

As the A's came to bat for their final chance in the bottom of the ninth inning, Matty had already retired the last seven batters to face him. Now he disposed of Lord on a weak grounder back to the box. Davis did the same, further dramatizing the futility of batting against Matty that afternoon. Cross ended it all by grounding out to Dahlen at short. The last ten A's had gone down in order. It took Matty just 95 minutes to capture his third shutout in six days, giving the Giants their first world title, four games to one.

Now the Polo Grounds rocked with noise, the crowd milling around for an hour after the game. Hats, umbrellas, canes, and seat cushions were flung into the air. Fans charged onto the diamond to carry their heroes to the clubhouse in right center field. From their safe vantage point, several Giants appeared on the second floor of the clubhouse to throw souvenir gloves and caps to fans waiting below. The band struck up its "Tammany, Tammany" victory march, as fans danced crazily to the song.

But the hero among all heroes—"the man who sparkled like a diamond in a coal mine," as Jonathan Yardley has written—was Matty. He had pitched 27 straight scoreless innings in winning three shutouts, walked only a single batter, struck out 18 and had a perfect 0.00 earned run average. Only one Philadelphian reached third base over the three games, an astonishing feat of preventive pitching. Few of those in attendance could recall a difficult play that Matty's fielders had been pressed to make. (A jarring note were two errors Matty himself made, fielding his position.)

The *New York Times*'s exultant description of the final game tried to put the deed in perspective. Like everybody else, the journalist got carried away. Here is how it went:

> Geological records show that Vesuvius disturbs the earth and that seismic demonstrations are felt by the greater number. But if that doctrine had been promulgated in the vicinity of the Polo Grounds yesterday, as Christy Mathewson and Roger Bresnahan of the New York Baseball Club unfurled their victorious yellow banner—"The GIANTS, WORLD'S CHAMPIONS, 1905"—it would have been minimized. For, as volcanoes assert themselves upon the earth's surface surely must that deafening, reverberating roar have lifted Manhattan's soil from its base. . . .
>
> Be it recorded here, New York possesses the pitching marvel of the century, Christy Mathewson, the Giant slabman, who made the world's championship possible for New York . . . he may be legitimately designated as the premier pitching wonder of all baseball records. The diamond has known its Clarksons, its Keefes, its Caruthers. Their records radiate. But to Mathewson belongs the palm, for his almost superhuman accomplishment . . . which will stand for all pitchers of the future as a mark . . . Baseball New York appreciates this work. That fact was amply demonstrated yesterday when it gave Mathewson a marvelous vocal panegyric and placed upon his modest brow a bellowed wreath that evoked only a half-suppressed smile and bow . . .

Such unstinted praise had rarely been bestowed on any baseball player, much less any other human being. Matty now stood bestride the baseball world, a hero, role model, paragon of the mound, presumably loved and respected by all those who came in contact with him (with the exception of the young lemonade vendor who went down under his punch.) Even the evil-tempered McGraw was an admirer of Big Six, wasn't he?

What's more, Matty had won money for McGraw, who bet a cool $500 with those Philadelphia rooters foolish enough to wager against the great Giant pitcher. Matty also helped each of his Giant teammates to earn an extra $1,142 in winner's shares, while the Philadelphia players settled for the loser's end of $382 each.

In 1905 Matty was the perfect pitching machine that McGraw had long envisioned, a man with impeccable control on the mound and in his private life. As baseball reigned without serious competition from football or basketball, with no television or radio to carry instant messages of ballplayer triumphs or failures, newspapers were left with a monopoly on spreading the word of Matty's magnificence. If there were warts and flaws in the makeup of the pitcher, nobody heard about them, or reported their existence.

A young reporter named Grantland Rice, who would become one of the most widely read and admired sportswriters of his day, was 25 years old in 1905, exactly Matty's age. Rice, covering the World Series that year for the Atlanta *Journal*, openly expressed his amazement at what he'd just witnessed.

"I marvel at what Matty has done," he wrote. "In those few days he was the greatest pitcher I've ever seen. I believe he could have continued to pitch shutouts until Christmas!"

Later the two men became fast friends, golfing together and playing poker, checkers, and chess—usually with Matty ending up on the winning side.

"I got to know him better than any of the other Giants," said Rice, the consort of many greats and near-greats of the sports world, "and he turned out to be as fine a companion as I ever knew." In his autobiography Rice provided a revealing insight into the pitching psychology that helped to place Matty above all others.

"An alibi is sound and needed in all competition," Matty told Rice, "I mean in the high-up brackets. One of the foundations of success in sport is confidence in yourself. So you can't afford to admit that an opponent is better than you are. So, if you lose to him, there must be a reason—a bad break; you must have an alibi to show why you lost. If you haven't one, you must fake one. Your self-confidence must be maintained. But *keep* that alibi to *yourself*. That's where it belongs, don't spread it around. Lose gracefully in the open. To yourself, lose bitterly, but learn. You can learn little from victory. You can learn everything from defeat."

It should come as no surprise that Matty always regarded his work in the 1905 World Series as his greatest achievement. Yet, oddly, he said that the Philadelphia team that he overwhelmed in '05 was not as good as other Athletic clubs that he would pitch against in future years.

⑨

JOY
AND
SORROW

F OLLOWING the canonization of Matty by an adoring press and fans he looked forward eagerly to the 1906 season. Jane had given birth during the off-season to John Christopher Mathewson, bringing further joy to the Mathewson household and pleasure to McGraw, who was proud that Matty's first-born was named for him.

However, the arrival of the blue-eyed, light-haired Christy Jr. meant that the close, off-the-field social relationship between the Mathewsons and McGraws would come temporarily to a halt. "We're still on speaking terms," Blanche McGraw said reassuringly. But before the season began the McGraws moved into quarters at the Washington Inn, a residential hotel near the Polo Grounds, while the Mathewsons remained in the furnished apartment which they'd previously shared with the McGraws. This arrangement permitted Little Napoleon to engage in his heavy thinking undisturbed by the caterwauling of Matty's infant.

On the field, McGraw, with a new three-year contract worth $15,000 a season under his belt, anticipated smooth sailing for his team. Blessed with his "pitching machine" Matty, plus a truculent, talented supporting cast—most of them Irish-Americans like himself—McGraw boasted that his team was too good to be headed off by Chicago. McGraw's celebrity was such that he invested some of his money in a pool hall on Herald Square with two partners, Jack Doyle, a gambler, and the well-known jockey Tod Sloan. At the midwinter opening of the hall the brilliant young billiards champ Willie Hoppe was a guest, along with several Giants players. But Matty begged off on the grounds that he was needed more at home with Christy Jr.

There were some problems in the Giants' world. But they didn't loom large. Mike Donlin, for one thing, had been thrown into jail in the off-season for disorderly conduct while under the influence of alcohol, and for waving a pistol around on a train from New York City to Troy. After cooling his heels in an Albany jail for a night, Donlin coughed up the fine and was released in sufficient time to join his teammates at their Memphis spring training headquarters. Other Giants, such as Bill Dahlen, were putting on age, and McGinnity was showing further reluctance at this stage for pitching both ends of double-headers. But, on the whole, McGraw had reason to be hopeful.

As the club marched north from Memphis to start the new season, McGraw added another touch: he instructed his tailors to sew "World's Champions" on the Giants' shirt-fronts, instead of "New York." In case people hadn't heard about it, of course.

However, the first sign that things were about to turn sour occurred just as the season got under way. Although the Giants got off to a good start, they did it without their star pitcher. Matty came down with what he thought was a cold. Suffering from fever, chills, and fatigue, he tried to fight it off. When his ailment was finally diagnosed as diphtheria, it became necessary for him to be quarantined from his family, as well as teammates.

For three weeks Matty's health was the subject of constant concern on the sports pages. After he was hospitalized crowds gathered to hear reports on his progress. Some newspapers published extras, going so far as to headline the news that: MATTY WALKS! To appease the curious the hospital presented almost hourly bulletins, detailing how high or low Matty's fever had fluctuated on that particular day.

McGraw's fears for his friend Matty were genuine, since he had seen so many in his own family succumb to the dreadful disease. Knowing at first-hand that diphtheria could often be fatal, he maintained daily contact with Jane and the people at the hospital who were tending to Matty.

After Matty's successful recovery he rejoined the team, somewhat weaker, and began to win games again. However, other mishaps were conspiring to ruin the Giants' season. Always a source of trouble for McGraw, Donlin broke his leg sliding against Cincinnati. The injury was especially vexing, for Mike had been leading the National League in hitting at the time. Making matters worse, Bresnahan was beaned by a pitched ball, Dan McGann broke his arm, and Gilbert, only 30, experienced a sharp decline in his batting. These misfortunes combined with the failure of pitchers McGinnity, George Wiltse, Leon Ames, and Taylor to fully compensate for Matty's diminished output. Big Six worked only 266 innings, about 100 less than his norm, while his victory total was down at 22, admittedly good for any normal pitcher—but not for a Matty.

Considering the adverse circumstances, Matty's performance was heart-warming, for there were those who didn't expect him to return so quickly.

The low point in Matty's year was reached in early June at the Polo Grounds, when he was the starting pitcher in a 19-0 rout suffered at the hands of the Cubs. He was pounded for nine runs in the first inning before McGraw showed mercy and removed him. By his own confession, Matty said, "I was hit as hard as any other time in my life." However, he was not the only guilty party in this massacre, for two other Giant pitchers followed him to the mound, each with little success.

In musing about his dismal showing that afternoon, Matty said: "After a disastrous inning of this kind, a pitcher, if left in the box, is often as good, just as invincible as he was before. I cite this as one of the most curious phenomena of baseball. Possibly it is only a sample of the mathematics of the game."

More curious was the appearance with the Giants of Henry, Matty's younger brother by six years. Taller than Christy, at 6'3", somewhat less bulky but also right-handed, Henry had also done some pitching in Pennsylvania, in and around Factoryville. Christy recommended Henry to McGraw for a tryout at a time when the Cubs were so far in front that it made scarce difference who pitched for the Giants.

Henry made his ill-fated start in September, as the Giants ended the season at the Polo Grounds. He pitched a full nine innings, gave up seven runs, while walking 14 and hitting one batter. Before the season was over Henry got into one more game, fared little better and managed to convince McGraw that pitching talent was hardly an inherited Mathewson characteristic. Although Henry reported to the Giants' spring training camp in Los Angeles the next year and appeared in one game during the regular season of 1907, he obviously didn't have the ability to help his brother. However, he became part of an eternal baseball trivia question: "Which two pitching brothers won more games than any other brother combination?" Henry, of course, contributed a zero to Christy's 373 victories.

So the 1906 season came down to a grindingly disappointing conclusion for the Giants. Under "The Peerless Leader," Frank Chance, also their first baseman, the Cubs galloped off with the National League flag. They took 116 games in a 152-game season, a major league record to this day. Chance, like his counterpart McGraw, was a savage driver of men, relentless in pursuit of victory. Unlike McGraw, Chance was noted for playing "clean ball," although both men inspired great loyalty from their janissaries.

More important, Chance was at the helm of a wonderfully talented group of ballplayers. The Cubs' infield of lyric fame—Tinker to Evers to Chance—was rounded out by a virtually anonymous third baseman, Harry Steinfeldt. Ironically, Steinfeldt batted .327, higher than all the others in that storied infield. Chance also had a first-rate outfield of Frank Schulte, Rabbit Slagle, and Jimmy Sheckard, plus an all-time catcher in Johnny Kling. The most dominant factor, however, was a pitching staff headed by Ed Reulbach, Orval Overall, Jack Pfeister, and Mordecai "Three-Finger" Brown, that allowed less than two runs per nine innings.

The most constructive note for the Giants in an otherwise disappointing year was that Bresnahan, still Matty's catcher, invented shin guards for catchers, an innovation that caused some of the more macho players to blush with shame. But others, like Bresnahan, who had to get behind the bat, welcomed such thoughtfulness.

The defeat in 1906, after such rousing success in 1905, made it apparent to McGraw that he had to make changes on his roster, replacing several of his aging heroes with fresh talent. True, Matty, now off the diphtheria anti-toxin that occasionally had caused him to go weak-kneed the previous year, was still there to be counted on. But Matty could not do it alone, even if at times it looked like he might do just that.

One of the changes turned out to be voluntary. Convinced that he had a budding acting career, Donlin, also newly married to actress Mabel Hite, threw down the gauntlet to McGraw: for a $600 raise he would consent to a non-alcoholic clause in his contract. McGraw grouchily refused, contending that his outfielder was trying to blackmail him. Turkey Mike proceeded to walk out on the club, depriving the Giants of a superb batter, when he wasn't putting in time at the corner saloon.

"Donlin was born on Memorial Day and has been parading around ever since," was how McGraw dismissively summed up his recalcitrant player.

McGraw called on Dick Kinsella, his one-man scouting staff, to come up with new faces for the Giants. Kinsella ordinarily made a living by running a thriving paint shop in Springfield, Illinois. But he reaped more enjoyment scouring the countryside, in his derby and high stiff collar, for raw talent on the hoof. One of his recruits was second baseman Larry Doyle, a gangly, ingenuous 20-year-old out of the mines of Caseyville, Illinois. The young man had been playing for Springfield, Illinois, in the Three-I League when Kinsella spotted him and passed the word along to McGraw. On Kinsella's say-so the Giants paid $4500 to Springfield for Doyle, an unheard-of sum for a minor leaguer.

When Doyle reported to the Giants in the midsummer of 1907, the purchase paid immediate reverse dividends, as Larry committed five errors in his first game. Oddly, McGraw felt compassion for Doyle, for he remembered his own faulty play when he first landed with Baltimore in 1891.

Another Kinsella nominee was 18-year-old Fred Merkle from Watertown, Wisconsin. McGraw put Merkle at second base late in the season but then decided the lad was cut out to be a first baseman. Both Merkle and Doyle, despite their rough indoctrination period, remained around long enough at the Polo Grounds to become immensely productive and famous.

There were others that McGraw called up: Otis "Doc" Crandall came from Cedar Rapids, a club that McGraw had played for at the start of his career. Doc would become a fine relief pitcher, often hustling to the rescue of anyone other than Matty, who generally finished what he started. Buck Herzog, an infielder, was also added to the Giants' roster from a Pennsylvania league.

Despite the incipient youth movement and a fast start in 1907, the Giants failed to be a contending team. By mid-season some even suspected that McGraw had gotten so tired of losing that he preferred journeying to the race tracks, where he bet heavily and often. For a man like McGraw to be accused of losing his ardor for baseball and his Giants, at the age of 34, was heresy. Yet, there was some reason to think that he was annoyed by the constant second-guessing of writers, the mercurial emotions of the fans, and the night-crawling of many of his players. They couldn't all be like Matty and McGraw knew it. But there were rumors that Roger Bresnahan was in line to succeed him as manager. That didn't sit well with McGraw, either.

However, McGraw appreciated that his team, losers of the last seven games of the season and mired in a fourth-place finish at 82-71, were better than they appeared to be. He chose to face down his detractors in 1908. Even if McGinnity was fading and others were growing older, there was still Matty to lead the way and the promising youngsters who he knew had the makings of excellent players.

There was no way that McGraw, under pressure from Brush to quit looking at horse flesh and get down to business, would back down from the job at hand.

10

A MEMORABLE
YEAR

I N 1908 the search for redemption by McGraw began by his selection of the little town of Marlin,
Texas, as the Giants' spring training site. He had soured on Los
Angeles as a training headquarters because he wanted a more spar-
tan environment in which he could supervise his men without distraction.

One of the most literate of sportswriters during Matty's time,
John Kieran, had described life in spring training camps as a series
of practical jokes. "The camps are crowded with ducks left swim-
ming in bathtubs, young alligators tucked under pillows of unsus-
pecting sleepers and snipe hunts all night long in the hills with
starry-eyed rookies left holding the bag," Kieran wrote.

But McGraw did not envision Marlin as a stomping grounds
for gags. To begin with, on each training day his players walked
from their hotel to the ball park along railroad tracks that were
nearby. Then they walked back to the Arlington Hotel, which was
about half a mile away. McGraw didn't care to encourage mineral
baths, which is what Marlin was known for, if known at all. In
fact, he had chosen Marlin, a town of 4000 in north-central Texas,
100 miles south of Dallas, because it was "out of the way." A perfect place, he figured, to impose stern discipline on the players.
"I'm going to put my heel down good and hard," he promised. Nobody had a reason to doubt him.

Also, Texas was far enough away from Manhattan and the rest

of the big-league map for the Giants to be regarded more kindly there than elsewhere. They were not yet pariahs in that vast cow country. The proximity of Marlin to larger Texas cities such as Houston and Fort Worth also assured that on weekends, at least, crowds would come out to see the Giants play their exhibition games.

As a youth Matty had viewed spring training as a pleasurable ritual: "I'd read about the big league clubs going south and used to think what a grand life it must be. Riding in Pullmans, some pleasant exercise which did not entail the responsibility of a ball game, and plenty of food, with a little social recreation, were all parts of my dream. A young ballplayer looks on his first spring training trip as a stage-struck young woman regards the theatre . . . She thinks only of the lobster suppers, the applause and the lights and the life, but nowhere in her dream is there a place for the raucous voice of the stage manager . . . As actors begin to dread the drudgery of rehearsing, so do baseball men detest the drill of spring training . . . What makes me maddest is that the fans up north imagine that we are having some kind of picnic in Marlin. But my idea of no setting for a pleasure party is Marlin!"

Of all the players, added Matty, the pitchers "have the hardest time of any specialists who go into a spring training camp. His work is of a more routine nature than that which attaches to any of the other branches of the baseball art . . . it's nothing but a steady grind." Marlin, in particular, complained Matty, had a skinned diamond, made of dirt, "where the ball gets wingy." Little pieces of the baseball, he continued, were torn loose by contact with the rough dirt, not at all like the smooth, grass-stained ball prevalent around the circuit in mid-season.

Even the Southern hospitality of Marlin Springs' merchants in setting up barbecues and fish fries for the players at the Falls of the Brazos, a lovely resort four miles away, didn't change Matty's perspective about the training ordeal. Furthermore, when Matty dared to straddle a bronco, he had difficulty sitting down afterward.

The only thing that stood up under the strain was his fadeaway. "He fairly made the ball talk down there," wrote Sam Crane. "He had perfect control all spring."

Regardless of what Matty may have thought about the rigors of Marlin near the over-heated Gulf of Mexico, McGraw seemed to have guessed right about the place. For within a couple of months after the season got under way the Giants found themselves in one of the most unusual four-team races anyone had ever seen. The young fellows on the club—McGraw's "Kiddie Corps" of Crandall, Merkle, Doyle, Herzog, and Al Bridwell, the shortstop obtained in an off-season deal with the Boston Braves—were doing splendidly. Obviously, they hadn't perished under the withering regimen at Marlin. The veterans, like Fred Tenney, the 13-year first baseman, another expatriate from the Braves in the deal involving Bridwell, were doing well, too. That also included Donlin, back again in the Giants' lineup, after his aborted dramatic career. Cy Seymour in the outfield, Devlin at third, and Bresnahan behind the plate thrived after the "deprivations" of Marlin.

As far as the pitchers were concerned, Ames, McGinnity, Wiltse, and Taylor, once considered to be declining, began to provide solid support for Matty.

Big Six knew in 1908 that teams that had once been tempted to throw away their bats when he strode to the mound had connected more regularly with his pitches in 1907. Now he was out to prove again that his mere presence could inspire the same fear among batters as it had earlier in his career. Reports of his pitching death, he argued, with merit, were grossly exaggerated.

Before the season began Matty experimented with still another pitch to add to his repertoire. This one was called a "dry spitter" because there simply wasn't any spit or other foreign substance on it. Nonetheless, it broke like a spitter, managing to fool several batters in spring training. The ball floated up to the plate without much force behind it. Just as the batter prepared to take a healthy swipe at it, the ball would suddenly waver, then drop dead in the catcher's mitt.

"It was just like a piece of paper fluttering along and encountering a puff of wind from the opposite direction," wrote Sid Mercer in the New York *Globe.*

The new freak pitch accented the fact that, in an era when the ball generally acted as if it was water-logged, something could be done to make it even deader.

Of all the various pitches that Matty had learned to master by 1908, there was his fastball, which sometimes finished with an inward shoot or upward shoot; the slowball, which did not curve or revolve; the drop curve, often his most successful pitch that could break abruptly or gradually; the out-curve; the under-hand curve; the celebrated fadeaway, which Matty preferred to call the fallaway; and the spitball, a damp pitch used infrequently.

As the National League race got ready for its April opening, three managers—McGraw, Chance of the Cubs, and Fred Clarke of the Pirates—shepherding teams that were expected to be in the running, issued their predictions.

"We have only one team to beat this year," said McGraw, "that's the Cubs. If we beat that outfit, with our changes in personnel, and I'm confident we will, New York will get another pennant."

Chance didn't even consider the Giants in his pronouncement. "There's only one thing for the world's champs to do this year, and that's repeat. We've taken two pennants in a row and there's nothing to indicate we will not make it three in a row."

Clarke's chief concern was that his as yet unsigned shortstop, Honus Wagner, was still not with the club. "I must admit I'm worried without Wagner," said Clarke. "The Dutchman's decision to leave may have a very bad effect on the team. Pittsburgh's team seems good enough to finish in the first division. As for reaching the top, I would have hopes if Wagner was with us." (Several days later, Wagner got Clarke's heart pumping regularly again when he attached his signature to a Pirates contract, assuring the baseball world that its premier shortstop would be around to have an impact on the pennant struggle. Matty had always found Wagner a difficult hitter to deal with, one of the few who caused him consistent trouble. The news of Wagner's return to duty was received non-committally.)

When the Giants opened their year in Philadelphia on a wind-blown April 14 before a throaty crowd of 17,000, Matty was on the mound. The Phillies couldn't touch him. Until the final inning of the 3-1 Giant victory, Matty had them buffaloed, fanning some of the more potent Phillies like Harvard Eddie Grant, Sherry Magee, and John Titus with ease.

So overwhelming was Matty's performance that the New York papers solemnly proclaimed that "this greatest pitcher in the land" was no longer "decadent." The New York *Evening Mail* suggested that "all the medical juice from antitoxing" that had been pumped into Matty to fight diphtheria had gone at last.

Four days later, working on three days of rest, Matty went all the way to shut out Brooklyn, despite the fact that he badly strained his ankle covering first base. It had become habitual by now for the more imaginative writers to invent new metaphors that described Matty in action. Hype Igoe's latest, in honor of the win over the Dodgers, declared that Matty stood out "like a crane on an ant hill." That was more picturesque than another encomium, at a later date, that declared that Matty "toyed with the sphere as a cat would with a ball of yarn."

In the Giants' home opener on April 22 Matty beat Brooklyn 3-2, as 25,000 fans worked themselves into a frenzy over a ball club that showed signs of being revivified. Public officials estimated that the crowd was the biggest ever to attend a game at the Polo Grounds. Long before the game's start hundreds of fans formed a crescent around the front of the grandstand, gradually working their way toward home plate. As a result, many of those sitting in the stands in the lower section rarely got more than a glimpse of the game.

Brooklyn scored single runs in the fourth and eighth innings, despite Matty's brilliance, leaving the Giants one run behind in the last of the ninth. McGraw sent up Merkle to bat for Matty, with the pitcher's acquiescence, for Matty didn't take kindly to being removed either for relief pitchers or pinch-hitters. Merkle thereupon doubled into the crowd in right field, confirming McGraw's genius as a manager. With one out and two strikes against him, Donlin followed with a game-winning home run into the hands of the bleacherites in right field. The crowd set up such a tumult that reporters remarked that they'd rarely seen anything like it.

It was often said that Chicago was a city that had gone completely mad over its baseball club. Nothing else much mattered—not business, home, or family—when it came to the city's beloved Cubs. At downtown bulletin boards, where the games at Chicago's West Side Grounds were reproduced in miniature, often as many as 40,000 people gathered to watch the progress of their Cubs. New Yorkers hadn't yet been carried away to this extent by the Giants. But their enthusiasm was growing daily; it was only a matter of time before McGraw's boys would rouse the same kind of support in their home town.

After a month of the season had gone by, five teams, including Boston, were bunched together in the National League; Matty hadn't yet lost a game; and, as always, McGraw's temper was rarely under control. Following a Giants loss to Boston, 7-6, Dan McGann, a Braves infielder who had been tossed overboard by McGraw after the 1907 season, searched the lobby of Boston's Copley Square Hotel for the Giants' manager. McGann had rammed into a double play against the Giants that afternoon, causing McGraw to reward him publicly with the slurring remark that he was "a damned ice wagon." In baseball language that meant a painfully slow runner.

When McGann finally located his tormentor in the hotel's billiard room, he threw a punch at him. Within seconds the two flailed at each other. Happening to be at McGraw's side, Matty tried to put a quick halt to the fisticuffs. But before he could separate the six-foot, 195-pound McGann from his smaller antagonist, blood was spilled, both the Kentucky variety (McGann's) and the New York variety (McGraw's). Still fuming, McGraw retreated to his hotel room, locking the door behind him.

The next day McGraw repaid Matty for his timely intervention. When pitcher Wiltse was yanked out of a game against Boston, Matty was not sufficiently warmed up in the bullpen to relieve him. So McGraw, announcing *himself* as the successor to Wiltse, claimed the customary privilege of five warmup pitches. After the manager threw one pitch, Matty came jogging onto the scene, presumably ready to work. (In today's game McGraw could not have pulled off such a delaying tactic, for he would have had to pitch to one batter.) When it came to employing his wits, McGraw was incomparable. "He should have figured in the tabulated box score as one of the Giants pitchers," wrote Sid Mercer of the New York *Globe.*

It wasn't until May 13, in Pittsburgh, that Matty lost his first game, 5-1, to the Pirates. In what was the fastest game of the season (85 minutes), Matty was knocked out in the fifth inning.

In the next series, played at Cincinnati, Matty started twice in three days, and was clobbered each time by the Reds batters. In the first game the Reds flattened him in two innings. Trying to explain how such a great hurler could have suffered such a manhandling, Jack Ryder of the Cincinnati *Enquirer* facetiously suggested that Matty's pre-game checkers playing might have deprived Matty of his concentration. As the best checkers player in the big leagues, Matty was occasionally the butt of such silly logic. Imagine, it was offered, how many games he could win if he didn't waste his time and energy on checkers!

Even those New York sportswriters who were hardly detractors of Matty speculated that over-indulgence in checkers might account for the downfall of their pitcher. Agonizing about Matty's recent losses, McGraw grumbled that "these checkers players come from near and far at all hours of the day and night and Matty accommodates them all. If he doesn't cut it out, he'll go to pieces as a pitcher."

Matty didn't cut it out. Neither did he go to pieces, although he did lose his next start to Three-Fingered Brown. With this latest defeat the mourner's bench was out in full cry. "Poor McGraw," they wailed. "McGinnity is washed up, Wiltse isn't more than fair, Ames is too wild, Taylor is too mediocre. Now Matty's blowing up, so what's going to happen to the Giants?"

On May 29 Matty put their minds at ease with a dazzling 1-0 victory over the Dodgers at Ebbets Field. The "soft mark" had been rejuvenated. McGraw's pals from Tammany, the boxing world, and the theatre, the usual suspects such as George M. Cohan, Gentleman Jim Corbett, and the rope-swinging Will Rogers, all expressed relief.

"They say those things about every great man," said Corbett, the former heavyweight champion. "They said them about me. They should learn to lay off Matty."

There was more ammunition for the nay-sayers when in an early June game at the Polo Grounds Matty walked two Cards in succession, an event that occurred as rarely as McGraw tipping his cap to an umpire. Matty won the game anyway, by 3-2, but the win didn't help too much, for the Giants by that time had fallen behind Chicago, Cincinnati, Pittsburgh, and Philadelphia. They were barely ahead of Boston. "The Giants have no chance to finish near the top," was Joe Vila's glum assessment in the New York *Sun*. Another writer sadly suggested that Christy had thrown his arm out in 1905 when he had mystified the Athletics for a week. "Now he's just a poor fellow depending on his fielders," said this disaffected reporter.

Befitting the mood around the Giants' clubhouse, McGraw drew a three-day suspension from National League president Harry Pulliam for calling umpire Jimmy Johnston a "piece of cheese." That seemed mild to most who had followed McGraw's verbalizing— but not to Pulliam. When McGraw's suspension ended and he was back in uniform, the Giants met the Cubs in three games in New York, with the Manager Chance of Chicago sniffing a ripe opportunity to put his club in front for good. But the Giants suddenly came to life, taking all three games, one a shutout by Matty. This feat restored some dignity to the Giants' cause, as well as launching them back into a race that had appeared to be settling into a two-way battle between the Cubs and Pirates.

Continuing their steady advance, the Giants journeyed across the Brooklyn Bridge to Ebbets Field for a double-header with the Dodgers. The largest crowd, including a contingent of diehards from Manhattan, ever to bulge the confines of the ballpark watched the New Yorkers walk off with both games. After rescuing Wiltse in the ninth inning of the first game, Matty went the route in the second game. "He just breezed along," wrote the New York *Press*, emphasizing that after the first game was over Matty continued to warm up with Bresnahan between games. Then he took the mound

again, without a breather, and picked up where he left off in the
first game.

Suspecting that additional transfusions were needed to keep
the Giants in the race, McGraw pried loose a young left-hander
named Richard "Rube" Marquard from the Indianapolis club of the
American Association for $11,000. It was said to be the largest price
ever paid for a minor-league player. Rube Marquard had been nicknamed after Rube Waddell—but was thought to be considerably
more moderate in his habits.

Inevitably, Marquard was tagged as "The $11,000 Beauty." But,
shortly, he also earned the less affectionate nickname of "$11,000
Lemon," following several failed starts for the Giants. In time,
however, he became a steady winner for the Giants, strongly complementing Matty.

The other purchase made by McGraw was a catcher, John Tortes
"Chief" Meyers, a Cahuilla Indian who had briefly attended Dartmouth College. With St. Paul, in the American Association, Meyers was highly touted, and McGraw dug deep again for $6000 to
add the youngster to the New York roster. A man of dignity and
intelligence, Meyers, like his fellow Indian Albert Bender of the
A's, loathed the nickname of "Chief," which was automatically
affixed in the baseball world to people of his heritage. It didn't take
long for Meyers to become not only an appendage on the field to
Matty but a firm admirer.

In Lawrence Ritter's book, *The Glory of Their Times*, Meyers
spoke with great warmth of his pitcher:

> What a pitcher he was! The greatest that ever lived. I don't think he
> ever walked a man in his life because of wildness. The only time he
> might walk a man was because he was pitching too fine to him, not
> letting him get a good ball to hit. But there was never a time he
> couldn't throw the ball over the plate if he wanted to. How we loved
> to play for him. We'd break our necks for the guy. If you made an
> error behind him or anything of that sort, he'd never get mad or sulk.
> He'd come over and pat you on the back. He had the sweetest, most
> gentle nature. Gentle in every way. He was a great checkers player
> and could play several men at once. Actually, that's what made him
> a great pitcher—his wonderful retentive memory. Any time you hit
> a ball hard off him, you never got a pitch in the same spot again.

From July on the National League race evolved into a three-
club brawl between the Cubs, Giants, and Pirates, even as the
American League chase boiled down to Cleveland, Chicago, and
Detroit. In such a close competition it was not unusual for Matty

to work on a steady diet of two days' rest. For example, he beat Cincinnati 2-1 on July 6 and won by the same score on July 9, with both games taking place in Cincinnati. Never questioning Mc-Graw's use of his right arm, Matty started games and finished them.

On July 7, playing at Chicago, the Giants went ahead 4-1 in the last of the ninth, with Otis Crandall holding the Cubs at bay. Then the roof collapsed on the rookie right-hander, as the Cubs walked three men on base after one out. Matty had been warming up during the early part of the game. But, feeling that Crandall had matters under control, he decided to go in to shower and dress. While he was under the water, the call went out from McGraw for Matty to rush to the mound. Wet as he was, Matty grabbed some-body else's baseball trousers, shirt and stockings. He couldn't squeeze his spikes over his wet feet, so he reached for a pair of street shoes. Forgetting his cap, he sloshed across the field to the mound. By that time, frantically stalling for Matty's arrival, McGraw had sent in McGinnity, who walked in a run, making the score 4-2.

After taking only two warmup pitches and nodding that he was ready—"Everybody who saw that nod knew that the stuff was off for Chicago"—Matty got the second out on a "love tap" to the infield, as a run scored. With the game in the balance, he fanned the last Cub batter, cementing a 4-3 Giants victory.

"The next time, damn it," shouted McGraw, "Don't take your shower in the middle of a pennant race!"

Two days later, playing before the usual noisy crowd in Chi-cago, Matty lost a brilliant pitcher's duel, 1-0, to his nemesis, Three-Fingered Brown. Brown's curve balls jerked like a trapped trout on a hook—but Charles Dryden of the Chicago *Tribune* insisted that the defeat for Matty was due to his staying up late the night before playing checkers. By this time, Matty was getting tired of respond-ing to such assertions.

Each game in the National League now took on the aspect of a crisis. On August 4, the Giants swept the Reds at the Polo Grounds in both games of a doubleheader. The first one went twelve in-nings, before the Giants pushed a run across to win, 4-3. They won the second, 4-1. Both victories went to Matty, and nobody regis-tered any remarks about checkers-playing.

When McGinnity weakened in the ninth inning of the opener, there was Matty, who had been cooling his heels waiting to start the second game, trudging in to the mound again to save the game—which he did. After the Reds tied the score, they never had a chance.

In the second game Matty showed no sign of the physical strain of having worked the last three innings of the first game.

Asked a few days later by the New York *American* how he thought this hectic race was going to end, Matty said: "I think the Giants will outgame the Cubs, even if the Cubs are a fast-fielding, heady, aggressive team . . . the Pirates must be reckoned with, but they are more or less a one-man organization—without Wagner they'd have a hard time getting into the first division. Our greatest chance, I believe, lies in the fact that we'll finish the season at home. The encouragement of a big, friendly city is no small factor in a team's success."

On August 10 the largest crowd ever to watch a Monday afternoon ball game in America—some 20,000—trekked to the Polo Grounds to watch Matty beat Orval Overall of the Cubs, 3-2. Monday traditionally was recognized as a poor baseball day. Blue Monday, working people called it. But they came to this one, knowing that Matty would be pitching and the Giants would be very much in the contest.

But when the Giants lost a doubleheader at St. Louis in mid-August, with McGinnity and Ames suffering the defeats, McGraw expressed his frustration. This was no way to challenge the Pirates and Cubs. However, the next day Matty made things right again, with a shutout victory over the Cards. With a storm threatening to curtail the game, and the Giants at bat in the fifth inning, McGraw encouraged Cy Seymour, who was perched on third base, to steal home—even though the Card catcher, Bill Ludwig, had the ball in his hands. Jack Barry, next up, was instructed to strike out as quickly as possible, in order to complete the half-inning.

"The team is filled with confidence with Matty in the box," said the St. Louis *Post-Dispatch*. The writer, Jim Crusinberry, might have added that McGraw was also filled with underhanded tricks. But nobody on the Giants bench was heard to complain, not even Matty.

The recent double loss to the Cards on a Sunday in St. Louis once again put in focus the subject of Matty's scruples about Sunday baseball. The "contract" that Matty had made with his mother before he entered professional baseball still held: he would play ball for money—but never on Sunday.

Some writers, such as Sam Crane, openly suggested that the Giants would have a much better chance to win the race if Matty decided to break his word. "Matty is loyal to the Giants," wrote

Crane, "but all of his fellow players—and I—wish he would step into the breach and help out on Sundays. Rivals take advantage of Matty's refusal to play on Sunday and crowd in double-headers at every opportunity. It places McGraw and his team at a disadvantage. If he is thoroughly conscientious, he deserves credit. But is he?"

Matty was aware of the rumblings about his intransigent stand on Sunday baseball. He'd also read some of the pot-shots that had been taken at him about his checkers-playing, as he went from city to city. When the club reached Cincinnati in late August, several champion checkers players from the state of Ohio threw out challenges to him. Invariably, he would accept such proposals, for he loved such competition, especially against the best. But now he refused. He agreed that everything should be strictly business on this trip; too much was at stake.

This switch of position pleased McGraw no end. But the manager was even more delighted when Matty came to him in Chicago and promised that, if double-headers started to pile up, with one possibly scheduled for that Sunday, he'd be willing to start in one of those games. Matty knew that the Giants' pitching was thinner than a pencil, and the whispering about McGinnity hinted that the Iron Man was drained. Except for Matty, there was no pitcher on the staff who would be able to carry the team through the last desperate month of the campaign. In the name of team spirit, he was now willing to abrogate his long-held principles.

As the summer wound down, it was impossible to predict how this most improbable of all pennant disputes would end up. The Giants found themselves on top on September 1, with a 69-45 record; Chicago was next with 70-47; and Pittsburgh was third with 69-47. For almost five months the teams had played hopscotch, causing jubilation, then despair among their supporters. But there still wasn't a clue as to who would emerge from all this fighting, clawing, and fuming.

Only one fact seemed apparent: without Matty the Giants' chances would long since have evaporated. He was experiencing the kind of year that made New York into one vast rooting section for him—he'd appeared in more than a third of his team's games, as a starter or finisher; struck out almost one in five batters; walked barely more than one hitter a game; threw shutouts in one of every three victories; and completed over two-thirds of his starts. When the game was in the balance, he wanted the ball, and McGraw was only too eager for him to have it. In 1908 there was only one appropriate word for his work: he was totally *dominant.*

There were a series of climaxes to this season, the first occurring in a hotly disputed game in Pittsburgh between the Pirates and Cubs. What happened on that September 4 afternoon was a harbinger of an event that would turn the Giants' season around, only in the wrong direction.

In the Pittsburgh home half of the tenth inning, with the score tied at 0-0 and two out, Manager Clarke of Pittsburgh reached third base after a single by Warren Gill. Three-Fingered Brown worked carefully on Honus Wagner, but the shortstop plunked a single into center field. Clarke came home on the blow, scoring the only run of the game. But instead of running down to second base and touching the bag, Gill ran just a few feet toward second, then headed gleefully for the clubhouse. He figured the game was over.

However, the alert Cub center-fielder, Artie Hofman, picked up the ball, as it bounced around in the grass, and tossed it quickly to second baseman Evers, who stepped on second base. Turning to umpire Hank O'Day, Evers loudly demanded that he declare Gill out for his failure to touch second base. In Evers's mind it was a simple forceout and the "winning run" was, therefore, nullified. The besieged O'Day, working alone that day, told Evers he hadn't seen the play. Whereupon the scrawny Cub threw a fit that would have made McGraw jealous. Other Cubs joined in the protest. But all to no avail. O'Day stood his shaky ground, refusing to invoke baseball rule 59, which called for a forceout in such a situation. Embarrassedly acknowledging that Evers's interpretation of the rule was correct, O'Day informed him that he was so occupied with the runner on third and the batter that he failed to note if Gill had gone into second base. If the play ever came up again, O'Day informed Evers, he'd be aware of it and call it. (When Matty first came into the league, only one umpire worked the games. Often when the ump, in this case O'Day, was out of position or blocked off from a play, Matty was actually asked by umpires for help in calling the play, for he had a widespread reputation for integrity and probity.)

An official protest was filed by Cubs owner Charles Murphy with National League president Pulliam, but the latter refused to honor the complaint. "I think the public prefers to see games settled on the field and not in this office," said Pulliam. The game went into the record books as a 1-0 Pirates victory, with the Cubs, at the time, falling unceremoniously into third place.

As a former pitcher who would spend 35 years as a major-league umpire listening to the bleats of players and managers, O'Day had received a jolting wake-up call. The next time, if, indeed, there was a next time, he'd be sure to be on the alert for negligent base-runners. That state of mind would come back to haunt the Giants before the season was over.

After the smoke had cleared from the incident in Pittsburgh, Matty kept the Giants on the right road with a 1-0 triumph over the Dodgers at the Polo Grounds. Al Bridwell sent the worried fans—worried because they feared the game might be called on account of darkness—home with a single that hurried Seymour across the plate with the winning run.

"Seldom have two hurlers, Matty and Nap Rucker of the Dodgers, fought such a gruelling fight," wrote Bill Kirk in the New York *American.* "Rucker pitched a masterly game and only caved in in the eleventh hour because he was pitted against the greatest twirler that ever threw a ball."

A week later Matty beat Brooklyn again, setting up the National League standings in this way: New York, 81-46; Chicago, 83-51; Pittsburgh, 82-51. Some clairvoyants already were conceding the flag to the Giants, even as others were sorely disappointed that McGraw and his hoodlums seemed about to win.

On September 18 in New York, the Giants bowled over the Pirates in two games, with Matty winning the opener, reinforcing the observation that he was as safe as the Bank of England. Tension permeated the atmosphere around New York, even as the sweet news of the double victory was carried over the bulletins. It was as if Giant rooters were waiting for painful messages from the bloody Civil War battlefields of Gettysburg and Antietam.

Neither was the continuing event local, for the *World* insisted that "the nation quivered and shook as 18 young men, most of whom will soon be quietly farming or running a cafe, played two games of baseball before the greatest throng (40,000) of humanity ever attracted to a baseball park . . . men talked and gibbered to themselves, women, forgetting all feminine reserve, leaped up to cry as tears rolled down their cheeks. 'Hit the ball, kill it, run,' they cried, 'for heaven's sakes, run!' "

But even "as the nation shook" the Giants' momentum stalled in the next ten days. Matty lost a 2-1 game to Pittsburgh and, in the process, even lost his temper momentarily when O'Day—always it was that man O'Day!—called a Pittsburgh player safe at first on a play that led to the winning run. Matty rushed O'Day, voiced his disbelief in the umpire's judgment, then nearly fell over in a swoon when he realized O'Day wasn't kidding.

When the Giants dropped a double-header on September 22 to the Cubs, 4-3, 2-1, in two fierce games, the Polo Grounds was engulfed in gloom. There were still two more games to be played in this series with the Cubs. And New Yorkers now dreaded the prospect, even if the contests would be played at home.

Each time in the last two years that the Giants had built new extensions to the Polo Grounds in order to provide more seating space, people quickly snapped up tickets. Those who couldn't squeeze into the ball park rushed to the city's newsstands to buy the latest editions of newspapers that carried the daily running story of this tense pennant race.

By the afternoon of Wednesday, September 23, the Giants still led the Cubs by six percentage points. Their chart read 87-50, with the Cubs at 90-53. The Pirates trailed both with 88-54. The stage had carefully been set for a game between the Cubs and Giants at the Polo Grounds that evolved into one of the most controversial episodes in the sport's history. Many considered it the most "famous" baseball game ever played. Depending on one's rooting inclinations, it could also have been rated infamous.

Long lines formed at the general admissions gate hours before the game began. Stores in the great city looked as if they'd been abandoned due to some freak of nature. Wherever people assembled at taverns, saloons, or barber shops, there was only a single subject of discussion. Didn't anyone work in this town?

Everywhere else in the country, in other big-league cities and, of course, in Chicago, and wherever the wires and papers carried the baseball message, minds and hearts focused on the event about to unfold at the Polo Grounds.

As the two teams completed their pre-game practice sessions, the crowd of over 30,000 stirred impatiently. Now they waited for McGraw, swelling at the belt line and paying the price for too many evenings at Dinty Moore's and Diamond Jim Brady's, to lead his charges onto the diamond. As was his calculated custom, Matty was the last to put in an appearance, fully aware that much of the drama of the day centered around his own presence. As cheers for him rumbled from the fans, Matty grinned broadly and removed his cap, waving it back and forth in semaphore.

Matty's mound foe was the left-hander Jack Pfiester (real name, Pfiestenberger), two years older than the Giant pitcher and scarcely as talented. Yet, since coming to the Cubs in 1906, Pfiester had been alarmingly successful against the Giants. So much so that he became known as "Jack the Giant-Killer."

Behind the plate was Hank O'Day. But this time he would have umpiring help from Bob Emslie, assigned to work the bases. When O'Day took up his position, McGraw snapped at him under his breath, as he headed for the Giants' dugout. All umpires were his natural enemies, even on a day when he could ill afford to antagonize those who controlled the drift of a ball game.

Evers opened the contest with a single. But Matty fanned Schulte to assure there'd be no early damage. Again in the fourth inning, Evers was a nuisance, as he rapped Matty for another base hit. But the other Cubs could add little to Evers's offense. "Players to whom the Cubs pay all sorts of fancy prices to knock the delivery of most pitchers," said the New York *World*, "where the fielders cannot get the ball, looked like 30 cents when Matty got through with them."

Through four innings, the Giants didn't fare very well with Pfiester either. So the score stood at zero for both sides in the fifth inning when Joe Tinker hit a fadeaway on a line into right center field. Donlin rushed for the ball, but when he grabbed for it it eluded his glove. Before Cy Seymour, playing center field, could retrieve the ball, Tinker sped around third base and headed for home. The play was close but Tinker slid in safely for the first Cub run. Credited with a home run, Tinker should have had no more than a double had the ball been played properly. "This boy—Donlin—should have been sent home without his supper, if this boy was our boy," said the *New York Times* caustically.

With the crowd restlessly urging their Giants on, the New Yorkers finally retaliated in the sixth inning. Steinfeldt, ordinarily a superb third baseman, took Herzog's bouncer and threw it past Chance at first base. As Buck chugged into second on the overthrow, the Polo Grounds came alive. Bresnahan bunted Herzog deftly over to third base, a tactic that McGraw taught his men until they almost hated him for it. Then the guilt-ridden Donlin cracked one through the middle, sending Herzog home with the tying run. Before the Giants could put together a big inning, Pfiester regained control of the situation, retiring the next two batters.

As the sixth, seventh, and eighth innings rolled by, Matty was masterful. The Cubs couldn't touch him, not even the pesty Evers, who flailed away at three pitches leading off the ninth. Schulte struck out, and Chance grounded out. As the Giants came to bat for their last licks, the crowd begged them to reward Matty with a run. All the while, McGraw, from the coacher's roost outside of third base, kept up a steady stream of exhortations for his men and abuse against the enemy.

It was now up to the Giants' offense to get something going before darkness could close down the affair. To start the last inning for the Giants Seymour hit one down to Evers, who made the play on it for the first out. Devlin, previously foiled by Pfiester's tosses, hit one into center field for a single, causing the large crowd to stir. Moose McCormick tried to bunt twice but hadn't learned his lessons properly from McGraw. He fouled off the ball each time. When he finally swung away with two strikes on him, McCormick hit a sharp ground ball to Evers, who threw to Tinker, forcing Devlin. The return throw to first by Tinker missed nailing McCormick by a whisker. Chance roared his disapproval of Emslie's decision, much as McGraw would have if such a verdict had gone against him. But Emslie stood his ground.

It was Fred Merkle's turn to bat. Although he'd played a handful of games in 1907, when he was just 18, he was still regarded as an untried kid. He was playing because necessity had forced McGraw's hand. Fred Tenney, the Giants' regular first baseman, had gotten out of bed that fateful morning with a painful backache and had trouble picking up his glove. So McGraw inserted Merkle into the lineup in his first starting assignment of the year. Previously, Merkle had been used as a fill-in at first, second, and in the outfield.

The first three times Merkle came to bat that day against Pfiester he was victimized by the pitcher's wicked curve balls. Now, after taking two strikes, Merkle ripped one over Chance's outstretched glove at first base. The ball sliced along the right-field foul line, an unlikely place for a right-handed batter such as Merkle to hit. As the crowd screamed in delight, McCormick tore around second and sped for third. The fans were unprepared for such production from Merkle and rewarded him with their screams.

With runners on first and third, the Giants needed only to advance McCormick 90 feet to present Matty with his victory. Sensing the kill, the crowd urged Bridwell, the next batter, to hit one safely. A skinny, left-handed batter from Friendship, Ohio, Bridwell dug in at home plate. Pfiester went into his set position. Then Bridwell's bat came around quickly on Pfiester's low pitch and the ball skipped right past the pitcher's box. Pfiester made a game but futile attempt to halt the ball's progress into the outfield. At second base, umpire Emslie almost somersaulted to avoid getting hit by the ball. He never even saw the ball hit the grass beyond the infield. But McCormick saw it as clearly as he'd ever seen anything in his baseball life, and he blazed home to score, followed all the way by McGraw, dancing crazily alongside him every step of the way.

Merkle had seen the flight of the ball, too. Running several feet toward second base, he looked across at McCormick halfway home, then headed for the Giants' clubhouse behind the bleachers in right center field. He had instinctively done what almost every other ballplayer of his time would have done: he didn't bother touching second base. In the excitement of the moment, as the fans flooded the field in their ecstasy, he didn't recall what had happened in Pittsburgh 19 days before.

Unfortunately for the Giants, the heads-up Evers, a party to the brouhaha in Pittsburgh, did. The baseball rule that hadn't been enforced against the Pirates was the same one he wanted enforced now. He knew that if he got the ball that Bridwell had hit he could make a forceout at second and invalidate the winning run. Spotting Merkle's failure to touch second, he raced out to center field and gestured to Art Hofman to return the ball to him. Hofman chased after it, then tossed it quickly back to Evers. But his throw went wild and past Evers toward first base. Iron Man McGinnity may or may not have been a conscientious student of the rule book, but he had the presence of mind to scoop up the ball. As he did, Tinker leaped on his back, challenging Iron Man for possession of the prize. Wrestling loose from Tinker's grip, McGinnity unleashed a throw that carried the ball toward the left-field grandstand.

At precisely that moment Matty, unaware of the mad scramble for the ball, was being carried off the field on the shoulders of the half-crazed crowd. But if someone had chanced to look out at second base, there was Evers, with a ball in his hands (where had he gotten it?), talking and gesticulating, first with Emslie, then O'Day. Emslie informed Evers he couldn't possibly have noticed what Merkle did or did not do at second base because he'd been too occupied in getting back on his feet and brushing himself off. However, O'Day, again in the eye of the storm, even if his vantage point had been from home plate, agreed with Evers that Merkle had not touched second base. This time O'Day made the call as he said he'd seen it. Thus, there was a forceout at second and the winning run didn't count.

The game should have continued from that point as a 1-1 tie.

Matty, as a little boy, in Factoryville. (National Baseball
Library, Cooperstown)

Growing up in the 1880s.
(National Baseball Library,
Cooperstown)

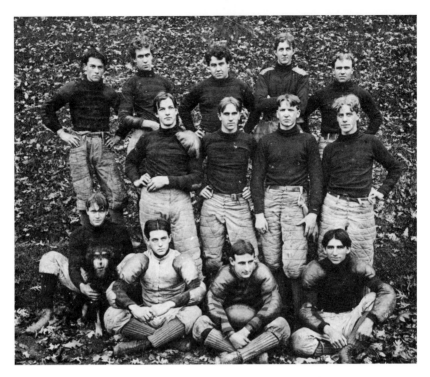

With Bucknell's football team, Matty *(middle row, far left)* was an expert at drop-kicking. (Bucknell University Archives)

One of three sports Matty played at Bucknell was basketball. He's in the first row *(far left)*. (Bucknell University Archives)

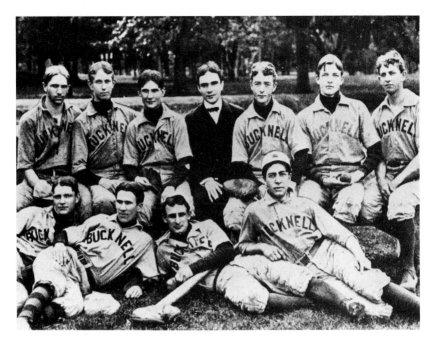

At the turn of the century Matty *(second row, second from right)* was a star pitcher for Bucknell. (Bucknell University Archives)

Always impeccably tailored,
Matty was handsome enough to
be on the stage. (National Baseball Library, Cooperstown)

Before Jane Stoughton married
Matty in 1903 she was part of
Lewisburg "high society."
(Bucknell University Archives)

The Mathewsons and the McGraws became inseparable friends, even sharing an apartment in New York together. (National Baseball Library, Cooperstown)

Matty *(on right)* went to Cuba for spring training with McGraw *(far left)* in the early 1900s. (National Baseball Library, Cooperstown)

During the 1912 Giants–Red Sox World Series Matty posed with his brilliant mound rival Smoky Joe Wood *(left)*. (National Baseball Library, Cooperstown)

Big Six, in his early years as the Giants' pitching mainstay. (National
Baseball Library, Cooperstown)

Christy, Jr. *(left)* grew up in a world that idolized his father. (National Baseball Library, Cooperstown)

Ty Cobb and Christy Mathewson, Taken at Third World's Series Game in Yor
October 17, 1911.

Though he never faced Ty Cobb *(left)* on the diamond, Matty got a chance at the 1911 World Series to chat with him. (National Baseball Library, Cooperstown)

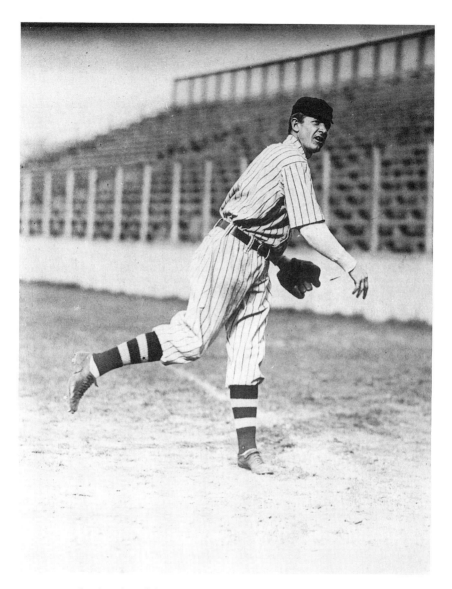

Matty, at the height of his pitching career with the New York Giants.
(Bucknell University Archives)

In 1916 Matty finally won his chance to manage the Cincinnati Reds, after he left New York. (National Baseball Library, Cooperstown)

The final mound duel in 1916 between Matty and Three-Finger Brown was heralded by a poster. (National Baseball Library, Cooperstown)

Matty served as a Chemical Warfare officer in World War I. (Note the misspelling of his last name.) (National Baseball Library, Cooperstown)

Ill with tuberculosis, Matty supported himself with a cane in front of his home in Saranac Lake, New York. (National Baseball Library, Cooperstown)

But with the crowd celebrating what they thought was a sure Giant victory—with thousands milling on the field and others heading joyously for the exits—O'Day realized the game couldn't possibly go on. Peremptorily, he ruled that the contest should be called on account of darkness. Then he made his hasty retreat to remove himself from sight.

"A flying squadron of police, reinforced by special men," wrote the New York *Herald*, "rushed O'Day under the grandstand and Chance was escorted off the field. Then the mob ran about the grounds throwing cushions and preparing for O'Day's reappearance, when it was known that the game might not be given to the Giants."

In the next few hours accounts of a Giants' 2-1 triumph over the Cubs actually hummed along the telegraph wires and circulated around the country. Indeed, some rumors spread that O'Day and Evers had departed from the Polo Grounds still in hot dispute over the game's outcome. But few of those present in the Polo Grounds were aware of exactly what had transpired. What's more, they didn't know what O'Day had purportedly said—or what he had ruled. Even many of the Giants themselves, who were raising pleasant hell inside their locker room, with its besmudged windows, unsteady milk stools, and nails that served as uniform-hangers, didn't know what had happened. Yelling and screaming, a steaming cauldron of naked young men, they flung good-natured insults at each other in the time-honored tradition of a team that has just won itself a close ball game.

In a corner of the rabbit warren sat McGraw, red-faced and sweaty, his stubby feet plunked across a desktop. Only seconds before he thought he had owned a victory over the Cubs. Now he knew better, for one of his loyal front-office aides had just finished whispering to him that the game had been ruled a tie because Merkle had failed to touch second base. The manager bolted from his position behind the desk. He couldn't believe what he was hearing.

"That dirty son of a bitch!" he screamed. "O'Day is trying to rob us of a game. How the hell did he know Merkle didn't touch second? He was at home plate and never saw a damn thing. The fucking ball was out in center field."

Little Napoleon's mouth was an active cannon of obscenities and threats. If he could have gotten his hands on O'Day at that moment, he probably would have choked the life out of him. The irony here was that McGraw, a man who often introduced technicalities and rule books to scheme his way to victory, was now wailing to the heavens about others who used legalisms to win an advantage.

There were many who agreed with McGraw. They said that if Merkle was out at second, it was O'Day's duty to clear the field and get on with the tie game. "But Merkle wasn't out," McGraw kept repeating. "They're just trying to take a ball game away from us. There's no set of fair-minded men in this land who would decide this game against us." When it came to the fate of his team, McGraw was always handy with broad generalizations. In this instance, however, he had gotten Matty to support him. "If this game goes to Chicago, by any trick or argument," Matty said, with uncharacteristic bitterness, "you can take it from me that if we lose the pennant thereby, I'll never play pro ball again!"

Matty's comment recalled to mind the general feeling he had about umpires. "Many fans look upon umpires," he said, "as a sort of necessary evil to the luxury of baseball, like the odor that follows an automobile." (A few days later when the tempest had cleared to a degree, Matty reflected more calmly on the issue. "I don't believe Merkle touched second base," he said, simply. "It could happen to anyone. There's no sense eating our hearts out. We'll just have to beat them again.")

On the night of the disputed game Pulliam asked O'Day to meet him at the New York Athletic Club, at Sixth Avenue and 59th Street, where the National League president lived. The umpire was assigned the chore of producing a coherent version of what had occurred. Before midnight O'Day made the official pronouncement: Merkle was out at second base; the game was thus a tie.

Meanwhile, Pulliam did not issue any further judgment on the matter. There was no indication from him whether or not the game should be replayed. He was following the least constructive course of action, leaving McGraw flirting with apoplexy and putting the pennant race on hold.

Since the two clubs were scheduled to play again the next day, Pulliam could have ruled that a double-header was in order. But he didn't. Some newspapers actually added a victory to the Giants in the standings of the teams, while others acknowledged the tie. Confusion was rampant.

Chance brought his Cubs to the Polo Grounds on September 24 before one o'clock, prepared to resume the previous day's game. When the Giants didn't show up, he crowed that his team should be awarded a forfeit. But no umpires were around to present the

Cubs with a triumph. Chance hadn't really expected to pull off his gambit. But it was so typical of him, as it was of McGraw, that he would utilize any trick to help his team win.

By four o'clock that afternoon, when the teams took the field, the Polo Grounds was aswarm with gnats, which seemed an appropriate prop to the madness of the past 24 hours. The 25,000 fans on hand jangled cow bells, blew horns, and screeched their disdain for the Cubs and the umpires. In general, they behaved disreputably enough to warrant the attention of 100 blue-coated policemen, who were called on to prevent mayhem. "Seldom has such partisan feeling been evidenced on a ball field," declared the New York *World.*

As for the game, which began in near darkness, the Giants banged out five runs early to please their vengeful supporters. But suddenly the Chicagoans pounced on Wiltse in the seventh inning—and again the call went out to Matty, even though he had pitched those fateful nine innings only the day before. With three runs already across, Kling prancing off third base, and a descending mist settling over the field that almost obscured the Giant outfielders, Matty went calmly to work. It got so dark that he had to walk close to the plate to study catcher Bresnahan's signals. At one point, a gnat lodged in Matty's eye, delaying the game. But overlooking such obstacles, including the failure of Emslie to call the game on account of darkness, Matty managed to save the day. The Giants won 5-4 to remain in first place.

Had the Giants continued to play winning baseball, the disputed game would have remained little more than a moot question; McGraw's tantrums also would have ceased.

But heading into the last weeks of the season the New Yorkers dropped a double-header to the Reds, with Marquard and McGinnity the losers on the mound. At this point only Matty and Ames were able to keep the Giants on an even keel. The schedule now seemed to look with favor on the Giants' chances, for they had eight games left with the Phillies, a team that finished fourth that year and was out of contention at this point, and three games with the sixth-place Braves.

The pennant race had grouped the Cubs, Giants, and Pirates like a tangled ball of yarn. But the Giants could have won without the Merkle indiscretion had they not fallen under the late-season spell of the Phillies' rookie left-hander Harry Coveleski. Three times in the final week of the season the Giants lost to this young man out of the coal mine area of Shamokin, Pennsylvania.

The final straw was Coveleski's win over Matty on October 3.

With this 3-2 victory over the Giants in the fading days of the campaign, Coveleski dropped McGraw's men into third place. Was there a limit, after all, to Matty's endurance? Had he been called on once too often by McGraw in this scorching pennant race?

"No one can stand such constant use and Matty has worked more than his share," sadly noted the New York *American*. "For half of the game with the Phillies Matty was the same cool, deliberate and unsolvable mystery of yore. Then the great strain told."

The previous summer Coveleski (the older brother of Stan Coveleski, a spitball pitcher who arrived in pro baseball a few years later) had been hurling for an amateur team in Wildwood, Pennsylvania. When he was brought up early in the 1908 season he'd been drubbed by the Giants, 14-2. But somehow, in those final days of the year, he'd learned to master the Giants—after winning only one other game that season.

On October 4 the Cubs beat the Pirates in Chicago, eliminating Pittsburgh from the race, before 31,000 wildly cheering Chicago fans. After dumping the Pirates into their coffin, Three-Fingered Brown was mobbed trying to leave the field. Back in New York with three less victories than the Cubs, but with 55 losses, the same number as the Cubs, the Giants faced the need to win their last three games against Boston, if they expected to tie Chicago.

Now regarded as stronger than Matty, Ames beat the Braves on October 5. With two games to go, would McGraw fall back on an exhausted Matty in the next game, or the last one? Or would he go with Wiltse, who had been shelled in the last two weeks of the season, but who was now reasonably well rested? He decided on Wiltse, who managed to turn back the Braves, 4-1, on the sixth, keeping the Giants' hopes alive.

But overriding this development at the Polo Grounds was the news emerging from the deliberations of the National League Board of Directors, composed of Charles Ebbets of Brooklyn, Garry Herrmann of Cincinnati, and George Dovey of Boston. This group, after much heat, decided to uphold the judgment of Pulliam and O'Day that the September 23 game was a tie. Thus, they ordered that game to be replayed on October 8, one day after the Giants were scheduled to close the season with the Braves. A coin flip put the playoff game into the Polo Grounds.

Nobody was pleased with this judgment. The Giants, led by McGraw, felt that they had been cheated, while the Cubs, anticipating a three-game series with the Giants, were incensed at the idea of having to play a single crucial game for the flag on the home territory of the Giants.

McGraw informed Matty that he didn't give a damn whether the Giants played the game or not. His own preference was to stay away. But he said that the players should get together and mull it over. When a vote was taken among the Giants several of them voted against participating—and in no mild terms. However, as the club's nominal leader, Matty headed up a small player committee to sound out the Giants' president on the matter. John Brush, ill at the time, told his players that they'd have to decide by themselves, although he underlined that it looked foolish for them to pull out of the replay after they'd played their hearts out all year. Matty and the others listened patiently to Brush and concluded that he made sense. They then persuaded the others that the Giants should play the game.

Ames pitched on one day of rest on October 7, as the Giants beat the Braves, 7-2, to clinch the tie with Chicago. Matty had been held out again by McGraw. Thus, this most bitterly contested of pennant chases would, indeed, come down to a replay of the September 23 game. The next day, with the nation's eyes fixed on the great outdoor bathtub in upper Manhattan, it would all start at three o'clock.

There was little doubt who would pitch this game for New York, for McGraw, despite his chip-on-the-shoulder grievances, was eager to face the Detroit Tigers, led by the fiery Ty Cobb, in the World Series. It was inevitable that Matty would be handed the ball. Manager Chance already had nominated Pfiester to oppose Matty, holding Brown in reserve should the left-hander show any signs of faltering.

New York's baseball fans were at fever pitch for the showdown. Baseball, the pastoral game, had now become an obsession for the big-city hicks. But it was no different among the players, whose own pre-game disposition was at an explosive level.

Adding to the emotions of the moment were rumors swirling around that attempts had been made to fix the outcome of the game. The press box buzzed with such tales, and reporters scurried to track them down. When the grapevine reached McGraw's ears, he flew into a rage. (A month later, after an investigation had been conducted in the National League offices, it was revealed that umpire-in-chief Bill Klem, a hard-nosed Gibraltar of rectitude in his strange trade, had, indeed, been approached by someone in the hours before the game. The "someone" turned out to be Dr. William Creamer, an unofficial physician for the Giants during the season. Klem said that Creamer had tried to put money into his hands, while hissing at him that "you needn't be afraid of anything." The umpire shoved Creamer out of the way. That, according to Klem, was the end of it. Considering Klem's reputation, nobody questioned that he was telling the whole truth.]

On the night before the game word leaked out where the Cubs were staying and crowds of ruffians gathered outside the hotel's windows. The unceasing noise made with horns and noisemakers was designed to deprive the enemy of sleep. Long before the ball park opened on October 8, thousands of unruly fans lined up outside. Some slept there until the early hours of the morning. Estimates of the number who actually viewed the game have ranged from 26,000 to 40,000, but that didn't include the hundreds who watched from the cliff overlooking the Manhattan field.

There was such a mad scramble to enter the Polo Grounds that many simply forced their way in by smashing down sections of the fence. At one stage it was necessary for fire hoses to be sprayed on fans in order to keep them from intruding onto the playing field.

An overflow in the press box caused some writers to cover the game while sitting in the laps of outsiders who had no legitimate reason for being there, other than the fact they were insane Giant fans. As a result, within the next year the Baseball Writers' Association of America was formed so as to properly police the press boxes in all of the major-league parks.

Two men were accidentally pushed—at least it was thought accidental—off the elevated structure beyond center field and died, while two others slid more than 75 feet off the grandstand roof and miraculously survived. In the crush, Jane Mathewson, carrying her two-year-old Christy Jr., escaped serious injury, only due to the attention of several policemen. Umpires Klem and Jimmy Johnston were late getting to the park. Though they were in civilian clothes, they were recognized and booed unmercifully, such was the mood of the occasion.

The Cubs contingent had to shove their way into the Polo Grounds. When they got inside they found there wasn't much time for batting practice. After an abbreviated session, the Cubs were brusquely informed that the Giants wanted the diamond to conduct a few minutes of their own infield drill. Chance refused to heed such orders, causing McGinnity to throw a punch at his jaw; Chance returned the compliment. As players from both teams milled around the combatants, angry epithets were exchanged, with many fans joining in the cheerless dialogue.

As things settled down to a mild tumult, the game was about to start. It was then that Matty, looking every inch the great bull-fighter, entered the arena wearing the familiar long linen duster over his uniform. Slowly he walked toward the Giants' dugout from the clubhouse in center field. Only a few moments before he began his promenade, McGraw had told him that he knew he was tired—close to 400 innings of pitching had taken their toll—but there was no one else he would dare trust with this mission. "I'll go as far as I can," Matty answered. As he took the mound to warm up, cries of affection from the fans echoed throughout the Polo Grounds. None of them knew that before Matty had left his home that morning he had told Jane that he wasn't "fit to pitch today."

When Matty fanned the first two Cubs and got Evers to ground out in the first inning, any fears that he might not be up to the task seemed put to rest. The excitement increased in the bottom of the inning when Pfiester's first pitch hit Tenney in the leg. The injured veteran almost crawled to first base; he was starting at first base that day only because poor Merkle's butterflies made him un-fit to play. Herzog walked, putting two runners on base with no-body out. But when Bresnahan was fooled on a third strike, Herzog was fooled, too, as Kling's arm rifled a throw to first to nail him as he roamed off the base.

The base-running blunder by Herzog would come back to haunt the Giants, for Donlin smashed one down the right-field line for a double. One run was across the plate, and a walk followed to Sey-mour. At this early moment, Chance walked to the mound to in-form Pfiester that he'd had enough. As the dispirited Pfiester shuf-fled off the mound, to be replaced by Three-Fingered Brown, the crowd booed lustily. Instead, they should have cheered Pfiester, for he was the best thing to happen to the Giants that afternoon. From here on, they would be at the mercy of Brown's darting curves. The indomitable Brown was fresher than Matty, too, for he'd pitched in some 80 fewer innings than the Giant, while winning 27 games.

That summer Matty had often made one run stand up. But this was the end of a long season for him, with his 37 victories and 10 losses. In the third inning Tinker, one of the few batters reputed to "own" Matty, hammered a long fly to center. Disregarding Matty's wig-wagging instructions from the mound to play deep on Tinker, Seymour was playing too shallow. The ball fell for a triple behind him. Kling singled, scoring Tinker. On Brown's bunt, Kling went to second. When Sheckard followed with a fly out, it appeared the assault had ended.

Unfortunately for Matty and the Giants, that was not the case. He walked Evers—his only pass of the day—and Schulte, who had fanned three times against Matty in their last game, doubled. Chance did the same thing, netting the Cubs four runs.

The silence in the Polo Grounds was like death. There was an ominous feeling that those runs would be unassailable; they were, though the Giants made one last-gasp try at getting to Brown in the seventh.

Devlin smacked a leadoff hit, McCormick followed with a single, and Bridwell, who got the hit that earned Merkle his reverse reputation, walked. The Polo Grounds came bursting alive, as Matty rose from the dugout to take his place at the plate. With the bases loaded and nobody out, Matty fully expected to be allowed to hit. But in one of the rare instances in all of his years with the Giants, Matty was removed for a pinch-hitter. Matty hardly ever disputed McGraw's decisions. When he was taken out of games with a big lead, he appreciated that McGraw's strategy was to preserve his energy for close contests. That was understandable, even if at times it deprived him of getting credit for victories.

But to be jettisoned now for a pinch-hitter didn't make too much sense to him, for he was rated as a respectable hitter in his own right (in 1908 he batted only .155 but in earlier seasons he'd hit well over .200). McGraw nominated Larry Doyle, who hadn't started at second base because his leg was bothering him, to hit for him. Matty turned to McGraw, quietly taking exception to the move. The manager listened, but wasn't sympathetic. Already a victim of the strange sorcery that Brown exercised over the Giants, Matty felt he was also being victimized by McGraw's judgment in favor of Larry Doyle.

Doyle fouled out to Kling behind the plate. Tenney connected for a long fly to score Devlin. But Herzog grounded out to shortstop. The rally was over, and for all intents and purposes, so was the game. In the last of the ninth, as the curtain came down on the controversial season for the Giants, Brown was magnificent. He retired the last three Giants on four pitches. The Cubs had won, 4-2, for their third consecutive National League pennant. The final standings showed Chicago at 99-55, New York at 98-56, Pittsburgh at 98-56, and Philadelphia at 83-71.

On leaving the field, Chance and his unpopular Cubs (unpopular in the Polo Grounds, that is) were lucky to escape serious injury at the hands of a sullen crowd. Some police drew their revolvers as they escorted the vilified athletes to safety. Brown was hardly exaggerating when he said that the Polo Grounds was "as close to a lunatic asylum as any place I've ever seen."

Although he generally accepted defeat with grace and calm, Matty was almost inconsolable. No member of the club, with the exception of McGraw, took the setback as keenly as he did. Hours later, after the clubhouse had emptied out and most Giants had departed for home, Matty sat on his stool, staring at the wet cement. The few players who remained tried to cheer him up but he didn't respond. At last, fully dressed, he walked slowly out of the park through the Eighth Avenue exit. When his familiar face was spotted by those who remained to applaud him, a cheer went up. He waved, bowed his head and smiled weakly. "I did the best I could," he told them, "but I guess fate was against me."

Several years later he supplied additional evidence as to why the Cubs beat him that afternoon. "I never had less on the ball in my life," he said. "What I can't understand to this day is why it took so long for them to hit me."

McGraw was bitter, yet somewhat philosophical. "My team lost something it should have won three weeks before," he said. "This cannot be put too strongly. It's criminal to say that Merkle is stupid and to blame the loss of the pennant on him. He didn't cost us the pennant—we lost a dozen games we should have won. We were robbed of it and you can't say that Merkle did that."

As far as Pulliam was concerned, McGraw was unforgiving. Shortly after the end of the season Pulliam was re-elected president of the National League, although the Giants cast the single vote against him. During the winter of 1909 Pulliam became emotionally ill and was granted a leave of absence from his job. He returned to his post in early summer but shortly after that shot himself, ending his life at the age of 40. Even at such a tragic moment, McGraw was unrelenting. "I didn't think a bullet to his head could hurt him," he growled.

Perhaps more unseemly was the post-mortem remark of Larry Doyle, who had failed as a pinch-hitter in that last game. In ensuing years Doyle evolved into an archetypical pepperpot second baseman. But in the winter of 1908 he was harsh about Merkle.

"He made a stupid play, a bonehead play," said Doyle about Merkle. Most surprising about this utterance was that Doyle had been Merkle's roommate and close friend. They often played pool together after games.

For the rest of a long and distinguished career (he was still playing in 1926), Merkle was the butt of derisive jokes and bench jockeying. Inevitably, fans and players tried to wound him by calling him "Bonehead." For a while "to merkle"—meaning to not arrive—was an expression that became part of the language wherever fans gathered to mourn the Giants. It took time for Merkle, who became a fine first baseman, to regain his shattered confidence. He lost weight over the incident and at one time pleaded with McGraw to get rid of him. Later, he felt, as did many others, that it was unfair that he had been defined by this ridiculous episode. Sensing Merkle's potential, McGraw shrewdly raised his salary by $500 for the 1909 season.

When questioned, Matty continued to acknowledge that he didn't think Merkle had touched second base. But he was insistent about putting the matter into a rational perspective. "It was just one of those things," he said. "It could have happened to anyone." He understood Merkle's anguish, just as McGraw did, and knew that he'd be pitching for many years with Merkle behind him in the infield.

Despite its sad conclusion, 1908 in every respect was Matty's greatest single year. What he accomplished was challenged by only one other pitcher in history. (Curiously, it was also in 1908 that Ed Walsh, the big spitballer for the Chicago White Sox, recorded 40 wins and 15 losses with a 1.42 ERA and 11 shutouts. He pitched an astounding 465 innings, which was truly Herculean. But his arm soon went dead.) Matty finished with a record of 37-11, an ERA of 1.43, and 12 shutouts. Working in 56 games in a total of 390.2 innings, he completed 34 of his 44 starts. He yielded a measly 42 walks, less than one a game, and struck out 259 batters, although the latter statistic was never something he emphasized. He gave up 285 hits, few of them for distance. In his eight years with the Giants Matty had won 200 games, an average of 25 a year. Yet, with all of these striking achievements, defeat had been his reward in 1908.

It also meant that Matty would never confront Cobb in a World Series or in any ball game. That two such transcendent performers of their era would never get to match their talents or test one another was baseball's loss.

Sharing Matty's disappointment, McGraw was eager to get away from it all at the season's end. Since he was an enthusiastic boxing fan, McGraw suggested to Matty that they travel to Australia at Christmas time to watch Canadian Tommy Burns, the shortest of all heavyweight champs at 5'7", 175 pounds, defend his title against the powerful black "tiger," Jack Johnson. The fight was scheduled for December 26, 1908, at Rushcutter's Bay outside of Sydney, about as far away from the Polo Grounds as one could get. Burns had been goaded into the fight by the author and reporter Jack London, who despised Johnson and was an advocate of white supremacy.

At the last minute, McGraw altered his plans. Instead, the two men and their wives settled for an evening at the theatre, in this instance Florenz Ziegfeld's Follies, with Irving Berlin's ragtime music and Fanny Brice's dialect jokes. They did not get to see Johnson knock out Burns in the fourteenth round, thus igniting the parade of "White Hopes" meant to unseat the dastardly "nigra."

With a black "too uppity" for the taste of a white man's country now the heavyweight champion, America also elected another heavyweight, William Howard Taft, president in 1908, an echo of the conservative instinct of the nation.

11

DEATH IN
THE FAMILY

O F the three Mathewson brothers—Christy, Henry, and Nicholas—the youngest was Nicholas, born in October 1889. According to family remembrance, Nicholas was also the best athlete of the three boys, and like his brothers, was tall, broad-shouldered, thick-bodied, and strikingly handsome.

Nicholas Wellington Mathewson was also a pitcher, just as Christy and Henry were. "Christy was a very good pitcher in his younger days," recalled Mathewson Senior, "but Nicholas had everything. He had a fast ball with a jump on it and had much greater speed than Christy could muster. I'm not the only one who has said this about Nicholas, either. All over our region he was recognized as a coming star."

A favorite of McGraw, Nick was often sent baskets of used Giants uniforms and other equipment. Nick then sold much of the stuff to kids in Factoryville, for the magnificent sum of 25 or 30 cents.

When he was in his late teens, Nicholas faced and defeated a crackerjack Scranton team. Hughey Jennings, manager of the Detroit club, and constantly on the lookout for talent, was so impressed with Nicholas's work that he offered Mathewson Senior three thousand dollars a year if he'd permit Nicholas to sign with the Tigers.

Mathewson Senior thought that Nicholas, not yet 18, was too young for such a commitment (though Christy had hardly been much older when he made his entry into the big leagues) and suggested that the Tigers might "spoil him."

"I won't work him hard," Jennings tried to assure Mr. Mathewson. "I'll let him sit on the bench for a year and give him his salary, while he's learning the fine points of pitching."

But Jennings's proposal failed to convince Mathewson Senior. At the time Nicholas was attending school, and his family thought there was no immediate need to rush him off to work. They felt he would be much better off delaying his entrance into baseball.

Instead, Mathewson Senior encouraged Nicholas to enroll in September 1908 at Lafayette College in Easton, Pennsylvania, even though Nicholas originally had intended to follow in his brother's footsteps at Bucknell. The decision to go to Lafayette, where the authorities were as familiar with his athletic abilities as they were with Christy's, suggests that Nicholas was not prepared to compete with Christy in every level of their lives. Did Nicholas also conclude that he would be under less pressure and would be able to establish his own identity at Lafayette?

As a member of the class of 1912, Nicholas joined the Phi Delta Theta fraternity, another break from Christy's tradition, since his brother was a member of Phi Gamma Delta at Bucknell. However, after a few months at Lafayette, in the fall and winter of 1908, during which time he didn't compete in any athletics, Nicholas returned home to Factoryville. At the time he complained that he felt ill. When the family encouraged him to visit a doctor, he didn't appear to be suffering any more serious ailment than a liver complication. But Nicholas continued to tell everyone that he felt run down.

While at home Nicholas began brooding over the classwork that he was missing. The fear of falling behind his classmates seemed to prey on his mind.

"We never realized just how much he was worried," said Mathewson Senior, "and we didn't appreciate that his mind was becoming so unsettled."

On January 15, 1909, Nick stopped by an elderly friend's house and presented him with two sizable pickerels he'd just caught. "You were always good to me when I cut your lawn and you paid me well," Nick said to his friend. With that, he went down the road to the Mathewson house. Walking into the back of the barn, he scrawled a few incoherent lines onto a sheet of note paper, climbed up onto the hayloft, and shot a bullet into his brain. He was not yet 20 years old.

Spending a few days with his family after the finish of the ill-fated 1908 season, Christy was the one who discovered his brother's body. He broke the heartbreaking message to his parents, who remained in a state of shock for months afterward. "I have awful news," Matty told them. "But all of us have to remain calm."

It was whispered before the 1909 baseball year began that the melancholy events of the preceding months had taken an emotional toll on Matty. That he might consider leaving the Giants, who now paid him $10,000 a year, was not given much credence. Yet, in weighing such a possibility, it was important to realize that he was intelligent and mature enough to enter the world of commerce. He had already been involved with McGraw in several business enterprises and had established an insurance business at 20 Vesey Street in downtown Manhattan. There were also rumors that he had been approached by some entrepreneurs who manufactured railroad ties. "When you see Christy Mathewson behind a desk," wrote Homer Croy, "it is hard to remember he is a baseball player . . . he dresses well and his voice is low and melodious . . . There is a note of honest clearness in the tone that makes a man feel comfortable . . . he talks like a Harvard graduate, looks like an actor, acts like a businessman and impresses you as an all-around gentleman."

Certainly these were credentials for business success. But Matty still was too young, at 29, and too much in love with baseball and athletic competition to retreat from the heat of the arena. If he had ever given thought to saying farewell to McGraw, there was no way of proving it.

So 1909 once again found Matty pitching in the Polo Grounds, satisfying those whose battle cry was "Let's go see Matty today!" But there were others from that embattled group from 1908 who were gone from the scene. McGinnity, one-half of the Matty–Iron Man tandem that was probably as potent a pitching force as was ever assembled in the big leagues, had pitched too much and too often. He was allowed to go to Newark, where he managed that club. Amazingly, he also began to pitch well again. For years he stayed in the minors—until he was 52 years old—thus confounding the experts. McGinnity attributed his longevity to the fact that he never warmed up for more than a few minutes.

Bresnahan, who always wanted to be a manager, was traded to the Cards in order to realize that ambition. In return the Giants received outfielder Red Murray, catcher Admiral Schlei, and right-hander Arthur "Bugs" Raymond, who had labored mightily in his young years to acquire his nickname. His boozy reputation preceded him; but McGraw's ego was such that he was convinced he could control Bugs's waywardness, just as he imagined that he had kept Mike Donlin under control. Donlin, the team's captain, also left the premises in 1909 in favor of a full-time career in vaudeville with his wife.

After an 8-5 season, Dummy Taylor, at 33, was given his release by McGraw, who was never a prisoner of sentiment. Others added to the cast in Marlin, where the Giants still trained, were shortstop Art Fletcher, Tillie Shafer, an infielder from the West Coast, and "Chief" Meyers, brought along, of course, to replace Bresnahan.

It wasn't long before Matty and Meyers worked so well together as a battery that Bresnahan was scarcely missed. But Meyers never claimed credit for such a welcome development. "Anybody in the world can catch Matty," he said. "You could catch him sitting in a rocking chair."

Matty's fly-speck control was such that even umpires became believers. When Matty pitched, their task, if it could be called that, was simple. Even when they called a pitch wrong, which they did on occasion, Matty never threw them a dirty glance or a harsh word.

Problems surfaced immediately with Raymond in spring training, forcing McGraw to make Bugs pitch the full nine innings of an exhibition game because of his "undue liberties with liquids." The experiment with the alcoholic pitcher failed to work out satisfactorily, despite the fact that Bugs ended the 1909 season with an 18-12 record, not bad for someone who haunted saloons. Raymond remained with the Giants for the next two years, often under surveillance of McGraw's private detectives. But he had little more than nuisance value for his manager. Not long after Bugs left the Giants, McGraw grumbled that the man "took five years off my life."

With a new look on the field, some repairs and additions were also made to the Polo Grounds. After bleachers were constructed to enclose the outfield, the capacity of the park went to 30,000. The grandstand was given a coat of roaring yellow, part of a scheme, some hinted, to give enemy outfielders trouble in picking up the ball; it was never clear why this didn't also bother the Giants' outfielders.

None of these alterations proved of much help in the 1909 race.

McGraw missed most of April and May due to an infected finger, giving Blanche McGraw her share of nursing chores at home. On the ballfield the Giants fell behind the Pirates and Cubs early and never were much of a threat. They finished in third place, 18½ games behind the Pirates, who beat the Cubs for the pennant by winning 110 games.

The Giants' failures were no distraction for Matty, who went along, as usual, winning ball games and pitching shutouts. He had eight of the latter, while winning 25, down from his 37 in 1908. But his ERA was at 1.14, his lowest ever and the third lowest posted in National League history. (Brown carved a 1.04 in 1906 and Bob Gibson of St. Louis ended with 1.12 in 1968.) His control was as precise as ever, with only 36 passes issued in 275 innings.

But the rumors that had aired during the pre-season suddenly emerged again as September rolled around. New York's newspapers headlined a story that said Matty was sure to quit baseball after the 1909 season, due to the call of business and money. It didn't sound like Matty, and there wasn't a single word of confirmation from either himself or McGraw. But there it was. People often believe what they read in the press, so they were tempted to give credibility to these gossamer yarns. When, a few weeks later, Matty assured his fans that he would certainly be back with the Giants in 1910, one could almost hear a sigh of relief from Coogan's Bluff to Madison Square Garden.

With Matty's certain return for his eleventh year, McGraw was convinced that his club was on the verge of revival. It had been five years since the glory days of the 1905 World Series, and he was eager to direct his team to the top again.

He now had Merkle, Doyle, Bridwell, and Herzog in the infield; Murray, Fred Snodgrass, and the diminutive Josh Devore in the outfield, with Meyers as the receiver. If only the "$11,000 Lemon," Marquard, could come into his own, McGraw felt the pitching, headed by Matty, would be enough to give his foes fits. Crandall, Ames, and Wiltse were there to round out the mound corps.

That spring McGraw worked his men harder than ever at Marlin. He split his team into A and B squads, an innovation, and played simultaneous exhibition games. He became more engaged than before in the conditioning process, pitching batting practice almost daily. He insisted that all hands had to participate in sliding practice, always feet first, for that was the best way to maneuver around a tag. He often demonstrated how it should be done, even if at 37, he was old in baseball terms.

Striving to obtain first-class accommodations for his players, who previously had to settle for cheap, flea-bag hotels, McGraw was determined to lift his players' self-regard, as well as their morale.

"To a man with daughters, ballplayers were dangerous," Eric Rolfe Greenberg wrote. It was exactly that image of his men that McGraw was trying to change. The behavior of many players in 1910 was still execrable. There were many practical jokesters, drunkards (McGraw always had his share of them), firecracker-tossers, and ill-educated hooligans. McGraw's own predilection for bridge and poker, pastimes that Matty enthusiastically shared with him, and his fondness for Broadway shows and ragtime music were not universally appreciated by ballplayers. The number of college men coming into the game was indeed growing, but they were still an invisible minority in a world that was dedicated to knocking an opponents' brains out. McGraw himself, coming from the old Oriole tradition, believed a man should rub his wound and get right back in there. Could that be expected from the more genteel college men?

Ever the psychologist, McGraw hired Arlie Latham, a third baseman from the 1880s, as a combination coach and court jester. Devoted to spreading good cheer, Latham was something of a counterpoint to McGraw, who was nothing if not sober and grumpy. Another old pal from Baltimore days, Wilbert Robinson, was also made a coach. Some 18 years before, as an Oriole, Robinson had delivered seven hits in seven times at bat, a feat now rarely associated with him. With his protruding belly, forgetfulness for players' names, and a more relaxed attitude toward the game than McGraw, Robbie was also supposed to be knowledgeable about the pitching trade. There was little, of course, that he could confide to Matty but McGraw had reason to think he could be helpful with Marquard. Between seasons Robbie had worked for a meat market, but he preferred the smell of green grass to raw beef. As different from McGraw as McGraw was from Matty, Robbie shared one trait with the manager—he loved a good pennant fight.

Operating with such a refurbished alignment, McGraw's Giants stayed in the pennant race for a healthy spell, until Chicago dashed past them for another pennant. Pittsburgh failed to repeat, falling into third place, behind the Giants. Matty was again brilliant with

27 victories and just nine losses. He worked 318 innings, more than he'd posted in 1909. If his skills were waning, he didn't show it, unless his total of two shutouts was a sign that he wasn't quite as overpowering as he'd been in the past.

But even if the Giants failed to win, a new spirit permeated the air. Broadway's luminaries still flocked to the Polo Grounds to see Matty pitch, and to watch McGraw's collection of the old and new play rousing baseball. Everyone, from New York's reform Mayor William James Gaynor, who had survived a bullet in his head fired by a disgruntled city worker, to George M. Cohan to former heavy-weight champ Corbett to John McCormack (the world-famed tenor who sang of the Irish countryside, much to the pleasure of Mc-Graw) to the gum-chewing Will Rogers to DeWolf Hopper, survivor of a thousand recitations of "Casey at the Bat," to the heavy-bosomed Lillian Russell, one of the first sex symbols, to stockbroker "Bet a Million" Gates, filled the pews at the Giants' ball park.

When the season ended it was generally conceded that things were on the rise at the Polo Grounds. What McGraw and Brush hadn't anticipated, however, was a shrill outcry for a post-season intra-city series between the Giants and the Highlanders of the American League. Up until now the Giants had chosen to ignore their upstart, parvenu baseball cousins at Hilltop Park, on a prom-ontory overlooking the Hudson River and New Jersey's Palisades.

Traditionally, the World Series had become the competition with the most crowd appeal. Yet, starting in 1882, when the Cleve-land Blues of the National League faced the Cincinnati Red Stock-ings of the new American Association, city and state regional games in the post-season period attracted a good deal of fan enthusiasm. In the early years of the twentieth century such rivalries as the National League Cards versus the American League Browns, vying for the championship of St. Louis; the Cubs and White Sox, bat-tling in Chicago; and the Athletics and Phillies, fighting it out in Philadelphia, were sometimes as heated as the regular games of the pennant race.

But now in 1910, deprived of a World Series, New York fans clamored for a round of battles between the Giants and the High-landers (soon to become known as the Yankees). Both teams were second-place finishers in their leagues. Under George Stallings, a Georgia plantation owner, then Hal Chase, the slick first baseman who had persuaded club president Frank Farrell to give Stallings a pink slip halfway through the season, the Highlanders surprised not a few people by coming in second. Led by two accomplished spitballers, Russ Ford from Canada and John Picus Quinn, the Highlanders represented a threat to the Giants' emotional dominance in New York.

At first McGraw grumbled that the two clubs didn't belong on the same field together. However, after a perusal of the economic possibilities of such a series (to be conducted on a best four-out-of-seven basis, just as the World Series was), Brush and McGraw concluded that it was worth the risk.

The Highlanders, naturally, had little to lose in such a confrontation and were delighted to show up for the first game at the Polo Grounds on October 13. McGraw wasn't going to take any chances, so he started Matty. It was good he did, for the game was tight from the beginning. Ford matched Matty almost pitch for pitch; by the eighth inning the two teams were deadlocked at 1-1 and the 25,000 fans who packed the Polo Grounds were besides themselves with joy at such an unexpectedly close ball game.

Matty batted for himself, as he always liked to do, in the bottom of the eighth, and singled to right field. Devore bunted for a single. Doyle bunted too, and the bases were loaded, when Chase's throw to third was misplayed by Jimmy Austin. With nobody out, Ford fanned Snodgrass and Murray, rising to the occasion. On Ford's next pitch, Bridwell, employing an old Oriole tactic learned from McGraw, "allowed" himself to be hit on the ankle, forcing in a run. Ford, a 26-game winner in his rookie season, then blew sky high, and the Giants went on to a 5-1 triumph. Not a single Highlander received a base on balls from Matty, as he struck out 14, a National League record at the time. The Highlanders had eight hits but didn't score an earned run.

The next afternoon, playing at Hilltop Park before another large crowd, the Highlanders trimmed Wiltse with a run in the ninth inning. The Giants led in the third game, 5-1, but the Highlanders kept whittling away, forcing McGraw to summon Matty late in the game. As usual, Matty did the job.

After a tie game called on account of darkness (no lights were turned on in those days), the Giants steam-rollered the Highlanders, with Matty getting credit for his second victory. The following day the Highlanders smacked around the rest of the Giants' pitching staff for a lopsided win, so McGraw wasn't about to take any chances. He started Matty again the next afternoon, with only one day of rest, to finish off the American League team.

Not since his masterful performance in the 1905 World Series had Matty been blessed with such an opportunity to show how effective he was. In this intense city duel, which the Giants could ill afford to lose—even if only for bragging rights—he came through, as McGraw knew he would. In his three complete game victories, Matty walked only one batter in 30 innings, saved a fourth game, and, by his presence, almost assured that the games would be a financial success.

Attendance was over 100,000 for the six games, allowing each Giant to pocket $1,110 out of the receipts of $85,000. The Highlanders benefited by $706 for each player.

The Giants' style of play in the intra-city series also tipped off the National League in advance on how they would play baseball in 1911. Always avid believers in the running game, McGraw's men stole bases with abandon against the Highlanders. Devore, fast as greased lightning, alone stole six bases out of his team's total of 19 steals.

Thereafter, it was rumored that the over-sized baby safety pin, to hold up the Giants' frayed pants, became the most important element in the Giant offense.

12

ON TOP AGAIN

WITH high expectations 30,000 people journeyed to the Polo Grounds on the blue-sky
afternoon of Thursday, April 13, 1911, to take in the opening game
of the season. The Phillies, managed by their catcher, Charles "Red"
Dooin, were the opposition—and on that day they turned out to be
tough ones. McGraw started "Red" Ames, since, for some inexplicable reason, he still preferred not to pitch Matty on opening days.
This superstition was attributed by some to the fact that he preferred to hold out Matty for the Saturday game, with the prospect
of a larger crowd on hand. Whatever the reason, Ames lost, despite
the colorful trappings of American flags flying, bands playing, red,
white, and blue bunting garnishing the grandstand, as well as other
manifestations of baseball patriotism.

It was precisely the type of day that Matty loved, even if his
own presence on the mound was denied him. "Baseball is always
played out in the sunshine, where the air is pure and the grass is
green," he wrote that year in *Pearson's Magazine*, "and there is
something about the game—or at least I have always found it so—
which teaches one to win or lose as a gentleman should, and that
is a very fine thing to learn."

On that afternoon of April 13 the Giants had to learn to lose.
But more bad news was to come.

Late that night, while the city dozed, a withering fire of un-
known origin swept through the wooden stands of the Polo Grounds,

setting up a flaring red sky over Harlem. Before New York's fire department, with its horsedrawn equipment, could rush to contain the blaze, the left-field bleachers and the entire grandstand burned to the ground. After the fire-fighters poured tons of water on the ruins, the only thing left standing was a section of the right-field and center-field bleachers. No adequate explanation was provided for the disaster but there were plenty of creative rumors circulating.

One such story insisted that a platoon of Chicago Cubs fans had put a match to a vendor's stand. Others hinted darkly that it was Cubs' manager, Frank Chance himself, who sparked off the deed. Those with a more conspiratorial bent said it was a Bolshevik plot. McGraw settled for Ban Johnson as the culprit.

But the immediate order of the day was for the Giants to keep on playing. Forced to go, cap in hand, to their much-despised foe, Frank Farrell, the Highlanders' boss, the Giants sought a temporary tenancy at Hilltop Park. In this case Farrell acted like a consummate gentleman. If the situation had been reversed it is unlikely that Brush and McGraw would have behaved with equal civility. Farrell gave the Giants the solution to their homelessness; they could stay at Hilltop until the Polo Grounds was ready for occupancy again. "That Farrell is a real white man to come to our aid like that," said Brush, in a typical expression of the day.

By that Saturday the Giants were playing at 168th Street at Hilltop, with its limited capacity of 15,000. Soon after they moved in—and started to win—plans were commissioned by Brush for a double-decker steel and concrete structure (which Brush dared to characterize as the Eighth Wonder of the World) to replace the burned-out sections of the Polo Grounds. Defying belief, the workers, who must have been Giants fans, reacted as swiftly to the emergency as the Giants were performing on the field. They got most of the job completed by June, by which time the Giants had already made good use of Mr. Farrell's hospitality at Hilltop. When McGraw's men returned to their home base they were well on their way to "stealing the pennant," with the help of daring baserunning of a type never before seen in the National League.

There wasn't a player on the Giants who wasn't capable of stealing a base if McGraw signaled for it—or even when he didn't (although it wasn't wise to steal if the manager hadn't specifically given his orders). As a team, the Giants stole 347 bases in 1911, a new major-league mark. Though he was supposed to be the slowest runner on the team, Doyle stole 38, not too far back of Devore, who had a total of 61. Eight Giants stole 19 or more bases during the season. "A man may as well be thrown out stealing," said McGraw, "as to be put out in some other way."

These Giants epitomized the kind of players McGraw had always dreamed of managing. Using the hit-and-run, the stolen base, and the bunt, going for the extra base, catching the foe asleep— these were the tactics constantly employed by Little Napoleon. This was the way baseball should be played, he thought. Certainly it was why he had won his reputation as a dynamic baseball leader, leaving aside for the moment whether anyone loved the man or not. To McGraw the home run was hardly important. The Giants hit only 41 in 1911, but they still scored four runs a game, a tribute mainly to their success on the basepaths.

Topping it all, of course, was the perpetual majestic display of Matty, as he won 26 games, lost 13, pitched in 307 innings, and held his ERA under 2.00. This was the "automatic Matty" that the fans cherished.

Until Doyle arrived with the Giants a few years before, Matty's firmest social relationship on the club had always been with McGraw. But Laughing Larry had also won the affection of the pitcher. On the road the two men invariably roomed together. By 1911 McGraw thought so well of the leadership qualities and maturity of Doyle that he named him team captain. By doing so, he bypassed Matty because the pitcher was not a daily performer.

"We were a rough, tough lot in those days," said Doyle, "all except Matty. But he was no nambypamby. He'd gamble, play cards, curse now and then and take a drink now and then, but he was always quiet and had a lot of dignity. I remember how fans would constantly rush up to him and pester him with questions. He hated it but he was always courteous. I never saw a man who could shake off those bugs so slick without hurting their feelings."

Doyle never ceased to marvel at how good Matty was. "There was no strain in the way he threw," he recalled. "He just let loose that easy, country boy pitch of his. He always respected his right arm, saving it whenever he could. Matty once told me, 'I always plan on throwing 75 or 80 times a game, instead of the usual 125 or so.' "

Matty's secret of pitching was in loafing when the pressure was off—when he wasn't "pitching in a pinch"—or when his team was way ahead. He was only great when he had to be. In tight games he was almost impossible to hit. But if the score was lop-sided Matty didn't seem to care a whit about his reputation. He'd toss in plenty of fat ones, just for the fun of it.

But McGraw never viewed what Matty did as fun. There were occasions when Matty almost drove McGraw out of his mind with such benevolent tactics. One day in mid-season in 1911, in St. Louis, the Giants galloped ahead with six runs in the first five innings. As a result, Matty began lobbing the ball toward the plate, throwing as if he were back in Factoryville, pitching against some farm-hand team. The Cards got three runs back in the seventh, causing McGraw to deliver a variety of his most choice epithets. He kept shaking his fist at Matty, as Matty returned to the dugout after each inning. In the eighth inning the Cards got two more, coming within one run of the Giants. Now McGraw could literally have choked Matty. "What the hell are you doing out there?" he screamed. "You're loafing!"

"Take it easy, Mac," replied Matty, softly. "Now we've got an interesting ball game. We'll win, don't worry."

In the ninth Matty struck out the last two batters as the Giants won, 6-5.

In many instances it was not unusual for Matty to ask his teammates to get him just one quick run at the start of the game. Not more than that. Just one run. Then he'd shut out the rival team over the distance and delight in the fact that it had been a wonderful, tight-squeeze ball game, the kind that he so much enjoyed playing.

Following a Matty victory over Cincinnati in a July game, Damon Runyon, coming into his own as a colorful interpreter of the roar of New York City, wrote in the *American:* "Mathewson pitched against Cincinnati yesterday. Another way of putting it is that Cincinnati lost a game of baseball. The first statement means the same as the second."

Along with Matty's continued brilliance in 1911, Marquard finally arrived as a full-fledged winning pitcher. Up until this year he'd had three lackluster seasons in which he won only nine games. For the metamorphosis of the lemon into a peach, Matty gave full credit to Wilbert Robinson.

"Robbie devoted himself almost entirely to Marquard in the spring of 1911 and he handed back to McGraw at the end of the rehearsal the man who turned out to be the premier pitcher in the league," said Matty. "He used to take Rube into some corner every day and talk to him for hours . . . this was the time when the papers were imploring McGraw to let Marquard go in exchange for some capable bat boy."

Robinson had emphasized to Marquard, said Matty, that he had to get the first ball over the plate on the batter. It seemed that one of Marquard's worst habits was also to get a couple of strikes on a batter and then let himself get caught up in a hole and not get the ball over.

"Robbie gave Rube the confidence he lacked," continued Matty. "Out there in the Texas sun, with much advice and lots of patience, Robbie showed why old catchers like himself can always have the best influence on pitchers. Robbie drilled the weaknesses of the batters into Marquard's head. He hadn't paid much attention before to such information."

At the end of 1911 Marquard had 23 victories against seven losses, and he led the league in strikeouts. Complementing Matty, as McGinnity had once done, he helped the Giants to stay in the race and then pass both the Cubs and Pirates.

Though Matty was willing to give Robinson the lion's share of credit for the evolution of Marquard into a superb southpaw, he played a role himself, perhaps unwittingly. One day in May the Giants battered the Cards for 13 runs in the first inning at Hilltop Park. With Matty on the mound, the umpires might as well have sent everyone home for the day. However, McGraw seized this moment to replace Matty, who had pitched only the first inning, with Marquard. Matty expressed astonishment at the move but McGraw explained what he was up to.

"I'm trying to get this fellow to pitch without pressure," he told Matty. "This is the kind of game he can do it in."

Matty agreed there was no pressure coming into a game with a 13-0 lead. He wasn't even miffed that the decision to bring in Marquard would deprive him of a victory. He just wasn't certain the strategy would be effective. Though he permitted five runs in the last eight innings, Marquard also struck out 14 batters, causing McGraw to believe the move had worked and that it was a watershed episode for the young pitcher.

By August the Giants took over first place, after knocking off both Chicago and Pittsburgh in five of seven games before large and approving crowds in the refurbished Polo Grounds. Johnny Evers, that eternally grumpy man, scoffed at the Giants, insisting they were a mediocre bunch, lucky to have a first-rate manager. Whatever the second baseman might have thought, the Giants were on their way to a first flag since 1905. In one last stretch of games they took 18 out of 22, clinching the pennant on October 4, against Brooklyn, thanks to one of Matty's five shutouts during the year.

In the American League Mack's A's were on top again. In the World Series of 1910 they had beaten Chicago. But now Mack was eager to add the Giants to his championship belt, for he still rankled over 1905 and how thoroughly Matty had dominated his club.

Philadelphia boasted of its "$100,000 infield," consisting of the hard-hitting J. Franklin Baker at third base, the jug-eared collegian Eddie Collins at second, where he was generally judged to be the best at his position, Stuffy McInnis at first, and Jack Barry at shortstop. (McInnis, due to an injury, would miss much of the Series and was replaced by Harry Davis.)

On the mound Mack had Jack Coombs, the "American League Matty," Chief Bender, and Eddie Plank, any one of whom could be a holy terror on a sharp afternoon. Mack's outfielders were a routine lot. He had to rely mainly on pitching and splendid infield play.

Aware of how much this confrontation meant to his own reputation, McGraw's competitive juices were flowing. He was so involved in preparing the Giants for the Series that Blanche McGraw scarcely ever saw him or spoke to him. "I doubt that he knew that I existed," complained Mrs. McGraw, but not within his hearing.

When the Polo Grounds opened its doors early on Saturday morning, October 14, an excited mob rushed the ticket booths. Special gendarmes were recruited to keep the citizens in line. Those who wormed their way into the ball park considered themselves privileged, for they would be attending an event that had seized most of the country with hysteria, not to mention the sweet parishes of New York and Philadelphia.

The regular season in 1911 had run to Columbus Day, October 12, causing a late start for the World Series. But that hadn't dampened anyone's enthusiasm. The natural pairing of such titans as McGraw and Mack only served to add an extra glow to the games.

The hoopla and flummery that preceded the Series was coaxed along by an emerging group of immensely talented sportswriters, all of whom were coming into their own at the same time. Look this way and that in the grandstand's cramped press box high above the Polo Grounds and you'd see the dandefied Runyon, with high forehead and thick glasses; the rumpled Heywood Broun, in his black felt hat slouched over one eye; handsome, affable Granny Rice, late of Vanderbilt; Sam Crane, inventor of Matty's nickname; mustached Fred Lieb, breaking in that summer; witty Boze Bulger of the *Evening Sun,* and the former farm boy from Illinois, Sid Mercer. And off there in a corner was the Chicago *American's* Ring Lardner, the dour-faced humorist and by-lined columnist who had penned a six-day series of verses that provided an alphabetical preview of the Series. These writers' Homeric phrases had stirred readers days before the Series began. Now they were digging in alongside 50 telegraphers who would carry the message of the game as far off as Havana and Los Angeles, the latter city still half a century removed from major-league baseball.

This Series would be the first in which assessments of each game would appear in newspaper columns under the names of various star players. In a daily story written for him by John N. Wheeler of the New York *Herald,* Matty's name was featured prominently as author. Matty received $500 for the use of his name on each article and, of course, made certain to express his opinions to Wheeler before and after each game. Already an old hand at this sort of spectral service, Wheeler had performed a similar stint with the Mexican revolutionary Pancho Villa. Later that same year Wheeler, also the founder of the North American Newspaper Alliance, would help Matty compose his instructive book, *Pitching in a Pinch.*

Wheeler and Matty made another odd couple. The sportswriter was part shrewd businessman, part Wizard of Oz, part devoted fan. Proficient at turning out such assembly-line prose, Wheeler regarded it as a coup to have lured Matty into print. When the book, which published three editions, plus a special Boy Scout edition, came out, Marianne Moore, the poet and baseball fan, read it and averred that "it's a pleasure to note how unerringly Matty's execution supports his theories."

There was high drama everywhere one turned on October 14. Never lacking the theatrical gesture, McGraw outfitted his men in the same baggy black broadcloth trousers, with white trimmings, that they had trotted out against the Athletics in 1905. A student of remembrance past, Little Napoleon was certain the "dangerous black" would intimidate the Philadelphians, or at least jostle their memory for the worst.

As Matty sauntered to the mound, "his head was held high and his eye, with slow, lordly contempt, swept the Athletics," as Lloyd Lewis, the Chicago historian recalled. At that moment an all-time record Series crowd of over 40,000 did everything but toss their straw hats into the air. Taking up where he left off in 1905, Matty retired leadoff batter Bristol Lord and the next two batters, continuing his streak of 27 scoreless innings through one more inning. But in the second inning, the Athletics finally scored a run off Big Six when Davis singled in Baker with the first tally of the Series.

The Giants came back to tie the game in the fourth, when Snodgrass scored on an error. The winning run came over for the Giants in the seventh, with Devore knocking in Meyers from second base. With a 2-1 victory in his pocket, Matty had now licked Mack's club four times in a row, yielding only one run in 36 innings. Certainly the outlook was promising for the Giants. Though he was six years older than he'd been in '05, Matty still looked invincible to the Athletics. What made his performance particularly convincing was that he issued only one walk and threw just 92 pitches. He hardly seemed to be falling apart, as some soothsayers suggested.

But the Athletics weren't going to concede the Series to the Giants. They had too many talented players for such a quick demise.

After a day off because both New York and Philadelphia continued to prohibit Sunday baseball, the Athletics showed they did indeed belong on the same diamond with the Giants. In a tight pitching duel on Monday at Shibe Park, before a noisy home-town crowd of 27,000, Coombs bested Marquard, 3-1. The coup de grace was delivered against Rube in the sixth inning by Baker, who picked up a chin-high fastball and sent it over the right-field fence.

In the pre-game strategy sessions McGraw pointedly had warned Rube not to throw such a succulent pitch to Baker. He reminded Marquard that Baker had hit eleven home runs that season to lead the American League and was, therefore, a dangerous adversary.

In Matty's column the next day, headlined "Marquard Made the Wrong Pitch," Rube was harshly criticized for disobeying McGraw's orders. The article, which Matty hadn't seen or endorsed before it appeared in print, took Rube to task for tossing the high outside pitch that Baker bombed for a home run. It wasn't politic to nail a teammate in print in such a way, but Matty refused to blame Wheeler. Engaging in a bit of team schadenfreude, the Athletics smartly clipped the column to their bulletin board, as a reminder that even the supposedly flawless Matty had his warts.

Marquard was privately burned up about the Matty-Wheeler castigation. It wasn't long before he had a chance to go public, for the next day another jam-packed Polo Grounds watched Matty do the unthinkable—yield a ninth-inning home run to—who else?—

Baker, on a high fastball. (Matty appeared to have the game won right before the home run, when Baker swung and seemingly missed a third strike pitch. However, the umpire ruled that Baker had ticked the ball, which rolled past catcher Meyers, and into the Giants' dugout.) The homer tied the score at 1-1, and, though Matty composed himself, his infielders didn't. In the eleventh inning, faulty play by Herzog and Fletcher blew the contest for the Giants.

Just what Marquard was thinking about this sequence of events isn't hard to guess. The next afternoon, in his own ghost-written essay (penned by Frank Menke, later to become a baseball encyclopedist), Rube reminded the world that Matty had chucked the same "wrong" pitch that he'd been accused of throwing.

"Will the great Mathewson tell us exactly what he pitched to Baker?" Marquard asked. "He was present at the same clubhouse meeting at which Mr. McGraw discussed Baker's weakness. Could it be that Matty, too, let go a careless pitch when it meant the ball game . . ."

Such exchanges were hardly conducive to producing tranquility among the Giants. What effect it had on the team in the rest of the Series is hard to figure, though it couldn't have helped. Clearly, the chief beneficiary of the two "wrong" pitches was Baker, the long-armed dead ball–era slugger, who forever after was known as "Home Run."

Following the third game, with the A's ahead, two games to one, the rains started to fall in Philadelphia, as if on McGraw's demand. It was one way to cool off Mack's ménage. For six days the rain pelted down, the likes of which the citizens of Philadelphia hadn't experienced in years. To get the field dry gasoline cans were set on fire around the infield and outfield grass. Finally, on October 24, the Series resumed, with the Athletics facing a presumably well-rested Matty. In a pre-game warmup under the first sun to peep from beneath the clouds in almost a week, Matty became agitated by the demands of a battery of cameramen who wanted him to pose for pictures. More prickly than usual, this man of "princely poise" grumbled at such an intrusion: "Who am I working for, the Giants or the photographers?"

In the first inning Matty struck out the side, leaving folks to think the rain had been good for him and the Giants. But in the fourth inning the roof fell in, as the A's tallied three off him. Baker started it with one of two doubles he'd make that day off Matty; Murphy doubled; Davis also doubled; and Ira Thomas hit a sacrifice fly. By the seventh, with the A's in front, 4-2, McGraw sent both Wiltse and Marquard to the bullpen to warm up. "Marquard strolled up and down with a great sardonic grin," wrote Lloyd Lewis. Could Rube have been thinking of Matty's ill-conceived column?

A pinch-hitter, Beals Becker, grounded out for Matty in the eighth, as the fans jeered Matty's removal from the game. It wasn't often that Philadelphia fans had had a chance to cheer for Matty's failures against them. Matty's departure marked his final appearance of the year. McGraw won the next game with three pitchers, Marquard, Ames, and Crandall, but lost the sixth with Ames. In this instance, McGraw had chosen not to come back with Matty in the sixth game with a day of rest. The move may have cost him, for the Giants ended up losing the world title to the Athletics.

Never a magnanimous soul, either in victory or defeat, Mc-Graw trudged into the Philadelphia dugout, after the A's had put the final touches on the Giant defeat, and congratulated the thin man who guided the Athletics.

"You have a great team," said McGraw to Mack. "They must be great because you beat a great team."

For a few moments McGraw had subdued his bitterness over the setback and his anger over the constant jeering from the Philadelphia crowd that had driven him off the coaching lines, after the fourth inning of the sixth game.

"I don't think that Tinker and Evers, in their best days with the Cubs, ever excelled Barry and Collins in teamwork and in guessing out defensive plays. They had great intuition and helped to stop our running game," admitted McGraw. In the six games the Giants stole only four bases, a dramatic drop-off from the regular season when the team ran the bases with impunity. In the third game alone five Giant base-runners were thrown out by A's catcher Jack Lapp, hardly much of a help to Matty in a close ball game.

With Philadelphia now at the top of the mountain, McGraw was also annoyed to learn that his old pal, George M. Cohan, knowing something that McGraw didn't, had staged a one-man coup by betting a few dollars on the Athletics to win. McGraw considered Cohan disloyal to the Giants and the city of New York. For the next few years he refused to acknowledge Cohan whenever he ran into him at the Lambs or other restaurants about town. However, the Giants' wounds were salved to a degree by the $2,346 that each player pocketed in defeat, about $1,000 less than each Athletic received. Despite the week of rain, which could have lessened enthusiasm for the Series, total attendance went over 180,000, another mark.

Within a month after the wreck of the Series, McGraw shepherded a group of his Giants to Havana, Cuba. He hadn't been there in over 20 years but had never lost his fascination for the country and its people. Going first to Jacksonville and then to Key West, the Giants took a boat to Havana, where they played a schedule of 12 games in a month. Jane went along with Matty, so that Blanche McGraw would have company. But Marquard, Merkle, and Meyers didn't choose to join the troupe. In Rube's case it may have been too soon for him to gulp down the column-inflicted sores of the 1911 Series.

(It wasn't until some years after that Marquard made a more gentle assessment of Matty: "He never thought he was better than anybody else. It was just the way he carried himself, the way we saw him. But it was okay, because, what the hell, when you come down to it, he *was* different, and on that mound, he *was* better than anybody else.")

When McGraw arrived in Havana he was pleasantly surprised to discover that the Cubans retained warm memories of him. He was still known among the Havana journalists as El Mono Amarillo (The Yellow Monkey). But that was a mark of affection, not a disparagement. Baseball had been in its infancy in Cuba when McGraw had first visited there as a teenager. But *beisbol* had since blossomed into a sport that had a strong hold on the Cuban population. Indeed, it could be said that Cubans regarded the pastime with the same obsessiveness that many Americans did.

They viewed their ballplayers with great pride and considered their homegrown players every bit as good as previous junketing teams from Philadelphia and Detroit. Now the Giants were included in such estimates. One such Cuban performer was a lithe, 150-pound, 24-year-old named Jose Mendez, who pitched for the Almendares club. At the start of their tour the Giants dropped their first two games to Almendares and Havana. When Matty and Mendez hooked up in a duel in the third game, Matty won, 3-0, but only after a first-rate performance by the Cuban. McGraw was pleased that the Giants won that contest. But he was seething over the first two setbacks, after which he ordered his troops out for a strenuous early morning workout. He made it clear, in no uncertain terms, that these games were not to be regarded lightly. "I don't relish losing to a bunch of coffee-colored Cubans," he barked.

Matty fared better in Cuba than he had in the late World Series. He lost only one game—that to Mendez, "the black Mathewson," as he was called—and won five. He must have been secretly grateful that baseball's color line prevented Mendez, a man he described as a "great pitcher," from coming to the United States to play against him.

While the Giants were in Havana Matty often accompanied McGraw to the American Club, on the corner of Prado and Virtudes, near the splendid capitol building. There McGraw's *yanquis* and their great *lanzador* could eat a daily lunch and gourmet dinners in the evening, featuring elaborately prepared Cuban dishes. Formal dances and social games were also held at the club. Just as he often did in New York at the Lambs and other clubs, Matty sat down in Havana opposite the best competitive checkers and card players, invariably beating them soundly. When Matty took on concurrently six players in checkers and licked them all, that brought gasps of astonishment from onlookers. After all, he'd had good practice back in the States, where his writer friends Runyon, Boze Bulger, and Heywood Broun often provided rugged opposition. (Broun, fresh out of Harvard, class of 1910, was first introduced to Matty by McGraw, who had gotten wind of Broun's reputation as a card and checkers shark. "You think you're pretty good?" asked McGraw of the young reporter. "I think so," responded Broun. "Okay, if you survive against Matty, you're telling the truth," said McGraw. Soon after the two men, Matty and Broun, sat down to play checkers in the Giants' clubhouse, with Matty taking two out of three games. "You're a very sound player," Matty told Broun. Thereafter, the two became bridge and whist partners, as well as mutual admirers.)

When the Giants returned to America, after their successful jaunt, Matty settled down with Wheeler to put the finishing touches on *Pitching in a Pinch*, his projected autobiography. His relationship with Wheeler obviously hadn't been damaged, even if it was unlikely that Marquard would be anxious to read Matty's gems of mound wisdom. The book evolved out of a series of articles on "inside baseball" that Matty had worked on for the McClure Syndicate, again with Wheeler spinning the words.

Throughout *Pitching in a Pinch*, Matty's distinctive voice was only barely present. (That didn't stop Walter "Red" Smith, a famous sports columnist of a later generation, from declaring that it was the first book he ever borrowed from the North Side Branch of the Kellogg Public Library in Green Bay, Wisconsin, where he grew up.) In his book Matty engaged himself in many areas of the game, including jinxes, luck, superstitions, strategy, umpires, sign-stealing personalities, observations about McGraw and others, his own pitching peculiarities, and "yellow streaks" among some athletes. Most memorable was his assessment of the 1908 pennant-losing game against the Cubs, an event that he said "stood out like the battle of Waterloo and the assassination of Abraham Lincoln."

Nothing in *Pitching in a Pinch* was designed to offend even Matty's worst enemies, if he had them. One reviewer in more recent years, the poet Donald Hall, mused that Matty's chef d'oeuvre supplied "anecdotes, but withheld sentence, image and metaphor." Such criticism suggests that Matty, equally as grammatical and literate as Wheeler, might have produced a better tome if he'd written it himself.

13

SNODGRASS
MUFFS ONE

O
N Monday, April 15, 1912, the Giants lost to Boston, despite a good effort by Matty, starting his thirteenth year in a New York uniform. With a mark of 1-2 after the end of the day, the team looked forward to evening its record.

The other news in the Giants' camp was that Merkle was still a holdout, as he demanded $4000 for the season. This caused some minor annoyance to McGraw, who said he wouldn't go past $3000.

But by late afternoon thoughts of baseball and the start of the new campaign quickly evaporated, as the grapevine spread the news of the hundreds of people who had congregated at the White Star Line's Broadway offices. They had been drawn there by the shocking headlines in that morning's *Herald:* "The New *Titanic* Strikes Iceberg and Calls for Aid." Friends and relatives of the 2000 passengers flocked with trepidation to the lower Manhattan building. Such financial titans as Isidor Straus, John Jacob Astor, and Benjamin Guggenheim were on board the *Titanic,* as well as other prominent New Yorkers.

By evening the dispatches had improved, with the optimistic suggestion that all on the liner had been saved. But hours after, the grim truth was revealed in the headlines of Tuesday's *Times:* "*Titanic* Sinks Four Hours After Hitting Iceberg, 866 Rescued, 1,250 Probably Perish."

The disaster on the high seas of the 42,328-ton, four-city-block-

long steamer, the largest and presumably the safest nautical creation in the world, struck a note of horror in the city and the country. Commercial activity in New York almost came to a standstill.
On the news that Straus and his wife went down with the *Titanic,*
R. H. Macy & Company and Abraham & Straus closed their stores
for a week. Though the pennant races went on, attendance was
down in the days following the tragedy and talk in the dugouts had
little to do with winning and losing.

When the fans' attention returned again to baseball, they voiced
confidence in the team McGraw was fielding that summer. There
were some major additions to the cast, if one excluded Charlie Faust,
who still remained on hand as a goofy talisman. Faust was anointed
with the name of "Victory," since the club continued winning when
he was on the bench. George Burns, a young outfielder from Utica
in the New York State League, became an instant favorite of
McGraw, who saw unlimited potential in him. Though Burns did
not play much in 1912 he was assigned the role of sitting next to
McGraw on the bench, to soak up the manager's wisdom. Burns
would become one of the better Giants in the next decade. The
other new face, one that contributed immensely to the Giants in
'12, was big Jeff Tesreau, a spitball pitcher from Ironton, Missouri.
McGraw obtained Tesreau from Toronto during the winter. In later
years Tesreau became Dartmouth's baseball coach; in 1912, after a
slow start, he took over as the third best pitcher on the team, behind Matty and Marquard. From July on he was hotter than a torched
stove.

McGraw once again had his club stealing bases (319 during the
season) and playing aggressively. Merkle, once he signed, Meyers,
Snodgrass, and Murray were steady batters who provided the kind
of hitting that the team needed to win games. The club took over
first place in mid-May. Though the Giants went through a late-
season slumber, they managed to complete a record of 103 victories and 48 defeats, to finish ten games ahead of the second-place
Pirates.

With his 23 wins Matty had another good season. But in 310
innings of pitching he failed to record a single shutout, something
that hadn't happened to him since his first year with the Giants.
McGraw still loyally looked upon Matty as the bellwether of his
staff, but he knew that the sharp-featured Marquard, a 24-game
winner in 1911, was truly responsible for carrying the team from
opening day. Marquard, who ended the year with 26 victories (with
only one shutout), ran off a remarkable string of 19 consecutive

triumphs, tying the record set by Tim Keefe in 1888. He beat Brooklyn on opening day, won two more in April, seven in May, eight in June, and one in July, as he beat every team in the league at least once. After he took number 19 on July 3 against Brooklyn, the team against whom it all began, he finally lost to the Cubs five days later at Chicago.

However, by that time the Giants had gained sufficient momentum to keep them on top. The Cubs put some last-minute pressure on them in September, when they moved within a few games of New York. But seven wins in nine games against Boston and Philadelphia, concluding with a victory over the Braves late in September, sewed things up for the Giants. They had won their second straight National League pennant and the third under McGraw.

The somewhat diminished performance by Matty in 1912 didn't dull his sparkling reputation. Off the field, he was purported to be the real-life inspiration for "Baseball Joe," a character in a new book written by author Lester Chadwick. The creator of Joe never denied that he had Matty in mind, although others figured that Joe was an amalgam of Matty and Frank Merriwell. In time Chadwick wrote an entire series about Baseball Joe, who was presented as a spotless, if unreal, role model for millions of baseball-mad youngsters.

The virtues of a game that men like Matty were popularizing continued to be acclaimed by people from every walk of life. Even Lillian Russell joined in the general kudos for baseball. "It gives one the chance to smile out loud under God's clear sky and to take in life-giving breaths of fresh air every time one empties the lungs with a lusty cheer," she said. But all was not as well as Russell suggested.

Increasingly, ballplayers felt they were being short-changed by penurious owners. Stellar performers and journeymen alike issued pronouncements concerning the basic unfairness of life in the big leagues. That other constant role model, Walter Johnson, the fast-balling pitcher of the Washington Senators, referred to his sport as a form of "slavery." He didn't argue that he should be making as much as the $10,000 a year that Matty got from the Giants, nor did he insist that he should make more than the $9500 that Ty Cobb eked out of Detroit. But he did say that he was worth more than the $6500 he was earning from the Senators. "The employer tries to starve out the laborer," he said. Coming from a man with such conservative Kansas roots, that was saying a Marxist mouthful.

Unrest among the "oppressed" reached such a point that the players threatened a general strike. Such collective action emanated from an incident involving Cobb, a man with only limited credentials for martyrdom. On an afternoon in May, 1912, Cobb leaped into the stands in New York to assault a fan who had been berating him. Johnson, the American League president, was at the game and witnessed Cobb's indelicate behavior. He promptly ruled that Cobb should be suspended ten days without pay.

Many of the Tigers, who found Cobb equally as distasteful as others did, still rallied around his cause. They voted to strike if he was not reinstated and given a fair hearing by the League office. They fulfilled their threat on May 18 by walking out en masse in a game against the Athletics. When a makeshift team of high-school kids, culls, baseball outcasts, and anybody else who could be rounded up by the Detroit front office took the field at Shibe Park, to replace the striking Tigers, a disgraceful 24-2 victory for the A's ensued. A storm of disapproval crashed down around the Tigers' heads, as newspaper editorials thundered at the ballplaying infidels. It got so heated that even Cobb beseeched his teammates to return to work. This they did, reluctantly.

However, the Cobb brouhaha produced a sense of solidarity among the players, who made up their minds to form a new ballplayer organization truly representative of their interests. The one man that they eagerly pursued to head up such a group was Matty. Almost unanimously ballplayers regarded him as a person with brains as well as integrity. That he had earned a high standing with the public was also a major consideration.

After much lobbying and imploring, however, Matty decided not to accept the post as president. He reasoned that he lacked both the time and independence to perform the role with thoroughness. He did assure the players that he would be pleased to serve along with the embattled Cobb as a vice president. Though the players were disappointed by Matty's rejection, they said they understood his position on the matter. Eventually, David Fultz, a former big-league center-fielder and an attorney in New York, was elected president of the group that called itself the Fraternity of Baseball Players of America. Only later in his career would Matty take on the mantle of baseball executive.

By 1912 Matty's relationship with the sportswriters, in New York and elsewhere, was consistently warm and cordial. Most of these men in the press boxes admired Matty not only for his skill as a pitcher but also for his varied abilities off the diamond. He was their homme engagé, the most unusual of all ballplayers, someone you wouldn't mind sharing an evening with at the theatre or at bridge or in just "shooting the bull." For a group often lacking in modesty about its own virtue and intelligence, many writers were willing to grant that Matty could compete with them in the former and possibly surpass them in the latter. In particular, Heywood Broun continually wrote and uttered things about his friend that could make one blush with embarrassment.

For example, in 1911, after Matty's opening game victory over the A's, Broun's flatulent prose reached stunning heights. "Matty's nerve was unruffled, his matchless courage unbroken," wrote Broun. "Thousands upon thousands, friend and enemy, paid tribute to the master who had toyed with Baker in the pinches, coddled Collins and sent the swift McInnis hitless through the struggles." (This was composed before Baker won his nickname of "Home Run," thanks to both Matty and Marquard.)

Broun acknowledged that there was nothing that he loved more than to watch Matty pitch—with the exception of teaming up with him in whist or bridge. The two always took several minutes to analyze hands, then played with lightning speed, a system that was jarring to opponents.

Constantly troubled about the state of his health, Broun once wrote a fake headline on a piece of paper and presented it to Eddie Brannick, the Giants' scrawny all-around assistant and confidant to McGraw. "Matty Pitches No Hitter as Baseball Writer Dies," the headline screamed. Broun was certain that if such an event occurred his heart would give out from the excitement.

For a brief period Broun acted as sports editor of the *Tribune*, making him responsible, among other things, for the selection of articles and photos that filled his pages. Such chores weren't as much to Broun's liking as writing about Matty from the press-box aerie. When an excess of stories came in, Broun just tossed them about in the same way that he indiscriminately packed his suitcase at Harvard. Often Broun just omitted whatever came to him last. If there weren't enough stories to fill the sports pages, Broun would invariably select a flattering photograph of Matty and insert it in one of the open slots.

There were few low moments for Matty that year, but toward the end of 1912 he suffered what was for him a minor humiliation. After being presented with a fine automobile by a group of fans in a Polo Grounds ceremony, Matty took the vehicle out for a spin on

Long Island. The outing was marred when Matty was arrested for speeding. The officer who detained Matty testified that he clocked him doing over 31 miles an hour, as he raced along the highway. The judge, having little use for baseball or Matty, fined the pitcher $100.

Another negative note before the World Series that fall between the Giants and the Boston Red Sox was the death of Mc-Graw's failed reclamation project, Bugs Raymond. Bugs had ceased to be a cog in the Giants' pitching wheel, yet there were some few who mourned his passing in a cheap Chicago hotel room. Bugs had gotten into a fight on the city's north side with a gang of toughs while watching two semi-pro teams playing ball. What remained of Bugs's alcohol-addled brain was battered into a skull fracture. Two days later he died at the age of 30. McGraw had tried hard to get Bugs to change his way of life. But even with such exemplary role models as Matty and Marquard, Bugs remained unregenerate.

The World Series between the Giants and the Red Sox was the ninth modern post-season clash and perhaps the most widely anticipated. "The country practically shut up shop for this national spectacle," wrote Fred Lieb. Newspaper coverage reached a peak, with endless stories evaluating the teams, players, and managers. There seemed to be more grainy pictures in the papers each day of the competing ballplayers than one could find of Teddy Roosevelt, the insurgent Bull Moose candidate for President, and the two men, Democrat Woodrow Wilson and Republican William Howard Taft, who were running against him in an election less than a month away.

Even a sensational trial in New York, in which police lieutenant Charles Becker was implicated in the murder of a notorious gambler, Herman Rosenthal, failed to attract as much attention as the event that was about to unfold at ball parks in New York and Boston.

In 1904 McGraw had refused to play Boston in the World Series. Now he had to face them in their new playground, Fenway Park, a bandbox that had quickly won a reputation among fans for its coziness and charm. Managed by Jake Stahl, a former Washington player-manager, the Red Sox had put together an extraordinary season of 105 victories. They finished 14 games ahead of the Senators, a club kept in the race through the exertions of Walter Johnson. They also vaulted past the Athletics, despite Philadelphia's vaunted "$100,000 infield." If Mack's foursome was valued at such a figure on the open market, what would an owner pay, hypothetically, for Stahl's premier outfield of Harry Hooper, Tris Speaker, and Duffy Lewis?

Speaker was easily the best center-fielder in baseball, the Joe DiMaggio of his era. By playing a daringly shallow center-field, Speaker challenged all batters to hit one over his head. Few ever could. Surrounding Speaker in the outfield, Hooper and Lewis could track down anything that Speaker couldn't. They loved these three men in Boston; the noisiest support they received was from the Royal Rooters of Boston, a grand fraternity of local Irishmen, who loathed one of their own, McGraw, as much as they worshipped their home team. Mayor John "Honey Fitz" Fitzgerald was on hand for most of the Red Sox games during the season and was certain to be present during the Series. (His yet unborn grandson, John F. Kennedy, would become President of the United States fifty years later.)

But it was on the mound that the Red Sox won their true edge, even over the Giants. The young right-hander, Smokey Joe Wood, at 23, and ten years younger than Matty, had put together a season of 34 wins and only five defeats, with 35 complete games and ten shutouts. In his best year of 1908 Matty had never been as successful. Johnson, even with his own locomotive pitch, admitted he never could throw as hard as Smokey Joe. He didn't think anyone else could, either.

During the 1912 season both Wood and Johnson ran off streaks of 16 straight victories, further evidence that nobody else could match their overwhelming speed. Matty certainly never said he could. His specialty, in variance with what Wood and Johnson threw, was to get the ball exactly where he wanted it to go. "He could shave you if he wanted to, if he had a razor blade to throw, instead of a ball," wrote Ring Lardner. Control was Matty's middle name; blinding speed was Wood's.

Despite proof of his dominance, Wood was deprecated by McGraw before the World Series began. "I'm not afraid of Wood's fastball," he announced. Needless to say, McGraw wasn't going to bat against it.

McGraw then resorted to another of his psychological ploys by holding Matty out of the first game at the Polo Grounds. His reasoning was that Matty would fare better in the hostile Fenway Park environment in the second game than rookie Tesreau, who had been nominated to oppose Wood, Stahl's choice to open the Series. McGraw's strategy played right into the hands of the Red Sox strategy, for Stahl preferred to have Wood pitch against a weaker opponent such as Tesreau.

The top-hatted Royal Rooters descended on the Polo Grounds in full force, slinging expletives and singing "Sweet Adeline" at the top of their lungs. Led by their ebullient mayor, they were part of a crowd of 36,000 that jammed every inch of the Giants' park.

Looking down on the mob from Coogan's Bluff one could see a wheat field of black derbies, punctuated only now and then by a woman's hat piled high with silk roses. There probably wasn't one man among the Royal Rooters who hadn't bet a dollar or two on the Red Sox, putting up five to win three. With Matty out of the opener, the Red Sox had to be favored, especially with Wood at the throttle.

For five innings of the first game, Tesreau held Boston without a score, making McGraw's illogical move seem logical. But the Giants' early two-run lead came down to one after a brief Red Sox rally in the sixth. In the seventh the Red Sox jumped on Tesreau for three more runs and the ball game, as the Royal Rooters screamed themselves hoarse. As expected, Wood was magnificent, striking out ten, including two straining Giants in the last of the ninth.

In Times Square enormous crowds followed the depressing circumstances at the Polo Grounds via a 17-foot-long electric scoreboard, which was perched on the façade of the Times Building. Lights blinked on and off to illuminate the progress of base-runners—but they didn't blink much for the Giants that afternoon.

The next day, October 9, before over 30,000 frenetic Boston partisans, Matty got his chance to even up matters with the Red Sox. In the first inning when the Sox crammed in three quick runs, mainly on Giant miscues, the braying of the Royal Rooters rattled the windows from Kenmore Square to Harvard Yard. Nobody had suspected such a speedy evisceration of the Great Matty to take place. But the Giants got back into the game with the help of some extra-duty hitting by Herzog and Murray. Matty kept things together, despite five errors by teammates (three by Fletcher at shortstop) and a momentary outburst of fisticuffs after Herzog tangled with Speaker on a play at third base.

In the eighth inning the Giants inched ahead, 5-4. But Fletcher's third error allowed the Red Sox to tie the score at 5-5. In the tenth the Giants scored in the top of the inning, producing ecstasy among their supporters, only to see the Red Sox take advantage of substitute center-fielder Beals Becker's misjudgment of Speaker's line drive. Tris went to third, where the relay was dropped, then scored the tying run when another substitute catcher, Art Wilson, in for Meyers, booted the throw to home plate. It wasn't very pretty—and appeared to be a painful prolongation of the misadventures that bedeviled Matty going back to Merkle's error of omission in 1908.

After another scoreless inning was rung up by both clubs in the eleventh, plate umpire Silk O'Loughlin gazed up at the darkening sky (the game was only two hours and 38 minutes old, having started at 3:30) and decreed that matters should come to a halt at 6-6. O'Loughlin, like the Great Arbitrator, Bill Klem, always professed that he'd "never missed one in my life." He even went one step further by comparing himself with the Pope. "He's for religion," said O'Loughlin, "O'Loughlin's for baseball. Both are infallible."

So Matty's eleven innings of intense effort, without a walk being issued, against three Red Sox pitchers, all went for nought. It was decided that the tie game should be replayed the next afternoon in Boston, with Marquard facing Boston's Bucky O'Brien. Rube was up to the task, defeating the Red Sox, 2-1, in another game marked by darkness and considerable rancor.

In the last of the ninth inning, with Boston fans screaming for blood, Lewis singled and Larry Gardner doubled, scoring Lewis. With the Red Sox needing one run to tie and two to win, Marquard was able to throw out Gardner on a play at third, for the second out. Searching for the third out, Marquard cringed when the Giant defense faltered, as it had so many times in the past. Before matters settled down, the Red Sox put men on second and third. A hit would win the game for them. The next batter, Forrest Cady, drove a ball deep into center field, where Josh Devore pursued it like a frightened terrier. Many of the Boston fans failed to see Devore make the catch in full stride, for an enshrouding mist was settling over the field at the time. Meanwhile, Devore triumphantly kept racing toward the center-field clubhouse, clutching the third-out ball close to his body. Thousands in the stands set up a Red Sox victory din, thinking the ball had eluded Devore. Only when they read in the next day's papers that Devore had caught the ball—O'Loughlin making the call—did they realize Boston hadn't won the game.

With the Series knotted at one game each, Boston surged into a three-to-one lead by snaring the next two games. Wood beat Tesreau 3-1 before 30,000 grouchy Giant fans in New York, then Matty lost to Hugh Bedient the next day in Boston, 2-1, on an error by Larry Doyle that permitted the winning run to come across. In the last five innings Matty didn't allow a runner to reach base but his team failed to score another run to get back into the game. The temper of the Boston fans was best illustrated by the fact that Giant players were constantly pelted with peanuts and varieties of fruit. Snodgrass winged a ball at one of the Royal Rooters when they attempted to interfere with Fred's progress toward a fly ball during outfield practice.

When the Series appeared to be lost for the Giants, McGraw rallied his forlorn troops. With Sunday an open date because of the religious prohibition, the teams waited for Monday to continue the Series at the Polo Grounds. The Giants won that one behind Marquard, 5-2, with the help of a first-inning offensive of five runs.

On Tuesday, when the Red Sox fans expected that Wood would wrap up the Series for them, the Giants broke out a first-inning attack that produced six runs on seven hits. Nobody was more shocked by this display than Wood himself. But there may have been an excuse for his disappointing performance. The start of the game had been delayed for thirty minutes by protesting Royal Rooters, who fought to occupy seats in which others were sitting. Finding themselves without seats, the Rooters battled a platoon of gendarmes, some of whom were on horses. Attacking the bleacher fence, the Royal Rooters knocked it down; then they dispersed into the crowd, to the accompaniment of brass bands that celebrated their anarchism, perhaps the most pernicious such display since the Boston Tea Party. While such activities were taking place, Wood, having already warmed up, found his arm tightening.

Whatever the reason for Wood's failure, the Giants, with Tesreau on the mound, won 11-4, to tie the Series at three games all. That set the stage for the final game, in this case an eighth contest. When the Red Sox won the toss of a coin to decide the venue, Fenway Park became the site of the ultimate battle.

McGraw was convinced that his comeback team, charging back from a two-game deficit, had momentum going for them. Also he had a well-rested Matty, who had just experienced three days off, practically a summer vacation for him. McGraw also felt there was no way that Matty could start three games in a Series and not come away with a single victory.

The day—October 16—turned out to be cold and forbidding in Boston, as Bedient took the mound for the Red Sox in the first inning. But it was more than weather that held the crowd down to 17,000. Many of the Royal Rooters, still in a state of pique over having been dispossessed of their seats the previous afternoon, refused to show up at Fenway. However, about 1500 Giant fans, hopeful about the outcome, took the train from New York, fully expecting to sing the praises of Matty and their Giants before the day was done.

This game may have meant as much to Matty as any he ever pitched. That morning, as he sat in the lobby of his Boston hotel, he chose to remain aloof from all passersby, including members of his own team. Even McGraw was not disposed to break Matty's introspective calm. Matty's face revealed long gullies of fatigue, his skin was tightly drawn over his jaw and his cheeks were more hollow than one might expect from a 32-year-old athlete. As he glanced at the morning's newspaper, with its endless speculations about that day's contest, Matty's body appeared gaunt.

When Matty started to warm up on the sidelines at Fenway, he employed no superfluous gestures, throwing only hard enough to allow his arm to feel supple. Again, he ignored all of those within hearing distance, preferring to concentrate on his tosses to Chief Meyers. To some observers he looked like the loneliest man in town—and may very well have been.

The Giants struck quickly in the third inning on a walk to Devore and a double by Red Murray. They came close to adding more in the fifth when Doyle was robbed of a home run by Hooper, who almost plunged over the right-field fence to catch the ball as it was about to disappear. Meanwhile, Matty was mowing down the Boston batters with regularity over the first six innings. His astounding drop curves, off-speed deliveries, and impeccable control had his strikes nipping at the edges of the plate and thudding into Meyers's mitt. But this wasn't going to be a day of many strikeouts, for Matty's intention was to conserve his energy. In the fifth he threw only three pitches, all for fly outs.

At the plate Matty stroked one long fly to center field that might have eluded an outfielder less capable than Speaker. There were two men on base at the time; a hit would have given Matty the comfortable lead he needed. In the sixth the Red Sox got a runner to third base. But when they tried to bunt the runner across with the tying run Matty delivered a pitch that sent the batter flying away from the plate. As a result, Meyers's throw to third caught the retreating runner flatfooted. In the seventh Matty began the inning with a single to left. On Devore's attempted sacrifice bunt, Matty hurtled into second base, where the umpire called him out on a close play. Matty picked himself up out of the dust and walked slowly back to the bench, as the rally was stillborn.

Boston started their seventh with an out, followed by Stahl's bloop over the infield for a single. Suddenly Matty's control went awry against Wagner, and the Red Sox shortstop walked on four pitches. With men on first and second and Red Sox fans imploring their team to come up with a hit, Cady popped out to Fletcher. It appeared that Matty had weathered the storm, even as Olaf "Swede" Henriksen, who was small (5'7", 155 pounds) and left-handed, was sent up to pinch-hit for Bedient.

Matty got two quick strikes over on Henriksen, who had never faced him before and thus should have suffered from such lack of experience. Now was the moment for Matty's fadeaway—the pitch in a pinch. But Henriksen swung late on it, causing the ball to barely strike the end of his bat. At third Herzog flung himself into the air as the ball went past him—an accidental hit, if ever there was one. The game was tied, with runners still located at second and third. Boston's fans roared for the kill. As Matty's shoulders sagged, McGraw glowered, suppressing the rage he felt at Henriksen's lucky hit.

But Matty wasn't ready to give up. Working carefully, he induced Hooper to hit one to Snodgrass in center, and Yerkes made the third out on a ground ball. At this point Stahl called on Wood, only twenty-four hours removed from a first-inning pasting by the Giants, to relieve Bedient. During this entire Series Matty and Smokey Joe had never gone head-to-head, a battle made to order for the country's baseball fans.

In the eighth Wood was up to the task, his fast balls banging relentlessly into Cady's mitt. However, Matty was also equal to the challenge. He got past the Red Sox in the eighth and again in the ninth, though the Sox gave the Giants a scare when Stahl's fly ball in the ninth dropped just over Murray's outstretched glove for a double. With one out, Matty then retired Wagner on a fly ball. Cady, up next, might have been passed intentionally to pitch to Wood, though the pitcher was rated as a fine batter (later in his career he played the outfield). But Matty and McGraw were certain that a pinch-hitter would appear for Wood. So the choice was to pitch to Cady, who conveniently popped up for the third out. The strategy assured that Wood would still be on the mound for Boston in the tenth. For the first time a World Series would be decided in extra innings, as the two best right-handers in the game jousted for the world title.

Wood began the tenth by getting Snodgrass out. Murray, batting in the cleanup spot, wasn't as easy. He launched a shot to left center field, where both Duffy Lewis and Speaker chased after it. They convened at the base of Duffy's Cliff, which is what that Fenway territory was called, but the ball was already past them and into the temporary bleachers for a double, Murray's fourth of the Series. Giant fans screamed that Murray was entitled to a home run. But under the ground rules set before the Series it went for only two bases.

Merkle dug in to face Wood. Still regarded as a failure based on a single mistake four years earlier, he had become a talented player, fulfilling all of McGraw's expectations. Leveling in on Wood's fast one, Merkle sent the ball screaming back through the box, a low white blur that not even the great Speaker could catch before it fell to the ground. Murray hustled around to score with the run that the Giants dearly hoped would bring them the championship.

But no further damage was inflicted on Wood. The score remained, 2-1, in favor of the Giants, as Matty walked to the mound in the bottom of the tenth inning. He turned to study the scoreboard that hung over the bleachers in right field, reassuring himself that he was ahead at this stage. He knew that all he needed were three outs to win the Series. Taking his warmup pitches with Meyers, he had the manner of one who had been through this meat-grinder before—in fact, many times before. And he was not going to be fazed by the rising crescendo of supplications from Boston fans. Ready for combat, he peered down at the batter, Clyde Engle, a heavy-set part-time player, chosen in this situation to pinch-hit for Wood. Engle, a right-handed batter, would be aiming to bash one against Fenway's enticing left-field wall.

Matty worked over Engle with two tantalizing curves. Then, with two strikes against him, Engle swung and lifted a Texas League fly that floated between center and right field. Snodgrass and Murray both were within easy reach of it. Yelling "I got it!" at Murray, Snodgrass took command—a routine procedure by center-fielders. Murray respectfully backed away, leaving it to his teammate to execute a simple catch. But instead of the ball settling for an out in Snodgrass's glove, it dribbled to the ground. On the play, Engle never stopped running until he reached second. Following his muff, Snodgrass threw the ball to Doyle,who returned it softly to the chagrined Matty. (In Los Angeles, where Snodgrass's mother was following the game on an electric scoreboard, she fainted.) Visibly stunned by Snodgrass's failure to make the catch, Matty swung his gloved hand in a gesture of despair. Or was it wrath?

He looked down at the earth around the mound and kicked it.

Trying to calm his pitcher, Meyers climbed out of his squat position and trotted out to Matty. Meyers knew now that Matty was
human after all, hardly the imperturbable man of legend. The pitcher
waved back at Meyers, indicating that he should go back to the
plate, where he belonged. Sensing Matty's dark mood, the crowd
set up a medley of catcalls and jeers that filled the small ball park.
Matty stepped off the mound for a moment, as he reached down
for the resin bag. His face, streaked with sweat, betrayed his discomfiture. Slamming the resin bag back to the ground, he faced
Hooper, the next batter.

Eager to take advantage of Matty's anger, Hooper lashed out at
the first pitch and sent it deep into right center field. This time
Snodgrass's outstretched glove held grimly to the ball, just as he
crashed into the wall. "Ninety-nine times in a hundred," Hooper
said later, "no outfielder could come close to the ball . . . but dang
if he didn't catch it. Robbed me of a sure triple." It seemed an easy
matter for Engle to advance to third after the catch—but he was so
surprised that Snodgrass made the grab that he had to retreat to
second, where he was almost doubled off by Snodgrass's return
throw.

With a man on second and one out, Matty was still in a good
position to rescue the game and Series for the Giants. Amazingly,
however, his control suddenly failed him, as he pitched to Steve
Yerkes, a second baseman of small stature who hadn't hit a homer
all season and had only six in his career. Watching four straight
errant pitches go by, Yerkes ambled down to first base, more surprised than anyone in the park. The crowd's animal roar trebled,
as Speaker walked to the plate. If there was any man a pitcher
would hate to face in such a situation it was "Spoke," a .383 hitter
with 222 hits during the season and ten home runs.

On Matty's first pitch, Speaker popped up a high foul near the
railing at first base, ordinarily a simple play. "Any schoolboy could
have caught it," wrote Fred Lieb, who covered the game, "but the
gremlins seem to have taken a hand." Merkle, at first base, circled
under it, so did Matty. But when Meyers also raced for it, Matty
hollered, "Chief, Chief," enough to cause Merkle to abstain from
the play. Meyers, who had been farthest from the ball, lunged fu-
tilely, as the ball dropped harmlessly to earth.

Was Matty's inopportune call influenced by Merkle's reputation? Hard to believe such a thing, for Matty's choice of Meyers
was more likely a reflex. But the question lingers. Whatever im-
pulse had caused him to bypass Merkle at that awful moment, Matty

knew he had made a mistake. Picking the ball off the grass, Matty spoke briefly to Merkle—was it a word of solace or confession?—and the first baseman nodded his head.

Facing Speaker again, Matty delivered a fast ball without any sting and the center-fielder, often rated in the same bracket as Cobb, cracked a liner to right field. Engle scored on the hit, to tie the game at 2-2. The other runners advanced to second and third, as Devore made a totally useless throw home.

Now there were few options open to McGraw. His choice was to walk Lewis intentionally to load the bases, to set up a force play or, hopefully, a double play. Third-baseman Gardner, another small man in the Boston infield—he was 5'7"—had the game in his hands. Batting from the left side, he pounced on Matty's second pitch and hit a long fly to Devore in right field. Matty knew from the crack of the bat that this was no ground ball, forceout, or popup. He turned to watch Devore go back to catch the drive, then make a desperate throw home to Meyers, trying to cut off Yerkes, who had tagged up. Even before Yerkes reached home with the decisive run, Matty started to walk off the diamond, toward the Giants' dugout.

The World Series was lost. The Red Sox had won a 3-2 victory in a game that ended the most thrilling Series that had been waged until that time. Two games down, the Giants had fought back gamely to tie the Series, only to see two pitifully played balls give the Series to the Red Sox. There was small compensation for the Giants in the loser's share of $2,566.47 for each player. The Red Sox took home $4,024.68 apiece.

In his account of the game, Ring Lardner wrote out of a sense of personal despair. "Just after Yerkes crossed the plate . . . there was seen one of the saddest sights in the history of a sport that is a strange and wonderful mixture of joy and gloom," he said. "It was the spectacle of a man, old as baseball players are reckoned, walking from the middle of the field to the New York players' bench with bowed head and drooping shoulders, with tears streaming from his eyes, a man on whom the team's fortune had been staked and lost, and a man who would have proved his clear title to the trust reposed in him if his mates had stood by him in the supreme test . . . the man was Christy Mathewson."

Some, like Speaker, felt that Matty, in his moment of defeat, had never been better. Writing in his autobiography, Speaker said that for six innings Matty was a perfect machine. "That one run looked awful big for a long while," he recalled.

When Matty finally retreated to the funereal atmosphere of the

Giants' locker room he sufficiently composed himself to declare quietly that nobody was to blame for the debacle. If anyone should be blamed, he insisted, it was himself, for failing to make the right call on Speaker's popup. He tried to console the unhappy Snodgrass by putting his arm around him and assuring him that "any man is likely to make an error." In such a situation other pitchers might have attacked the water bucket, in the tradition of the incendiary southpaw, Lefty Grove, the Athletics' superb pitcher of another generation, or butted their heads against the wall, in the manner of the tempestuous Wes Ferrell, a right-hander of the thirties. Any number of other less restrained hurlers might have at least verbally castigated Snodgrass. But that was never Matty's style.

Others in the Giants' household were more outspoken about the miscues that had derailed the team. "I know errors are a part of baseball," said Doyle, "but I wish Snodgrass had caught it. He feels worse than any of us and that's saying something."

The loss was as galling as any that McGraw had ever suffered. He knew that Snodgrass would be forever stigmatized as the villain of the defeat. The dropped fly ball immediately was institutionalized in baseball folklore as "The $30,000 Muff," the sum representing the difference between the winner's shares and the loser's take. What McGraw resented even more were the newspaper stories that blamed Snodgrass.

"If it hadn't been for Snodgrass," McGraw shouted, "we wouldn't have been in the game at all. He did a lot during the season that got us there. The game was lost when Speaker's foul wasn't caught. I'll tell you what I think of Snodgrass. I'm going to give him a better contract next year." It was no empty boast. McGraw did exactly that.

On the train returning to New York after the game, Matty walked up and down the aisle, trying to alter the rhythm of a sorrowful journey. "You can't blame a player for a physical error," he kept saying to his dispirited teammates. "The poor fellow feels miserable enough." Even in this hour of disgruntlement, Matty tried to focus his mind on a game of bridge with several writers.

Many years later, after a distinguished career as Yale's baseball coach, Joe Wood delivered a strangely unflattering and uncharitable assessment of his pitching adversary.

"You could be introduced to him a half-dozen times and he still wouldn't know you," said Smokey Joe about Matty. "I think he was a little 'high hat' and didn't want to remember you. Maybe because he was in the other league and went along with McGraw, who didn't care for the American League. I never actually talked to Mathewson but we all had the opinion, and I think it was true, that he thought himself quite a bit above the average player. It's true, of course, that we never had much to say to those fellows in the other league, so that may account for some of it . . . as a pitcher, I couldn't really tell you about Mathewson because I never saw him in his prime."

Wood was never known as a malicious man. To the contrary, he was a jovial storyteller, with a good head on his shoulders. What he had to say about Matty was remarkable, not because he may have found him "high hat" but because he felt that by 1912 Matty was no longer a great pitcher. How, then, was Matty able to pitch the game of his life in that last, luckless World Series contest?

A final lugubrious note attached to the Giants' 1912 season. Brush, after watching the Series from a wheelchair, in his automobile parked in center field at the Polo Grounds, set out for California in his private railroad car in an effort to restore his health. With two nurses and a valet attending to his needs, the Giants' president died as the train moved through Missouri on November 26. McGraw was deeply affected by the death of a man who had been his firm supporter, someone who had been loyally at his side through all the squabbles that characterized the manager's career. With Brush's death, control of the Giants passed to Brush's wife and daughters. A son-in-law, Harry Hempstead, became president. Hempstead knew relatively little about baseball. But that was unimportant, for McGraw knew enough for a dozen men. However, with the changing of the guard, McGraw felt somewhat isolated, for Brush had been his best friend, outside of his wife and Matty.

14

A LAST SERIES

BY 1913 Matty may have been past his prime, if one accepted Joe Wood's observation. Still, he was an extraordinary pitcher—and the team for which he played, despite their failure in two successive World Series, remained the ball club that aroused and fascinated fans everywhere. "The nation was Giant-conscious," Blanche McGraw averred. She was right. In New York the Giants were viewed as heroes and lovable bad boys. In the rest of the country, including those pits of hostility in Chicago, Boston, and Philadelphia, one could safely despise their manager, while still showing some respect for the icon Matty.

McGraw had hardly finished delivering the eulogy at John Brush's funeral in Indianapolis when he turned to the vaudeville stage. There had always been a slice of the ham in him, so it was not surprising that he took to the boards like a seasoned trouper. Though he was not the first sports personality to be sought out by theatrical promoters, he became the highest paid performer of them all. The B. F. Keith Circuit put him on the payroll for a reported $2500 a week, more than some of his own players earned for an entire season. McGraw toured through such appreciative cities as St. Louis, Boston, Philadelphia, Chicago, and, of course, New York. His act consisted mainly of a monologue about baseball, with anecdotes about players, umpires, himself, enemy teams, and any other miscellany that his scriptwriter, the estimable Boze Bulger of the *Evening World*, could conjure up for him. McGraw refused to rehearse his lines, certainly a denial of his own strict policy that his players be well prepared. But he had a sufficiently retentive memory so that he could speak his lines without any prompting. That his act often followed Odiva, "The Goldfish Lady," who had more diaphanous charms to offer in a glass tank than the pugnacious Giants' manager in black coat, tails, and gray trousers, failed to deter McGraw in the least. However, he acknowledged to Bulger that his act jolted his nerves more than any one-run ball game ever did.

For his part, Matty, with his book *Pitching in a Pinch* already on the market and doing well, was also much on the minds of theatre owners and producers. His clean-cut, heroic, and tousled looks, with his smooth, regular features and clear, blue eyes, plus an easy way with conversation, didn't hurt Matty's stage aspirations at all.

Following the 1912 season, he was made the star of a silent one-reeler produced by Kalem. The feature was called *Breaking into the Big Leagues*, and McGraw was also included in the cast. Posters were distributed, with photos of both men prominently displayed. Though Matty was deemed a modest man, he never revealed the slightest reservation about being exploited in such a manner.

During that winter he sat down with a playwright named Rida Johnson Young and wrote a baseball "comedy" in four acts. Several veteran stage performers such as Tully Marshall and Florence Reed were cast in *The Girl and the Pennant*, which ran for 20 performances at New York's Lyric Theatre. The plot concerned a scheming woman owner and her designing manager, vying for control of a ball club known as the Eagles. How much Matty contributed to the writing is not known, though he was quick to point out that Rida Young did less than John Wheeler on the project.

Such experiences in movies and theatre were not the first for Matty, however, for back in 1907 the Winthrop Moving Picture Company had made a film *about* him in action, using the earliest footage available. Such a film required no emoting on his part, as did future projects on which he worked. In 1910 he had teamed up with Chief Meyers in a vaudeville sketch, written by Bulger, called "Curves 1910." Curves had its premiere at the Hammerstein Theatre and ran for 17 weeks. Matty took down $1000 a week, about double what Meyers was paid.

In future years Matty tried to confine his extracurricular activities strictly to publishing, where the long, supple fingers of Wheeler again intruded. A series of children's baseball books, starting with *Pitcher Pollock* in 1914, was followed by *Catcher Craig* in 1915, *First Base Faulkner* in 1916, and *Second Base Sloan* in 1917. In these books players suffered "misadventures" in the field, while umpires never failed to say "Batter up, please!" Most players managed to write daily letters home, and some were commended for their "bully work," a phrase borrowed from Teddy Roosevelt. All of his publications were reasonably successful, but none of them enhanced Matty's reputation as a writer.

Before the Giants left for their Texas spring training camp in 1913, McGraw, ever the flamboyant impresario, pulled off another coup. He signed the part–American Indian Jim Thorpe, who had won the decathlon and pentathlon competition at the 1912 Olympic Games in Stockholm, Sweden. Thorpe also had run wild as a halfback at the Carlisle Institute in Pennsylvania, as well as playing a bit of semi-pro baseball for two summers. The latter employment cost him his Olympic medals, after the imperious American Athletic Union came down on him for his brief professionalism. It was never clear whether Thorpe's quiet acceptance of this rejection indicated deep hurt on his part or proof that he was proud to be known as the premier athlete in the world.

When McGraw signed Thorpe for one year at $5000, he was pleased about the widespread speculation that if Thorpe took the mound he would work with Chief Meyers, forming the first all-Indian battery in baseball history. However, most observers downplayed Thorpe's potential for baseball, attributing his signing as a raw publicity stunt to buttress the universal appeal of the Giants.

Ultimately, Thorpe spent several disastrous summers with New York, despite his speed and strong arm. Most of the time he remained on the bench, squinting into the sun and trying to figure out how to hit curve balls. "I felt like a sitting hen, not a ballplayer," Thorpe commented about his ill-fated apprenticeship with the Giants.

In one area, though, Thorpe was dominant. He developed a reputation as the best (against one, two, or three opponents) wrestler in the National League. Several of the more muscular players on the Giants, such as Edd Roush, Tesreau, and Merkle, challenged him for money—and lost. Prudently, Matty stayed out of such competition. When McGraw heard about the risks some of his players were taking with their bodies he threatened to levy $100 fines against anyone caught rough-housing with Thorpe.

As the season got under way, a dramatic architectural change took place in Brooklyn. The disastrously designed Ebbets Field, named for its owner, became the intimate new home of the Dodgers. At a cost of slightly more than a million dollars, it was shoe-horned into the malodorous slum section known as Pigtown. In the future the many boisterous tangles between the arch-rival Giants and Dodgers helped to foster the legend of the 32,000-seat ball park. Few games there between the two New York teams were ever played in anything but white heat.

There were changes, too, in the Giants, as 1913 approached. An infielder, Eddie Grant, educated at Harvard, was signed by McGraw and became one of the manager's favorites. Later in the season, Larry McLean came from St. Louis to help out Meyers behind the plate. George Burns replaced Devore in right field and as the team's leadoff batter, after a deal that sent Devore, Ames, and Heinie Groh to Cincinnati for right-hander Art Fromme. By winning 11 games Fromme proved to be of some help. But the rest of the pitching staff, again headed by Matty, was good enough to keep the Giants in the race all the way.

Matty again defied the gloom-sayers by registering 24 wins, with four shutouts. Marquard chipped in with 23 wins, despite a raging case of tonsilitis and sour public relations concerning his friendship with actress Blossom Seeley. Rube ended up marrying Blossom, and the two had a baby born ahead of schedule. Tesreau added 22 victories, and a rookie, Al Demaree, won 13. Demaree also proved to be a cartoonist of some talent. He drew accurate likenesses of many of the Giants, including Matty. After his career ended, he worked for *The Sporting News*, baseball's bible (or babble, to its detractors).

By late June the Giants got cooking in the pennant race, after the Phillies had broken from the pack to lead the league. McGraw persisted in believing the Phillies were not good enough to win. He continued at every opportunity to speak disparagingly of them, even when they were four games ahead of the Giants in early June. It was likely that McGraw was trying, with his vile tongue, to soften up his foes, for in reality they had some fine players. Their pitchers included Eppa Jephtha Rixey, a lanky Virginia southpaw who was good enough to stay in the majors until the 1930s, and Grover Cleveland Alexander, the hard-drinking epileptic right-hander who ended his long career with 373 victories, exactly the same number as Matty won. Gavvy Cravath was an able catcher, and Sherry Magee played the outfield well.

The Giants finally moved ahead of the Phillies on June 30,

after a bruising 11-inning 11-10 victory in Philadelphia. But the real story of that game was not the change in the standings but the embroilment of McGraw with Philly pitcher Ad Brennan. As McGraw headed for the clubhouse after the game, Brennan attacked him, presumably to get even for all of the abuse McGraw had heaped on him during the game. McGraw was knocked down, kicked, and shoved in the impromptu donnybrook. Although he wasn't hurt badly, it was his feelings that were at stake.

After the smoke cleared, with players pulling Brennan off McGraw and McGraw off Brennan, McGraw wound up with a $100 fine and a five-day suspension. Curiously, it was during those five days that the Giants took their next three games from Philadelphia, putting them in front by three and a half games. With the help of a 14-out-of-17 home stand, it was a lead they never relinquished.

Shortly before the Giants took over the lead, Matty embarked on a truly remarkable streak of control pitching. From June 19 to July 18 he worked 68 consecutive innings in which he didn't yield a base on balls. Overall, he gave up only 21 bases on balls, in 306 innings, about one for every 15 innings. This was about as close to perfection as one could achieve on the mound. "He seen what a good thing it was to have control and he went out and got it," explained Lardner, in one of his typically ungrammatical imitations of the baseball world he loved—as long as Matty was part of it.

Such needlepoint pitching, combined with the Giants' steady play for the rest of the season, enabled them to wrap up the flag with a mark of 101-51. The Phillies were left in the dust by 12½ games, with the Cubs third and the Pirates fourth. By winning the National League pennant for the third year in a row, the Giants were now in a position to wreak vengeance on the Athletics, who would be facing them in a World Series for the third time in nine years.

However, before the Series got under way, another controversy blossomed. Garry Herrmann, a member of baseball's National Commission, maintained that the World Series should be abolished. He subscribed to a feeling that was pervasive among social critics: that baseball and the cult surrounding the Series was a sign of national decadence. In fact, Herrmann's intentions were not as altruistic as they appeared, for he also proposed that all 16 teams in the two leagues should participate in an inter-league round-robin, with the best team to be crowned as champion. This was a transparent commercial ploy, one designed to allow the poorer teams to share in the post-season pool of money that was getting more swollen each year. Herrmann's idea was rejected, even though there was an acknowledgment that the Series had become a catalyst for heavy betting and ticket scalping, unfortunate evils of the free enterprise system.

Ban Johnson, on the commission with Herrmann, pointed out that the Series had become a truly national event that aroused enormous interest in almost every city, town, and village in the country. Thus, he said, it was silly to tinker with its structure. In such a controversy, men of stature in baseball, including Matty, Mack, Wagner, Plank, Baker, Lajoie, and others, were invoked in order to underline the basic purity and integrity of the sport. So much for Herrmann's argument.

McGraw eagerly looked forward to the 1913 clash with the Athletics, even if he realized he'd be operating from a disadvantage. He didn't care for alibis—but he had some handy ones, if he cared to exploit them. Matty, at 33, was getting old, as professional pitchers go; Snodgrass had a wicked charley horse; Merkle was nursing a leg injury; and Mack still had his celebrated infield intact. Under the circumstances, McGraw thought it would be wise to start Marquard in the first game, since he was younger than Matty and a fresher hand. However, the choice proved to be a disaster. In the top of the fourth inning, as 36,000 disappointed fans at the Polo Grounds looked on, the A's reached Marquard for three runs. They added two more in the fifth when Baker illustrated again why he was entitled to his nickname. He homered with one on, all but sewing up the game. Although the Giants reached Chief Bender for 11 hits, Mack's team won, 6-4.

Bad luck struck the Giants before the second game at Philadelphia. Meyers split a finger in practice and had to be shelved for Larry McLean. Matty, the starting pitcher, had always worked in excellent rhythm with Meyers, so it seemed he might be pitching with a disadvantage. Early in the game, as if McGraw hadn't suffered enough, Hooks Wiltse, the pitcher, was called on to replace Snodgrass, who had been shifted to first base because of his injury.

However, nothing could distract Matty that October afternoon as he held off the Athletics for eight innings without a run; he was at his best, an echo of his bravura performance against these same Athletics in 1905. Meanwhile, Plank was no slouch either, for the Giants could do nothing with him over the same span of innings.

As they waited for a break in the armor of either Matty or Plank, 20,000 fans in Shibe Park stayed glued to their seats.

In the last of the ninth inning, the A's got Amos Strunk to third and Jack Barry to second, with nobody out. Few thought Matty would survive. But one more time the master proved to be up to the occasion. And he did it with the help of Wiltse, of all people. Lapp shot one down to Wiltse, and the converted pitcher fired home, getting Strunk sliding in for the first out. Plank batted for himself and also hit one to Wiltse, the plot repeating itself. Wiltse again pegged home to get Barry trying to score with the winning run. Matty then got Murphy to bounce back to the mound, ending the Philadelphia threat.

Energized by this display, the Giants put together a three-run rally in the top of the tenth, sparked by Matty's own hit. With McLean on base, Matty cracked a hit to right center, scoring McLean with the first run of the game. Fletcher's two-run single gave the Giants three for the inning, enough for Matty to lean on as he completed his shutout in the bottom of the tenth. It turned out to be Matty's fifth and final World Series triumph.

The next time Matty faced Plank, in the fifth game at the Polo Grounds, the Giants were on the brink of defeat, down three games to one. Pitching with only two days' rest, Matty was trying desperately to keep the Giants' hopes alive. But this time he was cold as an ice wagon in the early innings, as the Giants fell behind, 3-1, by the fifth. Bad fielding also contributed to Philadelphia's lead, an epidemic that now seemed to plague Matty in important games. When no Giant rallies were brewed in the late innings, the Athletics won and the Series ended. Plank at last had beaten his old tormentor; the Giants got only two hits off him all day.

In the ninth inning of that last game McGraw punctured his friend's heart by sending up a pinch-hitter for him. Matty had already connected for three hits in the Series. But this time McGraw was not persuaded, either by his emotions or the fact that Matty was probably as good as anybody he could send up to hit.

After Crandall had grounded out for him and Doyle popped out to end the Series, Matty walked slowly, his head down, across the field, to the Giants' clubhouse in center field. Hundreds of fans, honoring his privacy, walked alongside him, without intruding on his thoughts. They sensed it was a painful time for him, and they acted with respect. As Matty neared the clubhouse entrance, one of the Giants who had accompanied him on his long walk placed a mackinaw across his weary shoulders. When he began to ascend the steps, the mackinaw slipped off its moorings and fell to the ground. Those who were present at that poignant moment never forgot the image of the great pitcher as he disappeared into the clubhouse, a loser in the last Series game he'd ever pitch.

Matty's final World Series docket of five wins and five losses was not brilliant, unless one looked at the details. Without such wretched luck it's conceivable he could have won at least two of the games he lost. He completed ten of the 11 Series games that he started, compiled an ERA of 1.15, gave up only ten walks in 101 innings, with four of his Series victories being shutouts. To this day no pitcher has ever equaled the shutout feat.

Now the author of three straight losing World Series, McGraw surprised everybody by congratulating Mack effusively. But one move he made in the last game revealed the depth of his bitterness. After a long relationship with Wilbert Robinson, who had been on the coaching lines during the Series, he accused his old pal of blunders and poor strategy. During a raucous beer-swilling party, McGraw fired his former Orioles teammate. When McGraw ordered Robinson to leave the party the two men almost came to blows.

For more than twenty years after this severance the two men never spoke a civil word to each other. After Robinson became manager of the Dodgers in 1914, their mutual hostility increased, accounting in part for the hateful combat that went on between the Giants and Dodgers.

Whatever else could be said about McGraw, he was resilient. During the 1913 season he was approached by the Old Roman, Charles Comiskey, owner of the Chicago White Sox, about a project that would take the White Sox and Giants on a world tour after the Series. With all of his rough edges, some of which had been smoothed over through his associations with Blanche and Matty, McGraw was both a shrewd and cosmopolitan citizen. He appreciated the value to baseball of such post-season exposure in different parts of the world. The trip was intended, in his opinion, as "a monument to the game" and part of his own motivation was to upgrade the image and social posture of big-league players. Matty had already contributed greatly to altering public attitudes about ballplayers—but more work was needed.

By plunging into preparations for the tour McGraw had found a constructive way to forget his disappointment over the 1913 World Series. Comiskey and McGraw underwrote half of the cost of the venture. By doing so McGraw made certain that he could choose the players that he wished to accompany him. He sought the guidance of Albert Goodwill Spalding, the sporting-goods businessman and millionaire who, as president of the Chicago franchise in 1888, had organized the first world tour of ballplayers. At that time Spalding sought to spread the word about the equipment he sold. His "missionary" endeavor also tried to introduce baseball to the world in "dramatic style." A more modest adventure in American imperialism than other ambitious efforts of that era, the trip failed to produce any major miracles. However, it did set a precedent for McGraw and Comiskey to follow, even as they figured to have a convivial time eating and drinking in places that ballplayers would ordinarily never see in their lifetime.

The three-month tour started just a week after Matty's loss to Plank in the Series. For the first leg of the tour Matty went along. He pitched and won the opening game of the long series in Cincinnati, but then, as he had previously advised McGraw, he chose to head back to Pennsylvania to be with Jane and Christy Jr., who was now 13 years old. Matty said he preferred to spend time in Lewisburg and Factoryville, the old home neighborhood that continued to have a strong pull on his loyalties.

What Matty neglected to add was that he suffered from a great fear of seasickness. "He might have gone, just to please McGraw and his other friends," Jane Mathewson once said. "But on our honeymoon we took a boat to Savannah, where the Giants were training, and Christy became terribly ill. He never forgot that, and people had a hard time getting him on a boat again."

With Matty absent from the tour, the project became less appealing for many fans. But there was still a formidable cast that had been assembled by the two promoters. Among the Giants going along on the 30,000-mile hegira were Meyers, Thorpe, Doyle, Merkle, Wiltse, and Donlin. McGraw also dipped into a pool of players from other clubs, including Speaker, Wahoo Sam Crawford of Detroit, Buck Weaver and Tom Daly of the White Sox, Lee Magee and Ivy Wingo of the Cardinals, Mike Doolin of the Phils, and Germany Schaefer of the Senators.

After the contingent of over 50 players, officials, and hangers-on toured Chicago, Kansas, Missouri, Texas, Oklahoma, Oregon, and Vancouver, the group boarded the *Empress* of Japan and set sail for Japan, China, the Philippines, Australia, Ceylon, Egypt, Italy, France, and Britain. They played under snowflakes in Illinois, before hundreds of reservation Indians in Sioux City, Iowa (where the two Indians on the Giants were greeted enthusiastically), had a visitation with the Pope in Rome, stared goggle-eyed at the Pyramids in Cairo, and finally performed before King George V and 35,000 other unappreciative British fans in London. Appropriately, Daly, a Canadian, who had never before connected for a home run in the majors, hit one for His Majesty.

When the group returned to New York in early March, sporting their newly acquired vocabularies in French, Italian, and Japanese, they were welcomed by Charlie Ebbets and McGraw's constant adversary, Ban Johnson.

That very day word was out in the newspapers that the structure of professional baseball was threatened by a bunch of recalcitrant ballplayers and ambitious businessmen, who opted to put together a rival Federal League to challenge the monopoly of the American and National leagues. The Federals had been making noises for several years and Chicago, St. Louis, Pittsburgh, Indianapolis, Kansas City, and Brooklyn were already in the Federals' tent. Now they were seeking to add franchises in Baltimore and Buffalo, which made sense, considering that America's population had grown vastly in a decade. In 1900 it had been 75 million, now it was close to 100 million—and some of the cities in organized baseball were smaller than those being invited into the act.

When the Giants players stepped off the British passenger liner *Lusitania* (sunk the following year by German submarines off the Irish Coast, in a grim prelude to America's entry into the Great War), chunks of money were tossed at them by agents of the Federals, who hitch-hiked on the brawny little tugboats pushing up New York harbor.

The Federal League's poachers included a hodge-podge of zealous capitalists such as Harry Sinclair, later to achieve an unpleasant niche in American history for his involvement in President Warren G. Harding's Teapot Dome Scandal; Phil Lamb, a St. Louis ice millionaire; the Ward Brothers, owners of the Tip-Top Bakery in Brooklyn; and Chicago restaurateur Charles Weeghman. What these men all had in common was an apparent indifference to throwing around their money, with all the beneficiaries being the players, who long had judged themselves to be just short of serfs.

The talent raids were now on in earnest, as many stars, as well as those who were slightly shopworn, were assiduously wooed by rich men scenting that it was open season on baseball. Tris Speaker talked openly about jumping, causing the Red Sox to cough up a two-year deal worth close to $40,000 to keep him in Boston. Joe Tinker signed a three-year contract to manage the Chicago entry

in the Federal League at $12,000 a year, plus stock. George Stovall
of the Browns was signed as a player-manager of Kansas City, and
Hal Chase, already marked as a shady and incorrigible character,
joined Buffalo. Others like Mordecai Brown, Chief Bender, Eddie
Plank, John Picus Quinn and Benny Kauff, who was nicknamed
"the Ty Cobb of the Feds," were also lured by the smell of cash.
Cobb and Walter Johnson stayed with their teams in the American
League, only because they were coaxed to return by handsome additions to their bank accounts.

McGraw himself was a prime target of the Feds. Already hailed
by kings and queens, princes, generals, tyrants, and Pope Pius X in
his recent trip around the world, he came home to discover a
$100,000 offer in his mailbox to manage one of the Federals.

"They offered me more money than I ever saw in my life," he
said. *"Saw?"* Blanche McGraw exclaimed, with surprise. Such a sum,
enormous in terms of what things cost (flour was four dollars a
barrel, coffee eleven cents a pound, and the best beef was less than
that), could have assured McGraw and his wife a life of wealth and
security. Even if the Federals had faltered he would have gotten his
money, under a guarantee.

But after several sleepless nights McGraw turned it down. He
envisioned that the Federals were on the road to failure, and perhaps baseball would be destroyed in the process. In order to insure
that none of his own players would jump to the scoundrels he ordered raises for most of his charges. In truth, few of the Giants
were interested anyway, for they were always among the better
paid of teams, and most had benefited from three straight years of
World Series lagniappes.

However, covetous eyes were cast, at Matty, in spite of general
acknowledgment that after 14 years of mighty striving he was on
the downside of his career. In seeking his services the Federals believed that Matty's presence in their ranks would add more than a
patina of prestige. It could also win them the legitimacy they craved,
after having missed out on Cobb, Johnson, and Speaker. Matty's
salary at the time was around $12,000 a year. Publicly he let it be
known that he was not interested in any entreaties from the Federals. But there were hints, here and there, that he might be listening. One such report, from columnist Jerome Beatty, writing that
spring in the *Los Angeles Press*, said this:

> The Brooklyn Federals are willing to pay Big Six any amount of money
> if he will become their manager . . . he is likely to be the next star

of organized baseball to jump to the Federals . . . Mathewson is in a receptive mood. "All morning I was thinking how it would be to be the manager of the Brooklyn Federals," Matty said. "Sometimes I thought it would be pretty fine, sometimes I thought it would be foolhardy to make the jump. The advantage of this sort of position would be that I would keep in baseball as long as I made good and making good would not depend on the condition of my arm. Of course I want to stay in baseball as long as I can."

If the Federals offer Matty enough money, will he jump? "I can't answer that very well until I hear the details from them," he answered. "But I will not use the offer to get more money from the Giants, I will not pit the clubs against each other." Matty is cautious. He does not want to open negotiations until he is sure the offer is not just a scheme to bring more advertising to the Federals. But his attitude when he left seemed to bode evil for organized baseball. He seems to see in the Brooklyn offer a chance to realize his managerial ambitions. Perhaps his only hesitation will be caused by a doubt that the Federals will last as long in baseball as he will.

In the end, Matty remained loyal to McGraw and the Giants. However, the year ended with a discordant note in the relationship between Matty and his manager. An article, published in *Everybody's Magazine* under Matty's name, openly speculated about McGraw's responsibility for the Giants' three straight World Series setbacks. The Giants, said the article, are a "team of puppets being manipulated from the bench on a string." The piece went on to imply that McGraw didn't permit his players to think for themselves, thus they were incapable of playing intelligently in a crisis.

There was never an open break between the two men as a result of the article. There is little doubt, however, that McGraw was familiar with its contents. Publicly, McGraw never rebuked his friend or uttered a syllable of criticism of Matty's putdown. But it must have rankled the thin-skinned McGraw, even if he was aware that such literary compositions often were the product of a ghost's handiwork.

15

DECLINING YEARS

ETURNING to Marlin Springs, Texas, for 1914 spring training, the Giants had every reason to feel that they could win the National League pennant for the fourth time in a row. Matty had rejected the sweet talk and sweeter money of the Federals, as only two lesser players, Art Wilson and Otis Crandall, had crossed over to the renegade league. McGraw proved his loyalty to the firm by turning down a fortune.

However, there was one disconcerting note, as the players gathered at Marlin. Harry Hempstead had traded Buck Herzog to Cincinnati for outfielder Bob Bescher while McGraw was traveling the globe. McGraw read about it while he was 5000 miles away, and it did little to bring his blood pressure down. Although McGraw despised Herzog, he still valued him as a player. The trade had been made by Hempstead to facilitate Herzog's desire to become the manager of the Reds.

"The next time a deal is going to be made on this club," McGraw roared, "I'm the one that's going to make it!"

McGraw had been bringing his Giants to Marlin for so long that the team had become an institution in the town. The Giants were even listed by *The Commercial Club*, a book telling everything about Marlin and what went on there, along with the mineral wells and the cotton gin. Marlin was democratic—as well as Democratic. The mayor, the sheriff, and all other prominent citizens were buddies of the Giant players, and old black people would

163

get off the sidewalks and take off their battered hats whenever "Marse Matty" walked down the streets. Such were the social mores of postbellum Texas.

During spring training Matty had other worries on his mind, in addition to the unusual cold weather. A man named E. C. Steart was the champion checkers player of these environs. The previous year Matty had soundly licked him but all winter long Steart studied up on strategy. He was determined to draw blood from his famous competitor. In one morning of play Steart lost three games but won two against Matty, as well as eking out a draw in two games.

When Matty left the checkers table and began to pitch in spring training games, it was said he looked as good as ever. But that sounded like the typical hyperbole of pre-season talk, the sort of thing that the teams had been dishing out to the members of the press for over a decade. Just a smidgen of spring training propaganda to get the home folks steamed up about the coming campaign.

Some nursed dubious feelings about Matty in 1914. But Lardner, as usual, insisted on speaking up for his friend in this way:

> So, give him a chanc't. The year's young yet. Leave him get warmed up, then give him a good look. This spring was hard on old soupers. You can't expect a bird that's been hurlin' the pill in the big show all these years to set the league afire. Don't talk like he was gone and ask me what kind of a pitcher he *was* . . . take him in a common, ordinary ball game, agin an average club, and what he's tryin' to do is stick the first one over so's he won't have to waste no more'n one ball on one batter . . . he'll go right on stickin' that first one over and maybe he'll allow a little scorin' . . . but there ain't nobody else in the world that can stick a ball as near where they want to stick it as he can . . .

In fact, when the season started, Matty did look pretty good— and the Federals were sorry that they hadn't been able to lure him from the Giants. "I never had the slightest idea of accepting their offers," Matty said, when the subject came up again.

Going into the year Matty had amassed 337 victories and 71 shutouts; 12 times he'd won 20 or more games; four times he'd gone over 30. McGraw probably would have settled for another 20-game season from the man on a reduced schedule of pitching. But it didn't work out that way.

The Giants began the year taking the lead, even though the Brooklyn team, now managed by Robinson, walloped the New

Yorkers in the opener. However, McGraw didn't anticipate that the Brooklyn team, soon to be called the "Robins," as a cheery tribute to their roly-poly manager, would give them further trouble during the season. For the most part, they didn't.

It wasn't until the last days of May that the Giants pushed into first place ahead of the Pirates and Reds, who soon were to fade from contention. When Herzog brought his Reds into New York in July, McGraw watched Matty, Tesreau, and Marquard bolt the door firmly against them. Although the Giants had their weaknesses, including the fact that Milt Stock wasn't turning out to be an adequate replacement for Herzog, while Marquard, the heir apparent to Matty, was suffering a dismal year, they looked to have matters under control. Marquard, in particular, was a disappointment. Having won over 20 the three previous years, his arm stopped producing victories. By the year's end he had only 12 wins against 22 losses, while Matty was again winning with metronomic regularity. He was pitching in more innings than he had expected and didn't seem to be hurt by it.

By July 4, which has traditionally been a date offered as a barometer to baseball finishes, the Giants nestled in first place, two games in front of the Cubs, the most serious contender at that stage. At the bottom of the league were the Boston Braves, who seemed primed for a cellar finish. Then, in mid-July two events occurred that were bound to have a large impact on the Giants, as well as baseball. In one, Marquard pitched all of 21 innings against Pittsburgh, winning 3-1. Opposing Marquard, Babe Adams also went the entire distance. This was the longest game played up until that time, and McGraw was delighted that Marquard had displayed such grit and durability. In truth, it may have been Marquard's undoing, for he dropped 12 straight games after completing his arduous task and never experienced another big season in his career. By midseason of the next year McGraw traded him off to Brooklyn, a particularly ignominious destiny for the left-hander.

In the same month as Marquard's feat, George Herman "Babe" Ruth, a product of St. Mary's Industrial (reform) School in Baltimore, launched his implausible career as the most dynamic personality in the game's history. It has been said that when Ruth was sold in 1920 to Colonel Jacob Ruppert's New York Yankees at the then unheard-of sum of $125,000, for the express purpose of hitting home runs and stimulating the gate, he saved the game from the wreckage of the 1919 Black Sox Scandal. But in 1914 he was just a raw, hell-raising 19-year-old southpaw pitcher for the Boston Red

Sox, a team still featuring many of the players who triumphed over the Giants in the 1912 World Series.

That two such imposing forces as Ruth and Matty never got to face each other on a diamond, as batter versus pitcher, is baseball's great misfortune. However, had they confronted each other it would hardly have been a fair test, for by 1915 Matty's career was in decline, while Ruth's phenomenal climb to center stage was just beginning.

That summer, as Americans watched the pennant races and laughed at silent-screen favorites Charlie Chaplin and Marie Dressler, a hungry young man from Colorado named Jack Dempsey, who often exceeded the bounds of propriety in order to win, began to get notices as a heavyweight prize-fighter. In Europe most people went about their daily lives, no more anxious than usual and paying scant attention to the comings and goings of soldiers, diplomats, and politicians—until June 28. On that date Archduke Franz Ferdinand of Austria-Hungary and his wife were murdered at Sarajevo by a Bosnian nationalist, setting off a series of actions, reactions, and ultimatums that by mid-August plunged all of the competing factions in Europe into a state of war.

Half a century of rancorous history and angry rivalries preceded the assassination of the Archduke. Now the terrible engines of mass destruction were wheeled into place for the opening rounds of the Great War. Inevitably, the war sent its ripples across the ocean to America. At first, President Woodrow Wilson flatly announced America's neutrality. But as more died, as more guns roared, as more German submarines prowled the Atlantic, even those men engaged in the frivolous pursuit of baseball pennants began to wonder about their own role. Would America be drawn into it?

One day when the Stock Exchange closed to avert panic, it was revealed that Matty was heavily invested in the market. The next day the poor fellow was called upon to assure the public, who regarded him as a prudent, honest man, that when the Exchange reopened the following day, he was definitely going to buy.

Most of the writers who covered baseball did not pretend to be historians or world thinkers, yet some of the more thoughtful, like Broun, worked references to the European war into their daily accounts of ball games. One such piece written by Broun was entitled "The Giants Hear the Hun at the Door." The thought of his favorites being called on to fight a war depressed Broun considerably—but the players themselves still were concerned more about the sudden emergence of the Braves as a threat to their dominance. By the first week in August, the Braves, led by their first-rate pitchers Dick Rudolph, Bill James, and Lefty Tyler, plus the acrobatic, impish shortstop named Rabbit Maranville and veteran Johnny Evers at second base, were perched in second place.

The Giants continued to do a fair amount of winning, but not enough. Matty kept adding to his victory column—by season's end he had 24, with five shutouts—but some insisted that the old magic was no longer there. Glowing phrases and brave words from the writers who loved him weren't much help.

As the Braves continued their astounding advance under George Tweedy Stallings, McGraw grew increasingly angry. His daily rage was directed at both the Giants' failure to hit and at the Braves' failure to lose. On September 2 the Braves swept two games from the Phillies, while the Giants lost to Brooklyn. The combination of events hurtled Boston into first place by a game. The press now hailed Stallings's team as "the Miracle Braves" and he, not Mc-Graw, was "the Miracle Manager," causing further aggravation to McGraw.

On Labor Day, September 7, two games in Boston with the Giants—in the morning and afternoon—attracted over 74,000 people, possibly the largest number of paid admissions for a single day of baseball in Boston. With Rudolph pitching in the morning, the Braves won when they rallied in the ninth for two runs off Matty. In the afternoon, behind Tesreau, the Giants came back to win, 10-1, tying up the race again. However, the next day, Marquard, already loser of eight straight games, was drubbed, 8-3. From that point on the rags-to-riches Braves were never headed.

The result of these dispiriting circumstances was that Mc-Graw caused enough fuss to get himself thrown out of several games. At one stage he was suspended for three days after getting evicted from three straight contests in Cincinnati, certainly a record in that department.

By mid-September the Giants fell two and a half games behind Boston. In one of these games Matty again failed to hold onto a lead, further adding to McGraw's discomfiture. Now, instead of rallying his forces, McGraw berated them and accused them of having been overconfident all along. In fact, that was McGraw's own sin. When Boston's lead galloped to eight games, it was clear that the Giants' pursuit of a fourth straight pennant had vanished in thin air.

The Braves officially clinched matters on October 1 at the Polo Grounds, as the Giants displayed such egregiously unsportsmanlike behavior that Umpire Bill Klem was forced to thumb most of the New York players out of the ball park. Even Matty was ordered off the premises, accompanied by 20 other Giants. McGraw was allowed to remain, though he had done nothing to persuade his players from acting so unprofessionally.

There was little reason for McGraw to hang around after the close of the 1914 season. But there was some clamor for another post-season city series between the Giants and Yankees. Slowly but surely, the Yankees were gaining a foothold in the New York area, even though McGraw would never acknowledge it, even in his nightmares. So the series was dutifully arranged; McGraw indicated his contempt for the whole process by not even being present on the Giants' bench. He chose, instead, to attend the World Series between Boston and Philadelphia, while his team, not good enough to beat the Braves, managed to win four games to one against the Yankees. Matty wasn't called on to pitch any of the contests against a team that had tied for sixth in the American League that year. He admitted to feeling tired, so the bulk of the pitching in this second intra-city series (also the last for many years) fell to Tesreau, Fromme, and Demaree.

Though all of the games were played at the Polo Grounds, the fans exhibited little affection for the home team. The Giants found themselves constantly booed, while the stands remained relatively empty. Only 40,000 showed up for the five games, with each Giant receiving a winning share of only $353. Meanwhile, the Braves took the Athletics apart in four straight games in the World Series, further adding to their reputation as a "miracle" team.

Going home to Factoryville, Matty promised he'd be back for his sixteenth summer in a New York uniform. He said he was looking forward to another spring training at Marlin, after a well-deserved rest in the winter.

A few voices were raised in the press hinting that Matty should retire, or perhaps find himself a manager's job somewhere. But most of his admirers were reluctant to face reality; they wanted to see him pitch again. They simply overlooked a fatigued arm and a body that could no longer respond as it had in the past. He had pitched in over 4700 innings in 623 games, enough to take a toll on the sturdiest of men.

Prior to spring training the Mathewsons went to Havana with the McGraws. They attended the horse races at the Marino track just outside of Havana, and Matty, who was a capable golfer, took

McGraw in hand on the golf course, trying to invest his manager with his own expertise in the sport.

When training got under way there were clear indications that Matty's career was in jeopardy. In early March he emerged from a friendly handball game with a sore shoulder, keeping him out for the rest of the week without throwing a ball.

"Matty is in no condition to pitch against any club right now," said one alarming story from Marlin. Some ten days later Matty worked a practice game for the first time and one paper reported that "a team of heartless hitters under Larry Doyle made ten runs and eight hits off him in one inning . . . Matty was throwing, not pitching."

There were constant signs that Matty was deteriorating. But always there was the rationalizing that, after all, this was only spring training. "He'll be the Big Six of old when the bell rings," was the cliched refrain of his admirers. Just a day before the Giants broke camp one writer assured the world that "Matty looks as good as he ever did . . . he made the Dallas batters roll over and play dead yesterday."

Sadly, the only thing that was dead in the 1915 season was the Giants ball club. That included Matty. Despite McGraw's altering the look of his team, by switching to horizontal pinstripes on their shirts and pants in place of the vertical pinstripes they had customarily worn, the club faltered almost from the start. After Tesreau and Marquard opened the season with wins (Rube's victory was a no-hitter against Brooklyn), Matty was badly bruised by the Phillies. If anything was premonitory, that was it.

Before long the club settled in last place, a neighborhood quite unfamiliar to McGraw; little could be done to energize the troops. Matty turned out to be a tired, losing pitcher for the first time since 1902, constantly troubled by shoulder pains and a back that tormented him on chilly days. Marquard, although much younger than Matty, faded so badly that McGraw was pleased to let him go to Brooklyn. Meyers was of little use, and Snodgrass lacked the zest and fire of earlier days. Curiously, Doyle, with 189 league-leading hits, compiled a .320 average to win the batting title, while Merkle matured into a capable outfielder. But their efforts couldn't counterbalance the general decline of the club. Losing 83 games while winning 69, the Giants were the worst club McGraw had ever managed and the only one that ever finished last under his banner. The Phillies, of all teams, won the National League flag;

the Red Sox took the American League pennant. Boston won the World Series in five games.

Only a year earlier Matty had been a 20-game winner. Now he appeared exhausted, mentally and physically. He ended the year with only eight victories against 14 defeats, with a lone shutout. His stingy issuance of 20 bases on balls in 186 innings was still remarkably low, but the year before his 23 walks had been spread over 312 innings. Such comparative figures tended to reveal a good deal about his diminishing powers as a pitcher.

That winter, as the Federal League was in its death throes, their unregenerate entrepreneurs brought an anti-trust action against the established leagues. The suit came before Judge Kenesaw Mountain Landis in an Illinois federal courtroom. In this instance, the judge failed to rule against organized baseball, as the Federals hoped he would. This was not forgotten half a dozen years later when baseball needed to polish its tarnished image, following the alleged Black Sox attempt to fix the 1919 World Series. Landis was rewarded by being chosen as baseball's commissioner.

But even as Landis pondered the fate of the Federals, Matty once again was pursued by them. In view of his dismal 1915 season, this was quite astonishing. Yet, an offer of $20,000 was made to him to pitch just one season for any team in the nearly bankrupt Federal League. At this stage, Matty was wise enough to appreciate he couldn't carry any team—much less a team in the Federal League. In addition, his business acumen informed him that the Federals were about to collapse. He rejected the offer.

16

"MY EYES ARE
VERY MISTY
FOR CHRISTY"

CONSIDERING the respect and affection Mc-
Graw still had for Matty, it is probable that
Matty could have remained with New York forever—in some capacity. Even at the end of the trail, in 1916, McGraw wanted him
around. After all, in McGraw's eyes Matty was a man whose
friendship he cherished, whether he was pitching, on the bench,
playing bridge or checkers, or just sitting across from him engaging
in polite repartee.

Unfortunately for Matty there was no opening for him to manage in New York. Now 43 and at the peak of his mental and physical powers, McGraw was still a compelling and kinetic figure. Nobody expected him to step aside at this moment, even for Matty,
who had expressed his desire many times to manage in the big
leagues.

As McGraw readied his club for the 1916 season, he was convinced that Matty had one more productive year in his arm. If he
didn't, there might be another way out—but that avenue could be
explored only when Matty showed that he could no longer pitch
winning baseball with regularity.

On paper the Giants of '16 were much the same team that
groveled in the cellar in 1915. But since McGraw had always felt
that the Phillies were an aberration the previous year, and thus
unlikely to repeat, his team didn't seem that feeble to him. In addition, four men had joined the Giants from the defunct Federal

League: Benny Kauff, who led the Federals with a .342 average and was spectacular on occasion; Edd Roush, a quiet outfielder known for hating spring training but who always played as if he didn't need it; catcher Bill Rariden; pitcher Fred Anderson.

Matty was one of a seven-man pitching corps that included Anderson, Tesreau, Pol Perritt, Ralph Stroud, Ferdie Schupp, and Rube Schaurer. Of that group he was rated now as only the third or fourth starter and would have to prove his entitlement even to that spot.

Soon after the season began it appeared as if the team was coming apart at the seams. After three dismal weeks their record was 1-13, compiled against the Phils, Braves, and Robins. Leaving New York in May, the Giants were in a state of shock; so were their grouchy fans. However, on the road a swift reversal of form took place, as the Giants swept the Pirates in four games, took three more from Chicago, then added three against the Cards. When they upended Cincinnati in three straight, then returned home to wallop Boston in four more, they boasted a most unlikely 17-game winning streak, at the time a major-league record.

The strange streak finally ended in a morning game against the Phillies on Memorial Day, even though they knocked Grover Cleveland Alexander, now the best right-hander in the league—the successor to Matty in that category—out of the box.

After such a winning surge, expectations for the club were aroused, only to plunge again when the off-again, on-again Giants failed to win at home. Floundering against the same western clubs that they had licked on their earlier road trip, McGraw finally came to grips with the fact that his inconsistent team was in need of surgery.

When the team reached Cincinnati Matty was enduring an embarrassing year, with a 3-4 mark in 66 innings. He had given up only seven bases on balls, still a very respectable level, but his ERA had gone up to 3.00, a true sign that he was no longer in command. Worse yet, every time he wound up to throw, he experienced knife-like pains in his left arm, shoulder and side. Something was radically wrong with his body. He knew it. So did McGraw and the fans, however reluctant they were to comprehend this reality.

Now the unthinkable was about to happen. For some weeks rumors had been swirling about Cincinnati's desire to depose its shortstop-manager Buck Herzog from his job. McGraw's old nemesis had a losing ball club on his hands. Such clubs are lightning rods for rumors, and the Reds were no exceptions. Despite owner

Herrmann's strenuous efforts to improve his club, things hadn't worked out. He had gone heavily into the Federal League market, adding a pitcher, Earl Mosely from Newark, for $5000 and second baseman Bill Louden from Buffalo. He also risked signing Buffalo first baseman Prince Hal Chase, who some considered the finest defensive first baseman who ever played the game. When Herrmann made the deal he was reminded about the questions that lingered concerning Chase's character, or lack of it. Chase had always been regarded as a contract-jumper and trouble-maker. A glib, handsome knave of diamonds, Chase played an ambiguous and "inconsistent" brand of baseball, another way of suggesting that he may have placed bets on games, as well as trying to fix them. This reputation had trailed him from the day he emerged from Santa Clara College, where he studied to be a civil engineer, to play in 1905 with the Highlanders.

Chase was having a wonderful year for the Reds in 1916, at one stage hitting in 19 consecutive games. He also demonstrated what was for him a rare quality of selflessness by playing in the outfield when several regular outfielders were sidelined because of injuries.

In late May the Reds were almost at .500, with a mark of 19-21. But after losing 28 of their next 41 games, they almost sunk out of sight to the cellar of the National League. It was then that Herzog's detractors demanded his head on a platter.

On July 13 the Reds' front office flatly denied a newspaper report that Herzog was out of his job, a sure sign in baseball circles that something dire was brewing for the man. A few days later, when the Giants arrived in Cincinnati for the second time, McGraw put through a call to Herrmann.

"I know you're not happy with your manager," McGraw began. "Well, I don't like Herzog personally, either. But I can use him. I'll give you two good players for him and you'll get a manager to take his place."

Herrmann instantly became curious. "Who's the manager?" he asked.

"Mathewson," responded McGraw.

Herrmann couldn't believe what he was hearing. Like everybody else in baseball the Cincinnati president was aware of the close relationship that existed between McGraw and his veteran pitcher.

"I don't like to part with Matty," McGraw continued. "He was not only the greatest pitcher I ever saw—but he is my good friend.

He could stay with the Giants as long as he wanted to but I'm convinced his pitching days are over and he'd like to be a manager. We've talked about it many times; I'd like to help him gratify that ambition."

Herrmann inquired about the names of the other players McGraw had in mind.

McGraw told him that Edd Roush and Bill McKechnie would also be in the deal. Roush, he said, was potentially a fine ballplayer but he hadn't been able to use him much, while McKechnie was steady as a rock and could fill in at all infield positions.

"You got a deal," said Herrmann.

However, McGraw added that one thing would have to be ironed out before they could shake hands on it. He reminded Herrmann that there was a mutual loathing between Herzog and himself and that this would have to be addressed between them. "I'll have to see if he's willing to play for me," said McGraw.

A meeting was immediately arranged between McGraw and Herzog in the hotel room of Sid Mercer, the writer for the New York *Globe* who had traveled for years with the Giants. When the two men met alone the chill in the air was remindful of an evening in the tundra. But Herzog realized the trade would be advantageous for him. He assured McGraw that he would give the Giants his best efforts, despite the friction between them. McGraw accepted that promise.

Getting back to Herrmann, McGraw said that he was now prepared for the exchange of the players, with Red Killefer also being thrown into the deal by the Reds. For his part, Herrmann also instantly agreed, yielding to his own quixotic notion that an icon like Matty would be bound to instill some of his magic into the struggling Cincinnatians.

Reports already were spreading in Cincinnati that Herzog had been traded, even before the official announcement was made. These rumors also hinted that Chase would become the new manager. On July 21, when the Reds took the field for a doubleheader, catcher Ivy Wingo was named acting manager. But the fans applauded Chase's every move, on the assumption that he was the next Reds' pilot. Later that day the word came through that it was Matty, and not Chase, who would succeed Herzog.

Herrmann rewarded Matty with a three-year contract. Not represented by an agent or lawyer, Matty drew up his own contract and sent it along to Herrmann, who he unfailingly addressed as

"Mr. Herrmann" in his letter of agreement. Matty's memorandum to Herrmann went as follows:

> This contract is drawn according to my own ideas of the kind of agreement I would like to have with the club. The reason I have executed the contracts before sending them to you is because the ten days time of which you spoke to me will expire on Monday, and there would not be enough time left to exchange views by mail . . . I suppose in addition to this contract as manager I should also sign a regular player's contract for a nominal consideration, in order that there be no question of my right to go on the field in uniform, and to take part in any game that I see fit . . .

As one might expect, the departure of Matty from the Giants was a melancholy episode. For 17 years Big Six had dominated the baseball scene at the Polo Grounds, always with the support of worshipful fans. Nobody ever doubted for a moment that he had given anything but his best, through all the exhilarating, as well as frustrating events that characterized his tenure.

Now it was time to say goodbye. Matty cleaned out his locker, removing battered old gloves, scuffed baseballs, and socks, playing cards, checker-boards, faded shirts and pants, all of the detritus accumulated over time by a ballplayer. As he completed his task, other Giants sat on their benches, silent and obeisant. Going from one player to another, Matty bid each of them farewell. Coming to Schupp, Matty was asked by Ferdie if he'd like to play one more hand of cards with him. Tears forming in Matty's eyes gave away his feelings.

"I don't know whether I want to become the manager of another club or not," said Matty to Ferdie. "This locker is the only one I've ever had in my life."

A few players pretended to be dealing cards. Matty stood and watched this charade for several minutes. But not a single card was played. Trying to break the morose mood, Matty asked the players to deal him in for one last hand. He sat down, played the game, then picked up his bag and walked out of the room.

Roush and McKechnie expressed their delight at leaving McGraw. But Matty didn't share their sentiment. He remained silent, until Roush asked him why he wasn't equally as pleased to be departing from his tyrannical mentor.

"I'll tell you something," said Matty. "It's been a mighty long time for me. The Giants have been my home. Leaving them like this, I feel the same as when I leave home in the spring of the year."

He admitted to the two players that he knew he was through as a pitcher and said he hoped Herrmann wouldn't ask him to pitch any more, even if that was the expectation of Cincinnati fans.

Curiously, by hiring Matty the Reds had also succeeded in eliminating him as their constant tormentor. He would no longer be facing them on the mound, and they were grateful for that. Through the years Matty had run roughshod over the Reds, more than any other pitcher in the league. The first time he'd ever pitched against Cincinnati he won, 1-0. That set the tone for the next 17 years, with Matty running up a record of 64 victories and only 18 defeats versus the Reds. At one time he put together a streak of 22 consecutive wins over Cincinnati.

The Reds had not done well against others, either. Their failures on the field provoked many jokes, including one that reminded baseball fans that though professional baseball had started in Cincinnati in 1869 that was the last time anyone had ever seen professional baseball played in the town. Herrmann figured he had hired Matty to set things right in his beleaguered village.

But Ring Lardner saw little chance for such a turnaround, even with his hero presiding. After Matty's departure from New York, Lardner typed six lugubrious lines memorializing the event. It went like this:

> My eyes are very misty
> As I pen these lines to Christy
> Oh, my heart is full of heaviness today.
> May the flowers ne'er wither, Matty
> On your grave at Cincinnati
> Which you've chosen for your final fadeaway.

17

A SENTIMENTAL DUEL

AT the outset of his managerial career in Cincinnati Matty reiterated his intention never to pitch again in a championship game. Herrmann tried to persuade Matty to change his mind but the pitcher was unmoved.

"I'll do my managing from the bench," Matty said. "No more pitching for me."

When Matty joined the Reds the club's record stood at 35-50. Few expected that he would be able to turn the Reds into a winner overnight, so the limited expectations gave him a chance to look over his talent and decide what to do about it.

He knew he had two good hitters in the unpredictable Chase, who must have been secretly amused that he was now playing under a man with such a reputation for strict adherence to the rules, and Roush. Chase was so good in 1916 that he led the National League in hitting. But the pitching, once one read past the names of Fred Toney and Pete Schneider, was lacking in depth. Oddly, the team's batting average of .254 turned out to be the second best in the league. But over the long haul the deficiencies on the mound and in defense kept the team from launching any form reversal.

As the season wound down the Reds played 25 games on the road, losing 15, while winning only 10. On the last day of 1916 the Reds played Pittsburgh at home, needing a victory to prevent them from finishing dead last. To avoid such ignominy, Matty awarded the pitching assignment to Toney, his big right-hander from Nashville. Toney shut out the Pirates, providing the Reds with a final mark of 60-93, enough to "clinch" a tie for seventh with the Cardinals. Under Matty the Reds had traveled at an unremarkable 25-45 pace, just about what they accomplished under Herzog.

But there were two events during the year that gladdened Matty's heart in an otherwise distressing season. Only days after he took over the club in July, the Reds came to New York to face the Giants. The return to the Polo Grounds, Matty's long-time home, attracted a larger crowd than usual.

When Matty made his first appearance of the afternoon in the unfamiliar Reds traveling uniform of red and gray, the fans stood and cheered for almost a minute, evidence that, at least for the moment, their old pitcher was still foremost in their affections. McGraw didn't even seem to mind losing this one to Cincinnati— but this benign reaction had to be placed in the overall perspective of the Giants' 16 victories in 21 games played that year against Cincinnati.

The other event that took place in the waning days of the season required Matty to break his pledge that he would never pitch again. Under the circumstances, he found it difficult to back away, for there was such a popular demand for one final mound duel between Matty and his arch-foe, Three-Fingered Brown, that he was forced to acquiesce to the arrangement.

The confrontation, if one could call it that, at a time when Matty was 36 years old and Brown was 40, took place in the second game of a Labor Day double-header in Chicago. It would be the twenty-fifth meeting between these warriors. In past match-ups Brown had won 13, with Matty winning 11, causing some commentators to rate Brown as a superior pitcher to Matty. "In the money or pressure games," Jimmy Powers of the New York *Daily News* wrote years later, "Brown was the better hurler. He had a great screwball which topped Matty's highly publicized fadeaway."

Leaving aside the question of which man was better, most baseball fans warmed to the prospect of these two taking the mound one last time. Even though the game was to be played on a foreign field, the Cincinnati papers promoted the game with great excitement. Other cities in the league also trumpeted the event, which served to underline the strong hold that these two competitors had on the baseball public. (Some years before, when the 300-pound William Howard Taft was the chief executive of the United States— and a big baseball fan in every respect—Taft had his private train attached to the train carrying the Giants to Chicago, so he could watch Matty pitch against Brown in a crucial game.)

Before festivities began that afternoon Matty and Brown were presented with dozens of American Beauty roses. Then they went about their work, proving that they had about as much left to their skills as two ancient, embarrassed heavyweight fighters who have long since lost their punch. The two pitchers staggered through the entire nine innings, with Matty emerging a 10-8 winner. The game was marked by 19 hits for the Reds (including three by Matty) and 15 hits for the Cubs (including two by Brown). Till the end Matty had his control, since he gave up only one walk while fanning three. The final out of Matty's career was a fly ball off the bat of the Cubs' Fritz Mollwitz, caught by outfielder Greasy Neale, who later won fame in professional football.

"Both of these great pitchers were finished and about all Matty had left was his wonderful ease of motion," wrote James T. Farrell, Chicago's literary troubadour, who was 12 years old at the time. "It was the most sentimental ball game I ever attended."

Though it was a game for which Matty hardly cared to be remembered, somehow the memory lingered on in baseball's record books. The final victory, Matty's 373rd of his life, was precisely the total ultimately hung up by Alexander, in another one of those priceless ironies of the game's history.

Following the game Matty repeated his promise never to pitch again. "Boys, I thought I could pitch some more games," he said, as the Reds clustered around him in the clubhouse, "but I just don't have the stuff any more. I'll never attempt to pitch in a league game again. If I ever go into the box again I'll buy every one of you a suit of clothes!"

18

AMERICA ENTERS THE WAR

O N the morning of April 8, 1917, America woke up to find itself in the European war. Reluctantly but forcefully, President Wilson, professing no quarrel with the German people, forged a case for military unity against Germany and its allies. Wilson saw this struggle as one to make the "world safe for democracy." Congress voted overwhelmingly to follow his leadership.

Within weeks thousands of young Americans—"doughboys" to the admiring public—were jammed onto troop ships to fight in places they had never heard of before: Verdun, Chateau-Thierry, Belleau Wood, and the Marne. Many considered it the adventure of their lives. In a year's time close to two million Americans reached European shores to pursue Mr. Wilson's vision.

At the age of 37 Matty didn't have to join up. Thirty-one years old was the cutoff point of the Selective Service Act. But the times were full of patriotic cries, stirring exhortations from the schoolmaster in the White House, rousing songs that never failed to stir a young soldier's heart, and unremitting propaganda against the tyranny of the German Kaiser. Those Americans who went had scant idea of what they were getting into—butchery on both sides brought about by cruel, demonic new weapons of destruction that were beyond imagination. By 1915 and 1916 almost an entire generation of British and French men were wiped from the face of the earth in brutal trench warfare, where poison gas was employed for

180

the first time. The dreaded Huns, as they were called by their enemies, also suffered enormous losses along the Western Front.

Despite the war fever, baseball managed to remain relatively untouched in 1917. The draft required that all men between 21 and 30 be registered the first week in June, with the first drawings to be made on July 20. Few ballplayers volunteered at the outset, fewer yet were called in the first draft. This led the owners to believe mistakenly that the entry of the United States into the war would cause hardly a ripple in their operations.

However, it soon became apparent from the diminishing attendance at ball games and editorial reactions around the country to baseball's ostrich-like, business-as-usual stance, that the national pastime would not escape the war's impact.

Matty was one who kept up with these developments, though for several weeks in July he was sadly distracted from his role with the Reds and the war by the death of his surviving brother, Henry. At the age of 31 Henry was the victim of tuberculosis, in Factoryville. The "White Plague," as it was called in those days, had taken Henry's life as well as other members of the Mathewson family.

In sizing up his ball club in 1917 Matty made the wise decision that he needed to bolster his sagging mound corps. Since the day that Connie Mack had declared that pitching represented about 85 percent of a team's strength, baseball men went around trying to prove that the grizzled tactician was correct in his assumption. Invariably when things went wrong with a club the managers, heeding Mack's admonition, sent out a call for fresh moundsmen. Matty was no different in this respect.

The spitball artist Clarence Mitchell was added to the cast from Denver. So was Al Schultz, who turned out to be a flop. Walter "Dutch" Ruether, considered canny even at the age of 24, was picked up on waivers from the Cubs, and fastballer Jimmy Ring was purchased from Buffalo. Horace "Hod" Eller, still putting paraffin wax on his "shineball," was drafted from Moline.

Aside from the improved pitching, Matty had Ivy Wingo to catch, the dubious Chase at first base, Dave Shean at second, Larry Kopf at shortstop, and "Heinie" Groh at third. Roush and Greasy Neale were in the outfield with Tommy Griffith. Due to the mounting anti-German hysteria, ballplayers like Groh and "Heinie" Zimmerman of the Giants chose not to be called by their nicknames, preferring instead to be addressed as Henry.

As the Reds got off to a slow start in 1917, the highlight of the early going was an unusual nine-inning double no-hitter on May 2.

In that game the Reds finally eked out a run in the tenth inning to give Toney a 1-0 no-hitter over the Cubs. Until the tenth Hippo Jim Vaughn of Chicago had matched Toney almost pitch for pitch on a dark, dreary day, with only 2500 people present to watch what was certainly one of baseball's finest moments. Kopf finally broke Vaughn's no-hit spell in the tenth with a single, followed by Chase's liner to center that was misplayed, permitting Kopf to advance to third. Jim Thorpe, now a Red after McGraw had let him go in April, bounced a high ball in front of the plate, giving Kopf a chance to run home with the winning score. Toney then completed his no-hitter by retiring three Cubs in a row in the bottom of the tenth. Watching the proceedings in the Cincinnati dugout, Matty reflected on his own no-hitter when he first joined the Giants many years before.

Toney's performance was an omen of good things to come for the Reds. Matty began using his young pitchers more frequently, experimenting, as McGraw had done with Iron Man McGinnity, by letting Toney and Eller work both ends of double-headers. Eller split his effort, while Toney won both games against the Pirates in July. Soon after Toney's display of durability, the Reds reached the .500 level, not an inconsiderable feat for a team that had done so poorly in 1916.

Matty's club split the 22 meetings with the Giants, and, as expected, McGraw's temper caused him to engage in battle against his own disciple. The brouhaha precipitated by McGraw occurred in a June game, after Chase broke up a double play at second base by rudely shouldering shortstop Fletcher to the ground. This was no legitimate rolling block; rather, it was outright interference, since Fletcher had possession of the ball.

When Fletcher appealed to umpire Ernie Quigley, his complaint was not honored. Plate umpire Lord Byron also paid no need to Fletcher, further aggravating McGraw. After the winning run trotted home a few moments later for the Reds, McGraw could restrain himself no longer. He barged out of the dugout to tell Byron exactly what he thought of his judgment. As he made physical contact with the umpire, McGraw encouraged players on both teams to enter the fray. Such a tumult ensued that it took the police to put an end to it. During the melee Matty attempted to play the role of peacemaker, even as he realized that, like all men, he was not exempt from the fury of his former manager.

Often as fast as McGraw's anger flared he would regain his equanimity, which sometimes made one suspect that there might have been a carefully calculated element of play-acting in his be-havior. In this case he didn't hold any grudges against Matty for long, especially since Matty had not played an active part in the fight.

By mid-August, when the Reds were in New York to meet the Giants, the two men united in a cause that ordinarily would not have been one of Matty's priorities. It was well known that Matty, since the day he entered professional baseball, had always been op-posed to playing baseball on Sunday. Now he was persuaded by McGraw that it made sense to play on Sunday, especially since it would give a well-earned day of relaxation to soldiers as well as working people.

On Sunday afternoon, August 19, in defiance of New York's established blue law prohibiting Sunday ball, the Reds and Giants played a regular season game at the Polo Grounds. That the game was staged as a benefit for the Army offered a further chance for Matty to rationalize his appearance in the ball park as Cincinnati's manager. Toney pitched a shutout, one of his 24 victories during the season. But after the game was over, Matty and McGraw were summoned to appear in a Washington Heights police court to ac-count for their nefarious actions.

The magistrate in charge of the proceedings dismissed the complaint, which had been brought by a group called the Sabbath Society. But he did more than that, as he praised the two managers for providing entertainment for people who might not otherwise be able to use their Sunday for such a worthwhile purpose. (Two years later the Walker Sunday baseball law, initiated by the fun-loving future mayor of New York City, permitted New York's first legal Sunday ball game to be played at the Polo Grounds on May 4, 1919.)

Matty didn't regret the active role he had played in bringing Sunday ball to New York, for he considered it a victory for democ-racy. *The Sporting News* had long felt that the minority was sti-fling the wishes of the majority on this issue. The paper frequently drew an analogy to the 18th Amendment that prohibited the sale of liquor and ultimately created an American crime wave. Others pointed out that the Bible, a book that Matty had read and re-spected, did not specifically forbid Sunday amusements. Baseball's owners, guided more by their venality than by any committed phi-losophy of life, insisted that it was time to take the matter out of the hands of the ministers. The latter group constantly warned that it was dangerous to allow large, unruly groups of lower-class work-ers to come together in one place on Sunday. Such reasoning particularly annoyed Matty, who felt this was exclusionary and anti-democratic.

As the season ended, the Reds managed to stay above the .500 level, with 78 wins and 76 defeats. Toney's work and Schneider's 20 victories helped Matty's team immeasurably, as did Roush, who won the National League batting title in his first full year in the big leagues. However, the Reds' only other .300 hitter was Groh, at .304. As the Reds finished fourth, McGraw's Giants were back on top for the first time since 1913. In the World Series, however, McGraw lost again, this time to the Chicago White Sox.

By losing the last four World Series in which they played, McGraw's team gave some credence to Matty's 1913 diagnosis for their failure. "Self-consciousness, over-anxiety and nervousness weigh on the Giants' shoulders like the Old Man of the Sea," Matty judged. "With a few exceptions the men were not of championship caliber. We won because the club is McGraw, because his brains directed the game from first inning to last. Now put these Mc-Grawized teams in a World Series, and they are stricken with a case of nerves. The system goes to pieces. For some reason they seem to think that they have to stand more on their own, that the hand of McGraw cannot aid them as it did during the regular campaign. Going ahead on their own they become nervous and blow up!"

It was quite an assessment, certainly a back-handed tribute to McGraw, but not his players.

Before the start of the 1918 season President Wilson was still encouraging baseball to go on "as usual." Rubbing their hands in response, the owners proudly proclaimed that the game was necessary for the country's morale. As well, they said, it was a great leveling influence in American society. They responded to Wilson by going ahead with a full playing schedule, with their club rosters remaining unsullied. Those who ruled the game decided retrenchment would take place only if events forced them to curtail their activities.

Under the circumstances, Matty led his men into spring training at Montgomery, Alabama, fully believing that his Cincinnati team had an excellent chance to win that year. The team was essentially the same as the one that had finished fourth in '17, with one important exception. Second baseman Lee Magee, who was born in Cincinnati as Leopold Christopher Hoernschemeyer, was obtained in a spring trade with the Giants. Obligingly, he had shortened his name to squeeze into the box scores. Matty expected him to provide better hitting than Shean.

With Magee in the lineup, the Reds nursed hopes that they'd contend for the pennant. This seemed a realistic ambition when, in May, the Reds launched an eight-game winning streak that enabled them to vie with the perennial favorites, the Giants and Cubs. However, two clouds now hovered over the team, threatening to dismantle the entire season for the Reds, and, incidentally, for baseball.

In late May the United States government issued a "work-or-fight" order setting a July 1 deadline for all eligible males either to enter the essential work force or face induction into the military. Secretary of War Newton D. Baker also said that baseball's 1918 season should end on September 2, with a period of grace for the World Series. That would give the Reds less than 130 games to play during the season, some 24 less than the schedule usually called for. Baker summarily rejected the notion that baseball should be considered essential, emphasizing that these were not normal times. The pleas from the owners to keep the sport going, without modification, were dismissed.

Increasingly, ballplayers had become targets of ridicule and criticism from the fans, who wondered, in a spasm of self-righteousness and patriotism, why such physically superior men were not getting into Army khaki. The May edict put this issue to rest quickly, as big-league players were forced to answer the call of their country. Ruether, so important to Matty, appeared in only two games in 1918, for a total of ten innings, before joining up; Kopf left to become a shipyard worker; Bressler went into the Army, as did outfielder Pat Duncan.

But Cincinnati was not alone in having its roster depleted, for players were now departing for "Over There" by the dozens or choosing to avoid the draft by going into steel mills, shipyards, airplane plants, or nitrate installations. (The prominent heavyweight fighter Jack Dempsey suffered embarrassment by having his picture snapped in a factory while wearing shiny patent-leather shoes.)

In all, over 255 players from both leagues went into the armed forces, following the example of Braves' catcher Hank Gowdy, the first to enlist. McGraw watched one of his favorites, Eddie Grant, depart to become a captain. In a few months Grant became the first casualty among baseball's warriors when he was cut down by machine-gun fire in the Argonne forest as he led a rescue mission for "The Lost Battalion."

As Matty's difficulties multiplied with the loss of personnel, another problem of equally serious dimensions developed for the Reds. Chase, often described as poetry in motion at his position, had again become suspect, a dirty story whispered about constantly in baseball clubhouses. In Matty's trained eyes Chase did not appear to be putting forth his best efforts. In short, he concluded that the first baseman was not playing to win at all times.

Matty knew how serious such a charge would be when leveled against a player. So, without openly voicing his suspicions, even to Herrmann, he kept observing Chase's actions. He noted that one day Chase would hustle like a mad dog, then the next he'd lie down dead. One day he'd scoop up a ground ball in his own inimitable way, starting a double play via a technique that he had invented: the quick throw to the short-stop, then the dash back to first base to receive the return throw. But the next afternoon, more than likely, he'd field the same sort of grounder, then stand immobile for a costly second, as if utterly baffled by the sudden return visit of a white ball.

For years players had been tuned in to Chase's curious inconsistencies. Surely nobody had ever played first base with more dexterity and grace—he was a veritable jaguar swooping down on bunts and grass-cutters. Grantland Rice often wrote of Chase's "magic hands, backed by amazing intuition and by both mental and muscular speed."

Yet the more Matty watched Chase, the more he was certain the man was up to something. He also noticed that Chase was spending more and more time with Magee, the newest Cincinnatian. Since Chase was generally a loner, who preferred his own company to that of other people, Matty's suspicions were further aroused, for the two men were often seen engaging in hushed conversations. Were they whispering about fixing games, or were they arranging to place bets for or against their own team?

One type of play above all others stoked the fires of Matty's troubled imagination. It was when Chase retrieved a ground ball wide of first base, then made the toss to the pitcher covering the bag. As a pitcher who had gone through this process hundreds of times, Matty understood the precise mechanics of this play. He also knew that Chase knew all about it, too, for he was capable of making the play with perfection. But Matty noticed that on too many occasions Chase's throws to the pitcher were not on target.

The result was that the batter was safe at first base, and the uninitiated would invariably blame the pitcher for a failure of execution. But Matty knew who was to blame.

However, it took two incidents, one in which Chase was not actively involved on the field, finally to rouse Matty to the point where he thumbed Chase out of the lineup indefinitely, suspending the miscreant without pay, for "indifferent playing and insubordination."

Before a July game against the Braves, the Reds' pitcher, Pete Schneider, approached Matty and asked him to start another pitcher that afternoon. Although Matty, in his brief experience as a manager, was never autocratic, he found the request made directly to him rather unusual. Schneider confided that his reason was based on the fact that he'd heard that Chase (who was not in the lineup that day) and his confederate Magee had put down bets on the Reds to lose the game.

Magee tried desperately to live up to his promise to the gamblers. On an inside-the-park home run by Roush, Magee, on base at the time, slowed down to such a crawl that the enraged Roush almost ran over him. "Run, you dirty son of a bitch!" Roush screamed at his flawed teammate.

Both men scored on the play, as the Reds won. However, it was later revealed that Magee stopped payment on a check that he'd given to a gambler named Jim Costello. A person of probity when it came to dealing with other con men, Chase ended up paying Magee's debt to Costello.

Matty didn't know the precise details of Chase's conspiracy, but nonetheless he smelled a rat lurking in the shadows. With Chase continuing to flub plays at first base, Matty's anger increased. Players on other teams now openly chided Chase, often asking him how much he'd bet on that day's game or requesting what the odds were. When it was reported that Chase had offered a bribe to right-hander Pol Perritt of the Giants before an August game at the Polo Grounds, Matty confronted the first baseman with his suspicions. Chase, always as good an actor as he was a fielder, denied everything. "It's just a bunch of damned lies," he said to his manager.

Chase also promised to sue the Reds for his unpaid salary, something close to $2000, which would have been his wages for the remainder of the year. But Matty was not about to give in to Chase's bluff. Though he'd been advised by a baseball writer that if charges of crookedness were brought against Chase—and not proven—that Chase would sue and probably reap heavy damages,

Matty was insistent on jettisoning the man. "Chase was an evil genius," Fred Lieb wrote. "Trouble always followed in his wake. It was an ill day for baseball when his name first appeared in a box-score."

Matty brought in Sherry Magee (no relation to Lee) from the outfield to play first base, as Chase was dropped from the club. Having won Herrmann's backing on the suspension, Matty then went about studiously collecting affidavits from several Reds players, who were as equally convinced as their manager that Chase was "not trying." At last the question of Chase's honesty and integrity was about to be resolved; certainly it appeared that way. But by the time the case was fully prepared for the perusal of National League president John A. Heydler, a former umpire and sportswriter, Matty had arrived at another important decision in his life. After much discussion with Jane, he decided to accept a commission as captain in the chemical warfare division of the Army.

On August 27 he managed his team for the last time in a double-header with the Braves in Cincinnati. The teams split, leaving Matty and the Reds with a record of 61–57 in 1918. The club was in third place when Matty said farewell to his men. Heinie Groh took over the reins with ten games to play, and the club won seven of the ten, even finishing up with six straight wins.

After the season was over, Herrmann brought formal charges against Chase, although he never really had much chance to convince Heydler, a man with little zeal at the time to nail Chase to the wall. With Matty absent from the proceedings, thus depriving Herrmann's case of Matty's strong moral authority, Heydler failed to be persuaded by affidavits from pitchers Jimmy Ring and Mike Regan. McGraw was called as a witness, as was Perritt. Sid Mercer also took the stand.

Heydler ended up exonerating Chase, insisting that Chase's performance in a game in which he was supposed to have bet against his own team was clear evidence that the player was trying. "In the sixth inning, with two men on base and the score two to nothing against the Reds, Chase hit a home run," remarked Heydler. "That put Cincinnati one run ahead." Obviously, Heydler felt Chase was trying that day—a man couldn't mistakenly hit a home run, could he?

During the inquiry, McGraw promised that if Chase was pronounced innocent by Heydler he would hire him to play first base

70   for the Giants. Did this represent a challenge to Matty's own code
71   of ethics or was it simply another example of McGraw's willing-
72   ness to put up with wayward souls as long as they could play win-
73   ning baseball? Sure enough, after the acquittal, McGraw dealt for
74   Chase in a trade for catcher Bill Rariden.

19

CAPTAIN MATTY

I N August 1918, when Matty joined up, the Great
War had been devastating Europe's population for
over four years. Eight million men in uniform had been slaugh-
tered, and hundreds of thousands more had been wounded and
maimed. In addition, a worldwide epidemic of flu during those same
years had caused millions of deaths. In the United States alone half
a million people died of the flu, including 25,000 soldiers at Army
camps.

There was no way of predicting in August how much longer
the war would go on, even as rumors circulated almost daily that
peace overtures had been made and that a cessation of hostilities
was at hand.

Like so many other patriotic Americans, Matty supported his
President, even if he didn't share Mr. Wilson's party affiliation. That
Matty chose to become involved in the military struggle at the age
of 38 was a decision that was not forced by either public opinion
or feelings of guilt. He could easily have remained out of it. Seemingly, he was more influenced by the number of his fellow players
who had flocked to enlist in the cause. He felt that he belonged
with them, rather than on the ballfields.

If anything, Matty's legend had now increased, with his new
managerial career making him the focus of admiration in the Midwest, as well as New York. There wasn't a single time when he

returned with the Reds to face the Giants that the fans in the Polo Grounds hadn't applauded him generously.

There is no evidence that Matty arrived at his decision to enlist based on an informed instinct that the war would soon end. Ten thousand Americans were leaving for France almost daily in midsummer of 1918, and it appeared that most of these men would sooner or later be engaged in combat. Many of those with substantial military knowledge concluded that the war might very well continue on through 1919. Though the Germans had taken enormous losses, even as hundreds of thousands of Yankees joined the French and the British in the bloody trenches and forests, they were unwilling to admit defeat.

In late September the German high command mustered much of its remaining strength for a massive attack at the Meuse-Argonne in Northeast France, for what evolved into the watershed battle of World War I. Had the Germans succeeded in their aims, they might have had an open path to Paris and the North Sea, thus altering the course of the war.

At such an unpredictable time did Matty, in his overseas cap, Sam Browne belt, high-necked khaki blouse, and roll puttees, join the newly organized Chemical Warfare Service. Already stocked with a complement of baseball luminaries, as well as others from the college gridiron and polo fields, the CWS was determined to train the inexperienced doughboys in the horrors of poison gas.

Major Branch Rickey, the president of the St. Louis Cardinals and the former University of Michigan baseball coach, was one of those already in the unit. Like Matty, he was, at 38, too old for military service and hardly a man addicted to violence. But he had been encouraged to join the CWS by Harvard's former football coach, Percy Haughton, who happened to be president of the Boston Braves. George Sisler, a player under Rickey at Michigan, and a first baseman with the St. Louis Browns, had also been made a lieutenant in the CWS.

Another captain in the CWS was Ty Cobb, who had just won his eleventh American League batting title, as well as a deferment from the military. At 32 Cobb was at the peak of his skills. But he also felt a strong duty to serve, being imbued with a brand of unquestioning patriotism, so characteristic of citizens from the South. Having passed up the deferment, Cobb, Matty, and the others were given accelerated training against the use of poisonous gas. Ultimately they would become instructors in what was to be called the "Gas and Flame Division."

The Germans first released chlorine gas against French troops in the Ypres salient in April 1915. Later in the war they used mustard gas, causing heavy casualties and a great outcry around the world.

The horrors of poison gas were dramatically underlined by the words of British poet Wilfred Owen, who died in 1918 at the age of 25 while commanding a company on the Western Front:

> Gas! Gas! Quick, boys—
> An ecstasy of fumbling
> Fitting the clumsy helmets just in time. . .
> His hanging face, like a devil's sick of sin,
> If you could hear, at every jolt, the blood
> Come gargling from the froth-corrupted lungs
> Bitten as the cud
> Of vile, incurable sores on innocent tongues
> My friend, you would not tell with such high zest
> To children ardent for some desperate glory,
> The Old Lie: Dulce et decorum est
> Pro patria mori.

In war, there is action, then reaction, so it wasn't long before the defensive gas mask was developed by the allies.

Grotesque in appearance, the anti–poison gas equipment consisted of a mask that fitted around the face, attached by a tube to a canister suspended around the doughboy's neck and hanging down in front of the body. The soldier was instructed to breathe air through a tube in his mouth, while the gas was filtered through charcoal and soda lime in the canister. A nose clip was designed to prevent breathing through the nostrils. However, there was no certainty that the soldier would be free of panic at such a moment.

A training technique developed by the CWS was to march a group of soldiers into an airtight chamber, then, without warning, release the deadly spray. This was to simulate battlefield conditions against the enemy. The emphasis was on the need for the soldier to act alertly, without hesitation.

Within weeks after Matty entered the Army, he left for France with his CWS contingent. Matty's fear of the ocean was already well known. When he volunteered for the CWS he knew he would have to face these anxieties again. As it turned out, he became dreadfully seasick during the voyage. More critical, he contracted flu, as did many others on board. From all accounts he was lucky to reach France alive.

The cold, damp autumn that greeted Matty in France also did

little to ameliorate his physical condition or his state of mind. But he was determined to fulfill his role of instructor. Here his story takes divergent paths, depending on whose version—Ty Cobb's or Branch Rickey's—one wants to believe.

Cobb's recollection of Matty's experience in the CWS was that Matty's lungs took on poison gas following a test exercise at Hanlon Field in Chaumont, France, near the Belgian border. In his memoirs, written with the aid of Al Stump, Cobb said that Matty missed the signal to snap on his mask to protect himself. (Jane Mathewson, however, said she'd been informed by one of Matty's fellow officers, a Captain Thomas, that her husband made it a point of always being the last man to put on his mask.)

"Men screamed to be let out when they got a sudden whiff of the sweet death in the air. They went crazy with fear and in the fight to get out jammed up in a hopeless tangle," Cobb recalled. "As soon as I realized what had happened, but only after inhaling some gas, I fixed my mask and groped my way to the wall and worked through the thrashing bodies to the door. Trying to lead the men out was hopeless. It was each one of us in there for himself. When I staggered out and gulped in fresh air, I didn't know how badly my lungs had been damaged. For weeks a colorless discharge drained from my chest and I had a hacking cough . . . I felt that Divine Providence had touched me, when the drainage stopped . . . I can recall Mathewson saying, 'Ty, when we were in there, I got a good dose of that stuff. I feel terrible.' He was wheezing and blowing out congested matter."

Cobb's memory appears to have been precise and dramatic. Yet Rickey's remembrance did not wholly support Cobb's version. "I went through the exact training that Matty did in France and I was with him immediately afterward," Rickey recalled, "and to my knowledge Matty had no mishap. In fact, Matty took part in an impromptu broad-jump contest, after the field training exposure, and outleaped everyone in our group who cared to try, by a comfortable margin."

However, there does seem to be agreement that at a later time Matty, as part of his duties, was engaged in examining ammunition dumps and other sites left behind by the Germans in Flanders Field. While performing this function he was exposed (again, if you would believe Cobb) to some residual deposits of mustard gas. His lungs already weakened by flu, Matty may have been more vulnerable to the gas fumes lurking in the trenches. However, though poison gas is terrible, as well as deadly to the lungs, it did not cause the tuberculosis which later struck Matty, as it had other members of his family.

As a result of these experiences, Matty was hospitalized in France before and after the long-awaited armistice, which finally came on November 11, 1918, at 11 a.m. The war had taken the lives of millions of the finest and most promising young men. Matty had not been among them, for he survived. But the war had left its deadly imprint on his health.

One of the young men who died was an American named Hobey Baker, a captain in the Air Force. A golden-haired 26-year-old, Baker had been acclaimed, much as Matty had been, as a gentleman and sportsman. An accidental crash of Baker's Spad plane after the armistice took his life, another needless tragedy that so marks wartime. To those who followed Baker's exploits at Princeton, where he excelled in ice hockey and football and anything else to which he turned his talents, he was a shining symbol. "He was like a legendary hero, a Sir Galahad, Richard The Lion-Hearted and even Paul Bunyan," wrote Al Laney of the New York *Herald Tribune*. In their behavior and values Matty and Baker were much alike. In 1951 the Cathedral of St. John the Divine in New York City dedicated its Sports Bay and Chapel to four great athletes who symbolized the highest ideals of character and sportsmanship. Matty and Baker were among them, along with Robert Wrenn in tennis and football's Walter Camp.

20

BACK WITH
THE GIANTS

D URING the winter of 1918–19 Garry Herrmann, never certain of how ill Matty had be-
come in Europe, wanted him back to manage the Reds. Though he
sent repeated messages and cables to Matty in Europe, Herrmann
failed to receive any response. Thus, he concluded it was hopeless
to expect Matty to return to Cincinnati "after he'd seen Paree" (as
the words of a popular war song of the day went). It was possible
that none of Herrmann's communications reached the former
pitcher.

By the time Matty returned to the United States, presumably
having recuperated from his exposure to poison gas, Herrmann had
already given up on him as his team's pilot. Instead, he signed a
former catcher, 43-year-old Pat Moran, who had led the Phillies to
a National League pennant in 1915. After a squabble with the Philadelphia front office, Moran, known affectionately as "Old Whis-
key Face," quit the club in 1918, then signed as a Giants coach.
McGraw was pleased to permit Moran to negotiate a managerial
contract with the Reds.

Realizing also that his old pal was now out of a job, McGraw
rode to the rescue, offering Matty a spot on the Giants as a coach.
It was a perfect opportunity to bring the two men together again,
even if it meant that Matty would find himself sitting on the same
bench as Chase, a man who was anathema to him. Despite his
clearance by Heydler, Chase was still regarded by Matty as an

amoral, incorrigible man, someone that McGraw never should have invited back into baseball.

The Giants went to spring training in Gainesville, Florida, in 1919 for four weeks, a shorter period than usual. McGraw felt that Marlin, the usual sunning spot for the New Yorkers, was too far to go for only a single month of training. On the first day at Gainesville, Larry Doyle's bat slipped out of his hands as he swung at a pitch. Standing close by, Matty fell over as he tried to avoid being hit by the bat. Nevertheless, he was cracked in the stomach, though not badly injured. Several Giants rushed to his side. But Chase, who had been standing there waiting for a turn at the plate, didn't move a muscle. A reporter at the scene noted wryly that "at least Chase had the grace not to laugh out loud. From that moment on Doyle could get anything he wanted out of Chase."

Those around Matty couldn't help but notice that his demeanor had changed. Most of the time he appeared subdued and fatigued. The color in his once handsome face was pasty, the vivid cornflower blue eyes had lost their glow. He coughed often, bringing beads of sweat to his forehead and around his mouth. When friends inquired if he felt all right, he'd invariably shrug off the query, with a wan smile. Jane, equally concerned, insisted that he go to see a specialist, who informed Matty he had chronic bronchitis.

It was evident that Matty had returned to the Giants because he still wanted to be close to the game and to McGraw. Perhaps he had never meant to respond to Herrmann because he thought his health precluded a full-time role as manager. No doubt he appreciated the cheers that always greeted him as he walked on the Polo Grounds diamond from the coach's box to the dugout. But his pace was noticeably slow and labored, his once-unflagging energy diminished to a point where he appeared to welcome sitting on the bench alongside his fellow coach, Jeff Tesreau.

McGraw's wife recalled that her husband spent many sleepless nights walking around their bedroom. Sometimes he would talk to himself about the steady, deepening cough that Matty had. "He was hoping this wasn't a sign that Matty was very sick," she said. McGraw wanted Matty to be around him, fully appreciating how much he meant as a living symbol of the Giants' colorful past.

Meanwhile, in Matty's former camp, Moran's Reds were doing well. Employing a roster made up largely of players recruited by Matty—Roush, Heinie Groh, Greasy Neale, Kopf, Rath, Daubert, Ruether, Ring, Slim Sallee, Eller—the manager had his team in the race from the start. The Reds won their first seven games, raising the hopes of Cincinnati's loyal fans, who hadn't had a winner since the old American Association days.

By the first of June the Giants were in first place, with a five-game edge on the Reds. But by mid-July the Reds had advanced to a few percentage points of the Giants, mainly by beating up on second-division teams, a trusted tactic of McGraw himself. In August the Reds won a series from the Giants in Cincinnati, and later that month they took four out of six from the New Yorkers, putting them in front. McGraw became so testy that he commented that he'd be glad to "get out of the home of the Huns," a pointed reference to the heavy German-American population of the city.

By September 2 the Reds boasted a seven-game margin on the Giants. On the fifteenth, as the Reds beat the Giants behind Sallee, McGraw didn't even bother to get into uniform. He chose, instead, to turn the team over to Matty, who looked on impassively, fully realizing that Moran had done the job with his former players. The next day Cincinnati clinched the flag, as Ruether beat the Giants again.

During the season Matty and Chase never exchanged a word, although Matty informed McGraw on a number of occasions that he thought Chase should have been as welcome as the bubonic plague at the Polo Grounds. McGraw would insist that the first baseman had learned his lesson at last and was playing the game of his life for him. For a while, in fact, it appeared that Chase was paying back McGraw for his trust. Even detractors of the manager were acknowledging that McGraw really knew his onions in handling men and that Matty was wrong in his harsh judgment of the man.

As late as July Chase's bat was winning games for the Giants. On July 19 he settled a tight, one-run game with a late-inning home run. Then in August, as the Giants played the Reds in a crucial series, the beginning of the end arrived for Chase. Fred Lieb reported one day that "Chase has been playing through these games as though he's in a trance."

McGraw must have sensed the same thing, for he began to remove Chase for pinch-hitters who were not half the batter Chase was. On August 16 Chase was dropped from the lineup with a "sore wrist." However, he remained with the team, coaching at first base with a bandaged wrist. Near the close of the season Chase failed to appear at the Polo Grounds one afternoon. When asked where his "rehabilitated player" was, McGraw growled that "he's sick." Chase never played another big-league game for the Giants—or anybody else.

It was later revealed that Chase had put in a good part of the season trying to manipulate the outcome of games. When Cincinnati wrapped up the pennant, Chase approached several Giants, including pitcher Rube Benton, confiding that there was "easy money" to be made by letting the Cubs win in a game that Benton was scheduled to pitch.

When Heydler finally banned Chase for life, he said, "I didn't have enough on him last year to convict him. But this does it. He's through as a player in the National League!" McGraw, with his strong loyalties to men as disparate as Matty and Chase, now confirmed that Chase had been working against the best interests of the Giants. "Chase deliberately let us down," he said. "I was never more deceived by a player." Matty had been right all along about this scoundrel, but it didn't bring him much joy that he was proven correct.

"Nobody can kill the game of baseball, except the public," Matty said not long after the Chase incident. "However, a baseball player who does not do his best every day—the best he can possibly do that day—should be disciplined and if he persists should be released."

With their first title ever in the National League, the Reds won the dubious privilege of facing the Chicago White Sox in the first postwar World Series. Under the aegis of their penurious owner, Charles "Old Roman" Comiskey, the White Sox were rated by many as one of the most powerful ball clubs ever assembled. They had practically the same roster that licked the Giants, four games to two, in the 1917 World Series.

However, the White Sox were also one of the most internally troubled and divisive teams in baseball history. Many of the players were at odds with each other. Columbia-educated Eddie "Cocky" Collins, the deft second baseman developed by Mack, headed up one clique that included the spirited catcher Ray Schalk, spitball pitcher Urban "Red" Faber, and Dickie Kerr, the undersized southpaw. All of these men shared an intense devotion to the game. Collins, the captain of the club, was rewarded handsomely in salary by Comiskey, while most of the other Sox players received less than half of Collins's $14,500 wages.

The disgruntled clique on the White Sox was led by first baseman Chick Gandil and third baseman Buck Weaver. Gandil had run away from his Minnesota home as a child and had been a heavyweight fighter and boilermaker. Weaver was good enough as a third baseman to discourage Cobb from bunting against him. Both men had a reputation for being surly and tough, especially Gandil.

Sectional and social animosity may have played a role, too. Shoeless Joe Jackson, an illiterate outfielder from South Carolina with skills as a batter second only to Cobb, and pitcher Claude Williams were rural Southerners, who shared little in common with Collins and company. Schalk was a Chicagoan, Kerr was from St. Louis, and Faber was an Iowan. Eddie Cicotte, the 29-game-winning right-hander, was from Detroit, but presumably lined up with the Gandil crowd because he considered himself vastly underpaid. Shortstop Swede Risberg, Happy Felsch, the outfielder, and utility man Fred McMullin were also drawn to the dissidents.

Despite their lack of esprit de corps, the White Sox dominated the league. The fans did not come to see the White Sox win, but *how* they won, wrote Eliot Asinof, in his classic *Eight Men Out*. Proper "chemistry" has always been considered a key element in a club's success. But in the case of the White Sox it seemed to mean little. The enormous talent of the White Sox compensated for the bitterness that permeated the locker-room atmosphere of manager William "Kid" Gleason's club.

As the World Series got under way in Cincinnati on the first day of October, the entire country seemed caught up once again in baseball fever. Every major city was wired up to receive details of the games; there wasn't a hotel room available in Cincinnati; scalpers asked and got $50 a ticket; and all that anyone talked about was how much of a chance did Moran's undermanned Reds have against the seemingly invincible White Sox.

At first the betting odds strongly favored the White Sox. Then strange fluctuations in the odds began to take place, causing informed people like Hugh Stuart Fullerton to sniff the air. Was something going on?

A native Ohioan, Fullerton had been writing about baseball for over 25 years for the Chicago *Tribune* and various syndicates. He had been one of the first to predict accurately the outcome of games, notably when he forecast how the World Series of 1906 would turn out. He took even greater pride in having discovered Ring Lardner and Cy Sanborn, two prominent citizens of the press box. Known as something of a pleasant windbag, Fullerton was covering the Series for the Chicago *Herald-American*. He'd already predicted that the White Sox were too good to lose this 1919 Series.

Working alongside him was Matty, who had been hired by the

New York *Evening World* to write stories about the games. Matty's heavy reputation as a baseball savant and his previous writing credits (with help from Wheeler) had won him the assignment. He took the job after a year of coaching for the Giants, feeling stronger than he had earlier in the year.

Thinking he might be helpful to the nouveau journalist, Fullerton recommended to Matty that they share a room in the Sinton Hotel. However, it turned out that Matty could be more helpful to Fullerton, for on the morning of the first game Fullerton told Matty that he was hearing all over town that the Series might be fixed. He had picked up whispers, he said, from many quarters that the underdog Reds were going to win because gamblers had gotten to some White Sox players.

Fullerton pressed Matty on the precise details of how ballplayers might throw ball games, without anybody picking up the clues. How did they do it, in front of thousands of people and observers like themselves, trained to spot every nuance and artifice that might betray a player's half-hearted efforts? Like Matty, Fullerton was a man of integrity who despised those who were spreading rumors about a game that he loved. Yet he felt deep in his bones that something rotten was going on. Not only had he heard that the Sox might be throwing the Series, but he'd also picked up from the grapevine that Chicago gamblers were trying to get Cincinnati players drunk to help the White Sox win. Under such chaotic conditions, said the baffled Fullerton, nobody would wind up on top!

Fullerton extracted a promise from Matty that they'd sit together in the press box (next to other celebrated wordsmiths of the time such as Runyon, Rice, Lardner, Lieb, and Taylor Spink of *The Sporting News*) and Matty would draw a red circle on his scorecard for every play he deemed suspect.

At the end of the Series, won by the Reds, five games to three, with Williams losing three times and Cicotte twice, Matty's scorecard was cluttered with red circles. On more than half a dozen occasions he raised his eyebrows skeptically about what he'd just viewed on the field. He had watched Cicotte slow-motion a throw to second base on a ground ball, dilatory enough to miss a double play at first base. He saw the bottom of Cincinnati's batting order produce unexpected hits to beat Cicotte and Williams. He brought to Fullerton's attention that Williams appeared to be hurling only fast balls, whereas his sweeping curve was his preferred pitch. He noticed how Schalk, red-faced with anger, kept shaking his fist at Williams. He watched in utter amazement as Felsch misplayed fly balls hit by Roush and Eller. He saw Risberg at shortstop back up on a grounder and questioned a stolen base that seemed unwise. An errant throw home by Shoeless Joe drew another red circle.

It was all down there on the scorecard—and Fullerton knew exactly what those baseball hieroglyphics meant. He knew, too, that what Matty was telling him was an honest appraisal—hadn't Matty been right on target in the case of Hal Chase?

Curiously, Matty did not express any of his suspicions in the articles that he wrote on the Series. The risk of being sued for libel may have intimidated him. However, Lardner, then writing for the Chicago *Tribune*, was so grievously disappointed in the play of his White Sox idols that he went around openly (while in his cups) singing, "I'm forever blowing ball games, pretty ball games in the air; I come from Chi, I hardly try, Just go to bat to fade and die; Fortune's coming my way, that's why I don't care. I'm forever blowing ball games, and the gamblers treat us fair." Lardner's song was a parody on a popular melody of 1919. Unfortunately, Matty wasn't as talented a writer of song lyrics as Lardner.

Not long after the end of the Series, Fullerton and millions of others knew that the White Sox had tarnished the game by attempting to pre-arrange the outcome of the World Series. The sell-out by eight of the White Sox, whether impelled by social, venal, or cultural reasons, threatened the foundation of baseball. The 1919 Series would forever after be known as the infamous Black Sox Scandal and the plea of a small boy to Shoeless Joe Jackson outside of a grand jury room, "Say it ain't so, Joe," would become part of American folklore.

Ultimately, the eight players were banned from baseball for life by Commissioner Kenesaw Mountain Landis, whose widely publicized toughness, was credited with saving the game. The save, of course, got a powerful assist from Babe Ruth, whose frequent homeruns helped the fans forget the skulduggery of 1919.

No man had been more concerned than Matty about the purity of baseball. Before 1919 even the most cynical of men preferred to reject the notion that ball games could be fixed. But Matty had learned his lessons through the bleak experience with Chase, then with his further education sitting in the press box of the 1919 Series, as he wearily gazed down at a cluster of players depriving the game of its innocence.

Yet, he continued to show broad tolerance for the alleged sins of those eight Black Sox. "There is such a thing as condemning the acts of these men and still forgiving the individuals," he said. "I don't think Kid Gleason and the rest of the White Sox wanted to see their former comrades sent to the penitentiary for violating the trust placed in them by the fans. They would not have been human if they did. Even a judge must dislike sentencing a man to jail, unless he is a most hardened criminal."

21

AT SARANAC LAKE

WITH McGraw's urging, Matty thought he could return to the Giants' coaching lines in 1920. However, his doctors, taking note of Matty's heavy, constant coughing and a body that appeared shrunken, thought otherwise. After an extensive examination, Matty was told that he had tuberculosis, a disease that was a scourge throughout the world and had become more endemic during the Great War. TB was damaging to the lungs and other organs and was generally accompanied by the very symptoms that Matty had exhibited: coughing, weight loss, diminished appetite, and fever. It was spread by airborne droplets and usually was contracted through close, daily contact with somebody who was infected. There was no likelihood that Matty had gotten TB from his exposure to mustard gas. However, such exposure could have weakened his resistance to the disease, decreasing his immunity to it.

At one time in the early 1800s 688 deaths per 100,000 people were attributed to TB. So infamous had the disease become that it was known as "The White Plague" or "The Captain of the Men of Death." At the start of the twentieth century it was also called "The Tailor's Disease," since tailors invariably toiled in cramped, dark environments.

By 1900 one in every nine deaths in the world was blamed on TB, and its victims came from all walks of life. Spinoza, Thoreau, Keats, Shelley, Voltaire, Mozart, Cecil Rhodes, Kant, Goethe, and

Robert Louis Stevenson all had suffered from it, though Stevenson actually succumbed to a stroke. Ironically, Branch Rickey, who had been in Matty's unit in France, suffered from TB in 1908. He made a successful recovery at Saranac Lake and by 1909 had enrolled at the University of Michigan.

The mortality rate in Germany from TB in 1918 went as high as 230 per 100,000, as compared with 142 deaths per 100,000 in 1914, when the war began. Between 1917 and 1919, 4,201 cases were reported in the U.S. Army. Of that number close to 500 died. Only a pre-draft screening managed to keep cases of TB down in the military service. By 1916 the French Army was so riddled with the disease that 86,000 men were said to have been discharged because of TB within twelve months' time. "TB is as integral to warfare as patriotism" was a maxim of the era. There is no doubt that desperate economic conditions prevailing in Europe, plus large food shortages, caused the serious rise in TB.

In order to provide Matty with a fair chance for recovery, in July 1920 his doctors insisted that he go to Saranac Lake. Some 60 miles from the Canadian border and nine miles from Lake Placid in northern New York State, Saranac Lake had become something of a haven for those who had contracted TB. Dr. Edward Livingston Trudeau visited there in 1873, preparing to die from TB, as his brother had. Exposed to the invigorating mountain air and sylvan ambiance, Dr. Trudeau recovered, then set about installing there in 1885 the first TB research laboratory and hospital sanatorium.

The mystique of Saranac—the "Adirondack cottage cure"—was based on a voluntary form of segregation, a closed society of consumptives. The formula for recovery encompassed bed rest, good diet, and the crisp air so typical of a region that had once only attracted poets and writers.

When Matty arrived at Saranac it was simply a nursing home (of some 700 private residences) where victims of TB could have peace, quiet, and nourishing food under medical supervision while they fought their private, often desperate struggles with the tuberclar bacillus. There were no drugs used at the time. The first measure taken in Matty's case was the drastic one of collapsing a lung and keeping the pleural cavity filled with air so the lung would stay deflated.

Because Matty was too well off financially, at first he was not admitted to the Trudeau Sanatorium. Instead, the Mathewsons, including Christy Jr., took an apartment in a prestigious building on

Church Street. His physician, Dr. Edward Packard, lived only three houses away and was always on call.

For the first six months little of accuracy was reported about Matty's condition, although from time to time the press would print alarmist accounts that he was failing or dying. Then the reports became more optimistic, suggesting that he was doing well. In fact, Matty was in great pain after the surgical procedure on his lung, and no visitors were permitted to see him outside of the immediate family. When Jane became highly distressed over Matty's seeming lack of progress, he would try to reassure her. "Never mind," said Matty. "That's all over and we can't do anything about it. Let's forget it and start over."

At Christmas time Dr. Packard explained that the pain was "like a drying-up process and was viewed with favor, adding chances to his recovery." However, Dr. Packard also noted that Matty was still bedridden and was not allowed to sit up.

Many believed that Matty would never emerge from Saranac alive. But he continued to remain more optimistic than most of those around him. With the aid of Jane, his doctors, and the strict regimen that had been prescribed for him, Matty slowly started to regain his strength. By February 1921, with his fever down and his drain tube removed, Matty was permitted to write letters and to sit in a chair for an hour a day, gazing out of the window at the dark green forests that surrounded his living quarters. He had taken up the study of natural history, becoming acquainted, at this stage only at a distance, with the trees, birds, and flowers of this beautiful region. Chess and checkers also were major diversions that kept him from brooding.

As the Giants battled for the National League pennant that year—ultimately defeating the upstart New York Yankees in the World Series (the first in which Babe Ruth played for the Yankees)—McGraw often telephoned Matty. He placed many long-distance calls to Saranac from hotel rooms all over the National League circuit, always enthusiastically chatting about the Giants' play and never failing to remind Matty that the Giants had a place for him when he returned. It must be remembered that in 1921 the long-distance call was an event. Matty couldn't help but be thrilled by the attentiveness of his friend.

By the time Matty was allowed to take brief walks and automobile rides in the countryside, he was also able to give limited interviews. In one he stated that as long as he had a chance to survive he'd keep fighting and plugging away. "In baseball we learn to obey orders and follow the rules," he said. "We try to make the plays that give us the most chance to win." He added that he had no alternative but to resign himself to what he couldn't help. "I try to keep cheerful, keep my mind busy, try not to worry and I don't kick on decisions, either by a doctor or an umpire. Kicking won't change anything." He strongly affirmed his feeling that you can't win if you quit.

"A fellow begins to feel that life is worth fighting for and to realize something of what it means to lose it. Oddly, a fellow thinks less and less of himself and more and more of others. He has less dread of death. He sees that life is good and that death isn't bad at all—if one is ready for it," he said.

Some homilies might have sounded false coming from others. But from Matty, a man always known for his indomitable nature, it rang true. When he said that after the first few days in the sick room he stopped feeling sorry for himself, it was credible. "I always think," he insisted, "how much better off I am than most other people."

In a demonstration of affection, the Giants played a double-header benefit for Matty on the last day of September. A crowd of over 20,000 showed up for the tribute, with all proceeds going to help their idol with his mounting expenses. An Old-Timers Game featured many men—Merkle, Tenney, Doyle, Murray, Devlin, McCormick, Dahlen, Wiltse, and Bresnahan (leaving a sickbed to put in an appearance)—who had played alongside Matty.

McGraw's Giants of 1921 played Matty's former teammates. The new breed included Frankie Frisch, George Burns, High Pockets Kelly, Emil Meusel, Ross Youngs, and Dave Bancroft, the nucleus of that year's pennant-winners. In five innings the Old-Timers licked the new Giants, 2–0. The second game, a regularly scheduled game with the Braves, was rained out. However, it had been insured against rain for $22,500. Between the receipts for the first game and the insured game Matty received almost $50,000, at the time the largest sum ever raised in a sporting event in behalf of one person.

Between games baseballs autographed by Matty were auctioned off for $620. One signed by President Warren Harding, Vice President Calvin Coolidge, Babe Ruth, and Matty went for $750, under the tender goading of Fred Lieb, who acted as auctioneer.

From his bed at Saranac Matty sent a message of appreciation: "On this day of days at the Polo Grounds I am glad to send heartiest greetings to my baseball friends. It is absolutely impossible for me to put into words my feeling of pleasure and gratitude at the manner in which the New York club and friends of baseball are honoring me, but it certainly is good to have friends who do not forget and who remember so substantially. With such support, I cannot fail to win my game. Here is hoping that the Giants win theirs."

By October, shortly after his 41st birthday, Matty was getting out into the Saranac countryside, exploring Adirondack's deep, black lakes, traveling over its rutted roads and russet mountains, always with Jane at his side. "These are some of the happiest days of my life," he said. Now he was allowed to ride in his automobile several times a week. Sometimes the weather flirted with the freezing mark but the Trudeau theory embraced the notion that it was beneficial to the patient, as long as he was properly dressed for the occasion.

When he appeared in public in Saranac Lake's downtown section for the first time to get a haircut, he was greeted enthusiastically, even though his neighbors made certain to respect his privacy. He still had the pallor of a sick man, his forehead was furrowed, and he'd lost forty pounds, but his manner was more jaunty than it had been for a year. This change was pleasing to Jane and Dr. Packard.

While Matty was at Saranac, hundreds of letters, usually addressed to "Big Six" or "Matty," were sent to him. The sentiments were always the same. They wished him a quick recovery. Sometimes the letter-writers suggested all sorts of remedies for him to beat TB. Most of these nostrums were preposterous—blowing a horn, for example, to clear his lungs—but they were all well meant.

As Matty became stronger he was encouraged to be more active, which did not displease him, for he admitted to being restless. He'd frequently visit the old St. Regis hotel in Saranac to reminisce and play checkers. Expert players came from all over the country to engage Matty in his sport. Now that he was getting around more, no longer did he have to "indulge in the violent exercise of having someone wheel me around in a chair."

By 1922 Matty was convinced that all of "the bugs were gone," even though he admitted feeling tired after walking for more than twenty minutes. His study of flowers, which was now more than a book exercise, including touring the village roads in search of his favorite wildflower, the blue gentian. The woods became his sanctuary, much as it had a hundred years before for the literary people who had first discovered the mysteries of the Adirondacks. He kept a careful record in longhand of all the flora that he had encountered on his walks, including such exotic flowers as the Hog Peanut, Maiden Pink, Ladies' Thumb and Monkey Flower.

"When I see the gleam of petals in the grass," he said, "I bend down eagerly to look and see if this is an old friend that I must study to find out about."

He also took up quail shooting, developing a way to enjoy it without exerting himself beyond permissible limits. Jane and he would drive along deserted mountain roads, looking for a covey of grouse or quail. When a collection was sighted, Matty would step out of the automobile and slowly approach the birds, shotgun in hand. However, he would shoot only when the birds flew off. He emphasized that the experience was pleasurable, not for the killing, but because it enabled him to get out into the fields where he felt very much alive.

Always community-minded, he lent his prestige to the cause of a local lumberman who was fighting to get a right-of-way across a huge preserve owned by William Rockefeller. In June he threw out the first ball in a season opener between Saranac Lake and Plattsburg. That fall his doctors consented to allow him to travel to Factoryville to visit his mother and father, who hadn't seen him for some time. These activities led him to feel that the "worst part of the battle is over."

In December he returned to New York City to inaugurate the annual Christmas Seal sale. His doctors now pointed to him as a prime example of the "Saranac Miracle," a man who had literally risen from his sick bed, without medicine, to make a remarkable recovery. "There stands our greatest victory over TB," they announced. "When a particularly stubborn case is encountered, we tell them about Mathewson."

Matty now began to give some thought to returning to his coaching post with the Giants, although he dismissed the notion of every going back to managing. "The managing end would take too much out of me," he said. "In the present state of my health, it wouldn't be the best way for me to get back into the game."

But McGraw had other ideas for Matty. He informed his friend that George Washington Grant was ready to sell the Boston Braves for half a million dollars and that he knew someone who might be interested in buying the club. If this could be accomplished, said McGraw, Matty would be the ideal choice to become president of the Braves, for the potential purchaser of the team was a warm admirer of Matty.

Matty inquired as to who this person was. McGraw told him it was Judge Emil E. Fuchs, who for some time had been an attorney representing the Giants. The matter was now up to Matty's doctors. But what they told him was scarcely encouraging. Dr. Edward Baldwin of New Haven, Connecticut, an assistant to Dr. Trudeau, warned Matty that he didn't think he'd live more than two years if he went back to baseball in such a role.

Alarmed by the doctors' statements, Jane reminded Matty that he'd have a difficult time holding back from giving his all on such a job. Wouldn't the Braves job, if offered, she asked, be too stressful? It was common knowledge to those who fought to restore TB patients to good health that a sudden, misleading glow of color to their cheeks was often only an aberration. TB, they knew, was insidious, its sufferers were often misled into thinking they were cured when they weren't.

However, Matty was not heeding such pleas. He yearned to be active again in baseball. He told McGraw that he'd be eager to meet with Judge Fuchs and his associates.

22

IN BOSTON'S
FRONT OFFICE

S INCE he was a boy growing up in New York City,
Judge Fuchs had loved baseball. He'd been a
catcher for the University Settlement team, afterward playing for
the Morristown Club of the Jersey State League. As a lawyer he
was appointed deputy state superintendent of elections in New York.
Two years later he became deputy attorney general of New York.
From 1916 to 1918 he served as a judge in the Magistrates Criminal
Court. A short, squat, overly polite man, Fuchs was not without
humor. "Since Prohibition," he remarked, during negotiations to
buy the Braves, "everyone wants to be in the cellar." One Boston
writer described Fuchs as a "sucker for a touch," though others
were not so charitable, preferring to call him "a stooge for Boston
politicians." What was absolutely certain about the Judge was that
he was an unstinted admirer of Christopher Mathewson.

In January 1923 Fuchs was host at the Lambs' Club in New
York to Harry M. Stevens, the food concessionaire, George M. Cohan, and McGraw for the purpose of discussing the Braves situation. After considerable talk about money and their mutual infat-
uation with baseball, Cohan, back on good terms with McGraw,
declared himself a dropout. "I prefer show business to baseball,"
said the renowned song-and-dance man, who had originally hinted
that he wanted to own a ball club.

However, Fuchs told McGraw he was ready to purchase the
Braves, provided he could get Matty to "help me run the opera-

tion." Delighted to hear such a proposal, McGraw promised that he'd bring Matty down from Saranac to hear Fuchs's plans. After Matty and Fuchs got together, with Matty trying to reassure Fuchs about his health, Fuchs came up with $50,000 for a thirty-day option on the Braves.

On February 23, 1923, an announcement was made that a New York syndicate headed by Fuchs and including Matty and James McDonough, a banker, had bought the Braves. The story was front-page news in most of the newspapers around the country, principally because of Matty's involvement. It was also suspected that a wealthy young sportsman named Charles A. Levine had played a role behind the scenes. (Four years later Levine flew across the Atlantic with Clarence Chamberlin, following Charles A. Lindbergh's celebrated solo flight from New York to Paris.)

The first act of the new owners was to reorganize the Boston bureaucracy. Matty was named president and Fuchs vice president, with Fred Mitchell staying on as manager. It was rare for a former player to ascend to executive status in the game; only a few others, such as Branch Rickey of St. Louis, McGraw, Washington's Clark Griffith, Chicago's Comiskey, A. G. Spalding, and John Montgomery Ward had followed that route.

"I never thought when I saw my first big league game in Boston back in 1899, when I paid 75 cents to see Kid Nichols pitch against Cy Young at the Old Walpole Street Grounds, that I'd one day be President of the Braves," said Matty. "For two years I've been trying to come back to baseball, living for the day, dreaming about it constantly. So when Judge Fuchs, whom I have known as someone who loves the game, gave me this opportunity, I grasped it."

Fuchs gave his assurance that Matty would be in no way a figurehead. He reminded everyone that Matty would have a financial interest in the team, and as somebody who had once run his own insurance firm, Matty was a shrewd businessman who knew how to get along with all kinds of people. Fuchs tried to downplay the notion that Matty's coming to Boston was nothing more than a dramatic gambit, designed to capitalize on Matty's popularity.

However, as things turned out, Matty was little more than a figurehead, due mainly to his limited energy. Less robust than he had hoped, Matty tried to work on a cure and at baseball at the same time—but the two objectives were incompatible. Matty's heart was in it, but his body wasn't. Most of the time he found himself going back and forth between Boston and Saranac Lake, where he got rest and further treatment. When he occasionally appeared at the Polo Grounds to watch his team play the Giants, Matty was pale and walked with a cane, always a shock to those who had known him during his days of athletic vigor.

In truth, Fuchs ran the Boston club. On the few occasions when Matty had some input it contributed to soiling the once impeccable reputation he'd had among his fellow players. The secretary of the Braves wanted to limit Braves' players to four-dollars-a-day meal money, a rather generous sum in those days. Fuchs thought they should even receive more. But having been raised in a parsimonious big-league atmosphere, Matty chose to maintain the four-dollar limit. He won his point. Inevitably, the players resented his stingy policy. Casey Stengel, on the Braves roster in 1924, was one of those who made his feelings known, for he rarely remained silent for any length of time.

Another judgment was made by Matty in regard to the team's manager. He removed Mitchell, whose deliberate style had brought sparse dividends (the Braves finished seventh in 1923), and replaced him with Dave Bancroft, the veteran shortstop of the Giants. Stengel and outfielder Bill Cunningham had been shipped with Bancroft from New York to the Braves for journeyman outfielder Billy Southworth, pitcher Joe Oeschger, and cash. The express purpose of the deal was to allow Bancroft to become manager of the Braves.

"I wanted to help Matty," explained McGraw, "and at the same time it gives Bancroft his chance at managing, something he's always wanted."

Bancroft was hardly more successful than Mitchell had been, for the Braves ended up in last place under his guidance. A strong contributing reason for the Braves' failure was an automobile accident that killed Tony "Elmer" Boeckel, Boston's hard-hitting third baseman. Matty's luck, as it had in so many instances, seemed to have run out again. However, in 1925, Bancroft pushed his club to a fifth-place finish, with a strikingly improved record.

THE LAST DAYS

WHILE Matty was spending less and less time on Braves duties, he cheerfully gave his attention to certain causes that he favored. He arranged for the proceeds of a game between the Braves and Pittsburgh to be given to the American Legion Post in Saranac Lake and the Massachusetts Department of the American Legion. The money was earmarked for those veterans under treatment for TB.

By 1924 Matty and Jane moved at Saranac Lake into a five-bedroom, three-bath colonial house with a living room, dining room, kitchen, and den, along with two ten-by-twenty-foot porches. Since Matty was a tall man, the bathtubs were six feet long, and mirrors were placed higher than average. The gray-shingled house, on a balsam-shrouded corner lot, came to be known as the Christy Mathewson Cottage, although it is not certain whether Matty actually owned it. The cottage was one of the most prominent structures in the Highland Park section of Saranac Lake, and its commanding position over Old Military Road and Park Avenue was evocative, said some observers with an eye for metaphor, of a pitcher on the mound.

Matty's surroundings were airy, comfortable, and uncramped. His favorite spot was the living room, where a great cozy chair and well-worn seat and footstool nudged close to a fireplace that crackled during the cold winter months. On the porch Matty loved to spend time in a large "cure" chair, on which sunlight fell and one could reap a magnificent view of Mount Pisgah, with its flaming fall colors.

In Matty's room there were many photographs of the old Giant days, including a picture of McGraw looking very magisterial. College photos of fraternity brothers and classmates from Bucknell also adorned the walls, a reflection of Matty's still strong attachment to his early associates. Three guns, now virtually unused, stood in a corner, and on a pipe-stand nearby was Matty's collection of meerschaums, burnished to a creamy beige.

In the summer of 1924 Matty was involved in an auto accident—a two-car collision—on the road between Saranac Lake and Lake Placid. Although the accident was not catastrophic, Matty suffered an arm injury. Since he had only limited vitality, the collision was a setback for him. When he was made the defendant in a legal action stemming from the mishap, Matty did not appear because Dr. Packard's affidavit underlined that "his recovery depends on freedom from cares and worries and any excitement would jeopardize his health."

However, against the advice of doctors Matty covered the 1924 World Series between the Giants, winning their tenth and last pennant under McGraw, and the Washington Senators. This Series was played under happier circumstances than the one in 1919. But the Senators, with pitching help from Walter Johnson, in the seventh game, toppled the Giants, causing Matty to feel great sadness for McGraw. Matty now wore glasses and walked with a heavy step. Most of the time during the Series he sat slumped in the press box, even as he remained an alert observer.

By the end of the year stories appeared again about Matty's failing health. But he still tried to perform his administrative duties for the Braves, especially when the welfare of his players was concerned. In January 1925 he wrote to the presidents of all the other National League clubs about the deteriorating condition from cancer of the stomach of Charlie "Duke" Farrell, a former catcher and scout for the Braves. "The limit for him to live is placed at three months," Matty informed them. "Would you be good enough to advise me what your attitude would be on a proposition to give Farrell financial assistance." A month later Farrell died in Boston at the age of 59.

In 1925 Matty decided to make a trip to St. Petersburg, Florida, where the Braves had their spring training camp. He thought the warmth in that sunny area would be salutary. Instead, he took cold. For someone in good health this would not have been a major affliction. But for Matty it was. He left St. Petersburg and returned at once to Saranac Lake in the hope that the Adirondacks would again give him respite from his weakened condition.

Sensing that Matty had taken a turn for the worse, Jane begged him to sever all relationship with the Boston club. But by this time such entreaties were unnecessary, for Matty had little strength to object to her advice.

Through the spring and early days of summer Matty battled for his life. From time to time newspapers ran stories about his "fight for recovery," always trying to put the best face on his plight. However, if one read between the lines it was apparent that Matty had regressed. He suffered great pain when he coughed, visitors were once again excluded, and he was rarely able to leave his bed.

In July, when Matty formally relinquished all duties with the Braves, rumors that he was dying spread in the baseball community. Dr. Packard was asked by his patient to tell people that although he was a sick man, he was going to come through again.

"Just say for me," he was quoted by Dr. Packard as saying, "that I'll fan Death again. He can't touch me, I'm sure of that. I want my friends to know that I am fighting and will continue until I come out on top."

The fight continued through early autumn. But the disease was relentless. On the morning of October 7, 1925, consumed by fever and barely able to talk, Matty told Jane, "It is nearly over. I know it and we must face it. Go out and have a good cry. Don't make it a long one. This is something we can't help."

That night at 11 o'clock, only hours after "Big Train" Walter Johnson, whose right-handed pitching feats had constantly been compared to Matty's, defeated the Pirates in the first game of the World Series, Matty died. He was 45 years old. The official cause of death was tuberculous pneumonia.

Word of his demise spread rapidly through the hotels, restaurants, barber shops, and saloons of Pittsburgh where the World Series was being played. By the morning of October 8 the news about Matty was in the headlines, although the *New York Times* misstated the case when they wrote "Christy Mathewson Dies Unexpectedly." After all, Matty had been seven years dying.

Before the start of the second game of the Series, before 44,000 fans, the flag was lowered to half-mast, and many in the crowd began to sing "Nearer My God to Thee." Each Pittsburgh and Washington player wore a black armband. After the game, McGraw, who had been in Pittsburgh to report on the Series for a syndicate, left immediately for New York, where he met Blanche. From there they traveled to Saranac Lake to be with Jane. Then the long, sad trip with Matty's body was made to Lewisburg. Matty, in his last hours, had requested that he be buried near the Mathewson house on Market Street, only a short walk from the Bucknell campus.

On October 10 his wishes were fulfilled, as he was put to rest in the little college town in which he had apprenticed for pitching fame. McGraw served as a pallbearer, and other celebrated figures of baseball, including Commissioner Landis, Judge Fuchs, John Heydler, Wilbert Robinson, and Davey Bancroft, looked on as Matty's coffin was lowered into a grave overlooking the green fields of Bucknell. Dozens of floral tributes were sent from "8,000 Knothole Boys of Boston," as well as from the American League, the National League, the National League Umpires, the Baseball Writers of America, and from his old catcher, Roger Bresnahan.

"I believe that he gave his life for his country, just as many boys like Eddie Grant, who was killed in action overseas," said Jane Mathewson.

24

THE MATTY LEGEND

THE outpouring of grief and praise for the departed Matty was almost unprecedented for an athlete. The morning after his death W. O. McGeehan wrote in the New York *Herald Tribune* that Matty was "the best loved and most popular of all American athletes . . . if baseball will hold to the ideals of this gentleman, sportsman and soldier, our national game will keep the younger generation clean and courageous and the future of the nation secure."

Grantland Rice, who watched Matty break 80 in golf for the first time years before at the Schenley course in Pittsburgh, wrote that he "was the only man I ever met who in spirit and inspiration was greater than his game." The New York *World* said that Matty's life was "a vindication of our love for sport." The Philadelphia *Inquirer* editorialized that he "was the symbol of the highest type of American sportsmanship."

"The country has lost one of its most valuable citizens," wrote the Boston *Telegram*. The Danville (Illinois) *Commercial News* said that "Matty trotted square . . . he was a man without guile and everybody loved him." Unable to restrain its hyperbole, *Commonweal* said that "no other pitcher loomed so majestically in young minds, quite overshadowing George Washington and his cherry tree or even that transcendent model of boyhood, Frank Merriwell." The New York *Telegram* thought he "was the greatest sportsman the game has ever produced."

Perhaps McGraw said it best of all in a tribute to Matty several days after the funeral. "I do not expect to see his like again but I do know that the example he set and the imprint he left on the sport that he loved and honored will remain long after I am gone," he said.

In the 68 years since Matty's death, he has become a legend, although these days only dimly seen. His enormous devotion to the game and to principle, his attractive physical appearance, his razor-sharp, eclectic intelligence, his sometimes frightening honesty that bordered, as some insisted, on unmitigated self-righteousness were the stuff of a "collaboration between the Almighty and a composer of fiction," as Donald Honig has written.

He was, indeed, the supreme pitching wonder of his time, allowing for supporters of Cy Young, Johnson, Waddell, Ed Walsh, and Brown. "A pitcher is not a ballplayer," Matty often said. Certainly he was not the kind of ballplayer—rough, crude, vulgar, often ignorant—that flourished in his era.

If in truth Matty was everything that was written and spoken about him he would have been insufferable. Countering this image, Jane was once moved to say that if her husband was the "goody-goody" and prig that they said he was, "I never would have married him!" He was hardly an abstemious man, for he liked his cup of wine and glass of beer, but always in moderation. He liked a good smoke, preferably his pipes and cigars. His face appeared on an endorsement for Tuxedo—the Perfect Tobacco. "A good, companionable tobacco—the kind 'to stick to,' " said Matty above his signature. He was able to handle profanity, although he wasn't a conspicuous user of it. Any man who formed such a beautiful partnership with McGraw must have had a high tolerance for such talk.

There were times when Matty spoke harshly about his teammates, even suggesting that some of the younger players were "choking" in the pinch. Though there is no evidence that Matty was a bigot, he went along with the unthinking mores of the time, blithely referring to the "Jew Kling" in his book, *Pitching in the Pinch.* (Ironically, there is some reason to believe that Kling wasn't even Jewish.)

On long train trips, with no air conditioning, cramped berths, and bitter coffee, the normally even-tempered pitcher could turn into a grouch. In card games, he could swear quietly under his breath when his cards ran cold, or Runyon or Broun got the better of him. As the beatification process insisted, he was an incorruptible man. He was also pragmatic, as witness his change of heart on the subject of Sunday baseball. But when he accepted a safety-razor endorsement for $200, Matty actually tested the razor before making the deal. "It works satisfactorily," he informed Boze Bulger, who had encouraged him to endorse the product. Would Matty have done so if his whiskers hadn't complied properly? Some took his shyness and reserve for aloofness. He was known for pulling down the shades of the Pullman car he was riding in so that people on the platform couldn't stare at him.

The popular "Gee whiz" journalists of the day were as responsible as anyone else for the creation of the Matty legend, for they were as worshipful of their hero as his fans. In the eyes of the mocking, irreverent Lardner, Matty could do no wrong. Lardner was completely won over by Matty's civility, selflessness, graciousness, and quick mind—all traits that set him apart from the tatterdemalion band that he played with. That éminence grise of sportswriting, Grantland Rice, regarded Matty as the greatest pitcher of them all. But more important, to Rice he was a role model for all men—and boys. In his profession Rice was adjudged as saintly as Matty was in his. When Rice penned his famous little poem, "When the great scorer comes to mark against your name, he writes not that you won or lost, but how you've played the game," he conceivably had Matty much in mind.

But in the realm of poetry there was nothing to match the lines of Lardner: "Who discovered the land of the brave and free; I don't know, I don't know. 'Twas Christy Columbus is what they tell me, maybe so, I don't know. There's only one Christy I know at all, one Christy that I ever saw. He's the one that discovered the fadeaway ball and he pitches for Muggsy McGraw."

Sportswriter John Kieran, every bit the cerebral man that Matty was, refused all qualifications in writing about him. "He was the greatest I ever saw. He was the greatest anybody ever saw. Let them name all the others. I don't care how good they were, Matty was better," Kieran wrote in the *New York Times*.

Even if Damon Runyon found inebriates like Bugs Raymond more interesting to hang around with and to write about (his bread-and-butter outpourings profited more from such associations), he still felt close to Matty, closer to him than any other athlete except Jack Dempsey. Runyon knew that he could talk seriously with Matty on many subjects. No other player in sight could do that with the iconoclastic, complex writer.

One startling dissenter from those who practically canonized Matty was one Walter St. Denis, who had been sports editor of the

New York *Globe* in the early 1900s. "In my book Mathewson was *not* the number one pitcher of all time," said St. Denis. "I traveled with the ball club for years. I knew Matty as well as anybody. I knew all of his virtues and faults. He didn't have all the courage in the world and he wasn't a team player. He was always looking out for Mr. Mathewson. I've often sat on a train and waited for him to go to McGraw with a 'sore arm' just before we were to open a series with a heavy-hitting team like St. Louis. He used that 'sore arm' stuff like a spoiled baby." (It's interesting to note that Matty beat St. Louis 52 times in his career, a higher total than he registered against Brooklyn and Chicago; he beat Pittsburgh 54 times, as a basis of comparison.)

St. Denis blamed Matty's reputation solely on the writers, "fellows who were sentimentalists of the worst sort." St. Denis pointed to the long, windy leads, in which they quoted the Bible to prove their point. "They polished up character traits that didn't exist. There were two Mathewsons—the human being and the newspaper invention," he said. "Novelists and newspaper men like Richard Harding Davis, were on the corny side."

Was St. Denis, in his harsh attack, closer to the truth than the Brouns, Runyons, Lardners, Craneses, Fullertons, Rices, Bulgers, and McGeehans? Did St. Denis feel wronged by Matty because he was one of those whom the pitcher ignored? At least one would think that St. Denis would have given his due to Matty as a pitcher. Instead, he settled by dismissing Matty as a man who had "a lot of stuff."

Official proof of Matty's greatness came in 1936 when, in the first election of modern (1900–1936) players, he was named to Baseball's Hall of Fame. The first four men chosen were, in order, Cobb, Ruth, Wagner, and Matty. Johnson, the only other pitcher, was fifth, with 16 less votes than Matty, who won 205 votes out of 226 ballots cast. The writers who voted had plenty of ammunition. They could point to Matty's 373 victories against only 188 defeats (one loss on August 5, 1905, was a forfeit of a game in the ninth inning to Pittsburgh). Only two other pitchers, Young with 511 wins and Johnson with 416, won more games than Matty, while Alexander was tied with Matty at 373.

Matty pitched 83 shutouts, the third highest behind Johnson and Alexander. He started 552 games, completing 435 of them. He worked in 4,779 innings, yielding only 838 bases on balls, while striking out 2,505 batters. He walked an average of 1.57 men a game and fanned almost five a game. In some years the walks he issued totaled less than his number of victories.

His 37 wins in 1908 was four behind Jack Chesbro's 41 in 1904 and three back of Walsh's 40 in 1908. He had the fifth lowest ERA for a single season—1.14 in 1909.

In 1913 Matty didn't issue a pass in 16 of his games and didn't hit a batter all season long. That same year he gave up 0.62 walks per nine innings, a record. His control was so immaculate that he once won a bet that he could throw twenty consecutive pitches to the same spot. The bet, in which he placed $50 at twelve-to-one odds, was made at West Point in 1907, where Matty often went to work out with the Army baseball team. There was one other condition to the wager: it was imperative that among the twenty pitches five would have to be fadeaways. Every ball Matty pitched wound up in the catcher's mitt, exactly where he had promised to pitch it.

In four seasons—1903, 1904, 1905, and 1908—Matty won 30 or more games, a feat unequaled by any other pitcher in history.

One can rationalize that Matty's years were highly favorable to pitchers. The ball was not lively, and they were often kept in use until they were as black as a threatening sky. Rogers Hornsby once said that "a ball stayed in play until it was ready to break apart." Certainly this condition helped a pitcher who knew his pitch wouldn't easily be hit for a home run.

But the other side of the story was that diamonds were invariably rough and poorly manicured. Balls behaved anarchically. Bad hops were common, and the gloves, not much bigger than the batting gloves players now wear, afforded poor opportunities for entrapment. If long hits were not commonplace, short hits were more frequent, and pitchers often had to work with men on base. Pitchers were usually called on by their managers to finish what they started, and Matty did exactly that.

Under these circumstances, Matty learned how to pitch with men on base. He understood the need to pace himself. When he found himself ahead in a game, more often than not he'd challenge the foe to hit his soft pitches. There are outfielders and infielders out there behind me, he argued.

After balancing all these elements of the game as it existed in Matty's era, one can still arguably reach the conclusion that he was the best, perhaps for all time.

Given the high esteem in which Matty was held in Lewisburg,

it was inevitable that professional baseball would erect the Christy Mathewson Memorial Gateway in 1928 at Bucknell's main entrance off U.S. Route 15. This was followed on September 30, 1989, by the rededication of the Christy Mathewson Memorial Stadium on the Bucknell campus, down the street from Matty's resting place in the Lewisburg Cemetery. This football and track facility had originally been dedicated in 1924 as Memorial Stadium. By rededicating it to Matty, Bucknell was underlining the school's commitment to a balance between scholarship and sports.

25

AFTER MATTY
WAS GONE

T WO weeks after Matty's death Jane informed the
press that her husband had never made a will.
This was surprising, considering Matty's responsible nature, yet it
is not unusual for lawyers, for example, to die intestate or for doctors to neglect their own health.

Electing to remain at Saranac Lake in the house that stored so
many memories, Jane stayed there for 25 years until 1950. For many
years Jane did not attend any baseball games. However, she remained close to the McGraws and other members of the Giant
family. Eddie Brannick, now an executive in the Giants' front office, visited her often. He never tired of reminding her of the many
times that Matty had taken tickets at the gate when the Giants ran
short of personnel. In order to pay for her upkeep at Saranac, Jane
became a shrewd investor in the stock market.

In 1939 she accepted an invitation to attend the inaugural ceremony of Baseball's Hall of Fame at Cooperstown, New York, where
she received Matty's plaque. She then declined all further invita-
tions to the Hall until 1955, when Betty L. Cook of Lewisburg urged
Jane to visit Cooperstown with her. Cook, a spirited woman with
an intense interest in baseball, lived just a few doors away from
Jane in a 160-year-old Victorian house on Market Street. The two
women traveled the 360 miles to Cooperstown by car each year for
the next 12 years for the annual induction ceremonies.

Despite her private personality, Jane, as a result of these ex-

223

cursions, became baseball's most celebrated and gracious widow. Not even the wives of Babe Ruth and Lou Gehrig attracted more favorable curiosity at Cooperstown. On each visit to the Hall of Fame Jane never failed to wear Matty's Phi Gamma Delta fraternity pin. She died in Lewisburg on May 29, 1967, at the age of 87.

Christy Jr., who never played baseball, majored in electrical engineering at Bucknell. He turned from engineering in 1928 to attend the Flying Cadet School of the Army Air Corps at Kelly Field, Texas. Thirty men out of a class of 120 won their wings. One of them was young Christy.

By 1930, when Christy Jr. was a second lieutenant in the Army Air Corps Reserve, he strongly resembled his father, but some who knew him felt he was "spoiled" and somewhat arrogant. But he had determined that he was not going to live in the shadow of his father.

When the Central Aviation School was established in Hangchow in the Chinese Republic, Christy Jr. won an assignment there to train Chinese pilots. On Christmas Day, 1933, in Shanghai, Christy married 23-year-old Margaret Phillips from Philadelphia. Two weeks later Christy took his bride for a flight—her first such experience—from the Shanghai Airport. After only thirty seconds in the air, the twin-motored plane owned by the finance minister of China suddenly nosed downward, crashing on a mudflat in the Whangpoo River. Chinese rivermen picked up Mrs. Mathewson but she had died instantly. When they got to Christy he was unaware that she was already dead. He pleaded with them to "Look after my wife!"

Given small chance to survive, with both arms badly injured and his left leg smashed, Christy gradually recovered. However, his leg had to be amputated. Striving to overcome the effects of the accident, Christy was later able to play excellent golf, and in 1936 he was married for a second time, to Mrs. Lee Morton, a British woman.

With the coming of World War II, Christy, once considered to be "crippled for life," fought to win an Air Force commission despite his disability. When he was put on active service, he was made a lieutenant colonel in the Air Transport Command, although confined to non-flying duties. While in London he met Lola Finch, another Britisher, whom he married in 1945, following a divorce from his second wife.

On August 16, 1950, Christy Jr. suffered severe burns over his entire body in a gas explosion at his home in Helotes, northwest of San Antonio, Texas. He managed to drive to the hospital, where he died. In what had become a tragic tradition among the Mathewson men—first Nick, then Henry, then Matty—Christy Jr., at 44, also met death when he was too young in years.

Index